# Confessing Excess

*SUNY Series in Gender and Society*
*Cornelia Butler Flora, Editor*

# Confessing Excess

## Women and the Politics of Body Reduction

CAROLE SPITZACK

State University of New York Press

Published by
State University of New York Press, Albany

Printed in the United States of America

For information, address State University of New York
Press, State University Plaza, Albany, N.Y., 12246

Library of Congress Cataloging-in-Publication Data

Spitzack, Carole.
   Confessing excess : women and the politics of body
reduction / Carole Spitzack.
      p.   cm. — (SUNY series in gender and society)
   Includes bibliographical references.
   ISBN 0-7914-0271-1. — ISBN 0-7914-0272-X (pbk.)
   1. Women—Health and hygiene—Social aspects.
2. Reducing—Social aspects.   3. Body image—Social
aspects.   4. Women—Psychology.
I. Title.   II. Series.
RA778.S734   1990                        89-36513
305.4—dc20                               CIP


10 9 8 7 6 5 4 3 2

*Dedicated to my Family*

# Contents

# Acknowledgments

I am deeply grateful to the women who so generously shared their lives with me in order to make this work possible. In addition to the women who allowed me to interview them, countless women have enriched my understanding of body experience and critical resistance through professional interactions as students and colleagues, the wonderfully complex communication in women's friendship, and intimate conversations.

Many colleagues, students, and friends listened and offered suggestions as I attempted to both clarify and resist my own position. With disciplinary backgrounds and experience in the domains of women's studies, feminism, Marxist and recent continental philosophy, rhetoric and persuasion, research design, interpersonal communication, social work and mass media, the following individuals provided alternative readings of women's body experience, support for my work, and inspiration: Bettina Bell, Donna Bersch, Jennifer Evans, James Hikins, Gaye LeMon, Jenny Nelson, Michael Presnell, William Sinda, Kathleen Turner, and Kittie Watson. I wish also to thank Ana Lopez, whose extensive involvement in the study of Latin American film and critical scholarship contributed significantly to my understandings of representation, otherness, political inscription, and the presentation of critical problematics. I am indebted particularly to Kathryn Carter for her careful reading of an earlier draft of the manuscript, her generosity in talking with me endlessly about critical readings of body issues, and her unwaivering friendship.

Others assisted in providing a supportive institutional climate in which to work on the manuscript. The Newcomb College Center for Research on Women gave me access to formats in which to present and receive responses to various arguments and ideas in the manuscript. Debra Thomas and Linda Harold worked laboriously and painstakingly to aid in the transcription of recorded interview documents. John Patton, chair of the Department of Communication at Tulane, made possible the acquisition of expanded computing facilities and research funds. My dear friend and colleague Nicholas Buchdahl provided facilities in which to make the production and printing of the manuscript efficient. Rosalie Robertson and Diane Ganeles, at the State University of New York Press, offered enthusiastic support for the project and expert editorial assistance.

# Introduction

Contemporary American culture has witnessed and promoted an increasing interest in women's health. Specialized clinics are prevalent in the treatment of particularly female medical problems ranging from sagging eyelids to infertility; gyms and spas designed for the pursuit of female strength are pervasive; countless weight reduction programs are promoted in the name of greater fitness; the cosmetic industry proliferates innumerable products for the accomplishment of a "natural," healthy appearance; and an endless array of relational advice books enable women to form and sustain healthy relationships, to name only a few. Invariably, the selling of women's health is informed by a rhetoric of appreciation—a desire on the part of cultural members to acknowledge the "special" needs of women. Here, the lives and bodies of women are no longer blended seamlessly with those of men because females and males are presumed to be different, requiring different forms of diagnosis and treatment in the accomplishment of health.

A willingness on the part of experts to appreciate the health concerns of women is often promoted as an accolade to women's liberation. Because women ought to be seen as fully functioning and independent members of society, they are worthy of considerable acknowledgment in consumer markets. Women are not portrayed as persons open to deception by false claims and inaccurate information, but as informed and knowledgeable individuals. Discourses of women's health invite all women to become liberated, overriding a past history of gullibility, by taking control of existence, refusing the repression and distortion of those who fail to see female capacities for strength, influence, and success. To refuse participation in the domain of women's health, for both promoters and consumers, is to appear nonprogressive. Opponents to women's health are viewed as barriers to liberation because they wish to preserve backward images of women, sustaining women's oppression.

1

Central to the politics of women's efforts to achieve body liberation is an *aesthetics* of health. Body fitness and overall well-being are primarily determined visually, through the gazes of self and others. Advertising imagery, for example, entices female consumers through tributes in which "natural beauty" is combined with a "healthy glow," both of which can be obtained with products ranging from liquid foundation to breakfast cereal. Here, former beauty regimes founded on a masking/fabrication of women give way to an acceptance of the "natural" strength and attractiveness of women. An attractive body, in turn, signifies a healthy attitude. Jane Fonda's (1981) hugely successful *Workout*, for example, proposes a streetwise castigation of oppressive capitalist practices as a means by which to achieve greater female health. The author's current body signifies health, unlike the Jane Fonda whose body was exploited and objectified in *Barbarella*, because she has taken control of her life by refusing the manipulation of others. Writing about the period surrounding the making of *Barbarella*, Fonda writes, "I did not even realize that I had been [a sex symbol]. The burgeoning new women's consciousness had not yet found its way into my mind and heart" (p. 18).

Freedom from cultural dictates is no longer simply a matter of ridding oneself of excess poundage or learning to select colors suited to one's complexion, but is bound up with mental functioning and personal politics. Rosalind Coward (1985) observes, "The old ideas told us our bodies weren't in good shape. But at least we could blame that on nature . . . now our minds are the problem" (p. 24). Women who follow in Fonda's footsteps, or those of other health promoters, are obliged to reassess the whole of existence, to scrutinize life choices, and to make individual freedom from constraint the goal of healthy women. Mind over matter, control, and transcendence are signified by the "naturally" healthy female body. In order for this gambit to work, female consumers must gaze at Fonda's body—slim, beautiful, erased of physical flaws— and determine that, indeed, she is healthy and strong.

If mental problems and regressive politics are at the root of women's efforts to achieve a version of health that is written on the body as increased attractiveness, then by implication, unattractive women are associated with deficient thinking and repression. In the chronicles of their past lives, for example, female diet book authors, now thin and healthy, often recount a history of decadent blindness and conservatism. Judy Mazel (1981), author of the best-selling *Beverly Hills Diet*, notes "I was killing myself . . . The health revolution had started, but I thought the people who shopped in health-food stores and didn't eat meat were weirdos and hippies" (p. 11). Mazel's rebellion, her "revolution" against disease, entails alignment with political activists; through resistance, she manages to achieve "an ideal weight of 102" (p. 10). Conversely, women such as Andrea Dworkin, a feminist writer and political activist who has militantly rejected cultural standards for female attractiveness, is now aligned publicly with Edwin Meese, head of the anti-pornography commission. Both Dworkin and Meese can be seen to represent censorship, conservative politics, constraint on human liberties.

The notion of liberty through culturally defined beauty comprises the central paradox in contemporary discourses of women's health. If women were truly beautiful "naturally," there would be no need for products, books, and services designed to achieve natural beauty. If women are freed from oppressive cultural constraints, freedom would encompass the advice of "experts" who delineate the parameters of feminine health. Following in the footsteps of Jane Fonda (1981), for instance, underscores a reliance on experts, masters, scripture—all of which bespeak enmeshment in cultural prescriptions. Efforts to replicate the bodies of other liberated women underscore the interchangeability of female bodies, not a so-called appreciation for women's individuality.

A demand for self-examination as a prelude to images of freedom works effectively to realign women with traditional visions of femininity. Not only does the activist woman begin to look like her conservative counterpart, but both women suggest the need for a continuous surveillance of female actions and bodies. If all women engage in a constant struggle against disease, and female struggles are recorded and reproduced endlessly, the bodies of women are seen to require careful attention, unceasing examination. Further, when responsibility for liberation is thought to rest with the individual, women do not profit from a preoccupation with oppressive *societal* standards, but from a preoccupation with the personal or individual nature of feminine disease. Ultimately, as Coward (1985) notes, "Health is presented as something which calls for individual hard work, not social solutions" (p. 25).

The contradictory forces that underpin discourses of female health are epitomized in strategies designed to aid women in a reduction of the body. Reducing one's body, or becoming less of oneself in order to become more of oneself, pervades health discourses in general, but functions with pronounced blatancy in the domain of weight loss. Contemporary weight loss diets appeal to health rather than disease, individuality rather than conformity, and supplant in each consumer the necessity of self-examination. The fantasy woman who represents health is seen to be only temporarily hidden underneath the surface. She is "imprisoned" in her body, but holds the promise of release as long as she probes deeply enough, thoroughly enough, into every dimension of personal existence. Each dieting failure is replaced by another diet, each presenting a new angle or issue in need of scrutiny, each purporting to eliminate the barriers to an emergence of natural, permanent health.

Body reduction/health discourses encourage examination, and guarantee a permanently "in progress" actualization of women's freedom through confession. Healthy women are those who confess a multitude of misguided actions, deviant sensibilities, transgressive moral propensities, all in the name of salvation, the successful accomplishment of an afterlife. In Michael Foucault's (1985) examination of the Christian confessional, two "ensembles of obligation" are foregrounded (p. 367). First, there is an "obligation to hold as truth a set of propositions which constitute dogma, the obligation to hold certain books as a permanent source of truth, obligations to accept the decisions of certain authorities in matters of truth," and second, each individual "has the duty to explore who he is, what is happening within himself, the faults he may have committed, the temptations to which he is exposed" (p. 367). The obligations described by Foucault can be seen in virtually every contemporary body reduction technique; each act of truth telling works toward permanent resolution and calls for increased controls, further examination, greater confessional capabilities.

Discourses of female body reduction can be said to operate as a political site wherein "subjects become objects of knowledge and at the same time objects of domination" (Foucault, p. 366). The activities undertaken in the name of self-knowledge preserve images of feminine disease over which society must retain control. Each effort to rise above political strategies and strategists brings further inscription in discursive terrains which endorse the sickness of women. A normalization of female bodies proceeds by revealing disease, repeatedly, so that the "normal" state of women's bodies is a diseased, troubled state.

My analysis takes up the terrain of women's body reduction/health as a confessional discourse. I depart from some tenets of post-structuralist and deconstructionist work because I see critical value in considering the voices of women who have lived the paradoxes in the domain of women's health, Foucault (1980a) observes, for example, that "power relations can materially penetrate the body in depth, without depending even on the mediation of the subject's own representations" (p. 186). I agree that power operates materially, not from a position of transcendence or as a foundation, but I am not prepared to abandon the subject's mediation of representations. Without privileging or sacrificing the everyday experience of women, I wish to show how the systems of domination *materialize* in voices of women. Central to the accomplishment of women's health is a capacity to engage in constant mediation between body and intellect, a continuous displacement of closure which depends on undermining and reinstantiating the centrality of body appearance. Voices which display the gaps, discontinuities, and displaced desires within the domain of women's health, from my perspective, are rich in critical potential.

In the examination to follow, I exact a confrontation between discourses of female body reduction and data from fifty tape-recorded interviews in which women talk about body experience in American culture (see Appendix). The voices of women, the ways in which women take up discourses of body reduction, serve to both underscore and deconstruct women's excesses and the need for confession. Women are shown to mediate between sickness and disease, never quite sure of condemnation or salvation. Yet, in the same act of precarious mediation, women's voices give attention to the artificially constructed character of cultural oppositions, the impossibility of women's health, and by implication, these voices open avenues for political critique.

My examination proceeds in three parts. Part one provides a description of the terrain of women's health/weight loss discourse. Specifically, chapter 1 offers a general analysis of the blending of body reduction and women's health, and shows how "experts" encourage resistance to cultural images of femininity through the promotion of weight loss. The next chapter focuses on women's experience of "expert" wisdom in the context of the gaze. That is, I consider how the gazes of experts are supplanted in women so that women come to both see and not see themselves as they are seen within polarities of health and disease. Further, I consider the expansion of territory opened to examination through the politics of body reduction/liberation. Chapter 3 takes up the notion of "speaking transgressions" or confession as mandated by body reduction/health discourse.

Part two examines women's relationships with others in the context of body issues. Central to the accomplishment of women's health, discursively defined, is a scrutiny of personal relationships. Women are required to investigate and override the negative and constraining influences of family, friends, and romantic partners who attempt to undermine feminine health and beauty. In reflecting on the body's relation to and with others, women's relational experience adds considerable complexity to the mandate for an escape from relational influences. In many respects, women reproduce cultural views concerning female participation in varying relational arrangements, and in particular the part played by a woman's body, but in numerous ways, women also provide a strikingly different portrayal of relational involvements.

In the third part of my analysis, I consider the lack of fit, along with the points of cohesion, between women's body experience and cultural discourse. Chapter 7 places women's speech within the domain of symbolic and ideological oppositions which construct and reproduce cultural representations of female and male sexuality. Resting on a symbolic opposition of health and disease, women are positioned to fail in their efforts to establish closure or finality, but also positioned to resist dominant truths. For example, women often describe themselves as "experts" on matters of health and beauty, claiming with considerable frequency, "I could write a book about this." Finally, chapter 8 returns to the question of solutions, to the problem of women's health as a political project.

# Part I

Transgressions and Cures

# Chapter 1

## Curative Voices: Anti-Diets and Experts

Weight loss diets represent a pervasive activity in the lives of Americans, generating billions of dollars in annual revenues for the diet industry.[1] Edwin Bayrd (1978) estimates that 79 million Americans are "significantly overweight," and that "at any given time, 52 million of them are either dieting or contemplating a diet" (p. 10). Bodies that exceed socially determined dimensions of acceptability are often subjected to a variety of "normalization" efforts, including, among others, memberships in organizations such as Weight Watchers or Overeaters Anonymous, reductions in the intake of calories carbohydrates, fasts, "combination" diets, vigorous forms of exercise, cosmetic surgeries, numerous forms of therapeutic and medical intervention, and prescription drugs. In addition, mass media, most notably television and magazines, are pervaded by advertisements for slimming devices and formulas, designed to assist in efforts to reshape body boundaries. Bayrd concludes, "We are, in short, a nation of compulsive dieters, given to periodic bouts of systematic fasting and punishing self-denial aimed at achieving—and then maintaining—significant weight loss" (p. 10).

Formulas for a visible reduction in body size are drawn from innumerable sources. Medical and mental health professionals, media celebrities, astute entrepreneurs, professional athletes, and everyday people who have devised their own experiential strategies, to name only a few, participate in a cultural consumer market devoted to curing the disease of excess weight. Perhaps singular as a disease category, obesity is overtly diagnosed and "treated" by countless individuals and organizations that have no medical credentials. Although most Americans would not solicit the aid of a movie star or a businessperson to correct a kidney malfunction, cures for obesity are often readily marketed and consumed, with little concern for expertise by consumers or governmental agencies. With a degree of business sense and an enticing cure,

9

every member of American society is permitted to be an "expert" on weight reduction. The complement to mass expertise is that every member of society is capable of diagnosing and judging the disease of obesity, establishing a collective "eye" to govern the body boundaries of all citizens.

That anyone with enough industry and perseverance stands to make large profits in the weight loss industry underscores obesity as a largely *visible* or external disease. As an "illness," obesity can be diagnosed visually. The overweight body may signify internal malfunctions—thyroid problems, a reduction in heart and lung capacity—but the initial judgment of disease is based on external appearance. Further, there is no absolute correlation between body weight and internal body functions, except, perhaps, in cases of morbid obesity. The precarious nature of obesity as a purely physiological disease can be seen by considering, for example, that most forms of medical insurance preclude its treatment (Millman, 1981, p. 83). Losing weight is akin to "cosmetic" surgery; both are comprehended socially as elective procedures because most often they cure aesthetic rather than physiological deficiencies. Only in a small number of cases do consumers in either market *require* the procedures in question for the continuation of life.

The "voluntary" character of weight reduction is further apparent when considering that most people who embark on weight loss diets are *not* seriously obese. Typically, they are between twenty and thirty pounds over average weight as determined by clinicians, which hardly poses a threat of major health complications (Watson, 1985, p. 8). Moreover, as Marcia Millman (1981) points out, cures for obesity are often more dangerous than the disease: "there is little health benefit in the activities of most dieters who repeatedly lose and regain weight, a stress on the body that is itself probably more unhealthy than staying overweight" (p. 83). In essence, weight reduction is a business within American culture that speaks to persons who, in spite of little evidence of physiological disease and in the face of methods that may cause more damage than the disease itself, seek to "cure" culturally defined defects in appearance.

Culturally, obesity is constructed not only as an affront to aesthetic sensibilities, but as an indicator of overall character deficiencies. A curious mix of science, aesthetics, and character judgment, as components of weight loss discourse, acquires particular significance with the realization that more women than men are thought to be significantly overweight. Bruce Shephard and Carroll Shephard (1985) indicate, "Women consistently outnumber men two to one in obesity and exceed men in the amount of weight gained" (p. 381). Women's bodies, within clinical accounts, are medically predisposed to the illness of obesity. And indeed, female physiology is conducive to weight gain, particularly as women's bodies move through advanced stages of maturation. The female tendency toward weight gain, Paula Caplan (1985) explains, is due to "the extra layer of fat in women's bodies and the physical changes related to menstruation, childbearing, and menopause, including the effects of female hormones on water retention and weight gain" (p. 120). Invariably, weight loss experts implicate women's reproductive capabilities as the principal cause of female fatness. It is, in effect, women's sexual functioning that predisposes them to the "illness" of obesity and the resulting moral jeopardy.

Feminine sexuality underpins cultural and clinical diagnoses of excess flesh, leading to countless "cures" for female body/moral deficiencies. The convergence of voices within the domain of weight loss discourse presents a challenging analytic task for anyone who is interested in dismantling the operations that link female sexuality and aesthetics under the guise of disease. Most curative voices present slenderness as liberation from a physical and psychological disease, as freedom from the culturally imposed constraints on feminine sexuality. A woman is seen to take control of her body through weight loss, rather than allowing the body, others, or dogma to control her. Further-more, liberation discourses are typically resistive; thus they appear to challenge, instead of support, dominant ideology. Women are encouraged to abandon re-straints on feminine sexuality by challenging traditional visions of female physiology. Representatives of so-called female body liberation within the weight loss industry do not originate in a single source, such as the medical community or the mental health profession. Rather, the power of weight loss discourse rests in its *dispersed* character, its multiple and varied points of resis-tance which all point to a single vision of female beauty/health/liberation.

Below, I lay the groundwork for an analysis of the political and ideological dimensions of female weight reduction within American cultural practices by tracing the convergence of voices that insures conformity in the domain of female body appearance. Proponents of what I call an *anti-diet* orientation both offer particular diets as cures for body oppression *and* condemn dieting as an activity. In the first section of my analysis, I do not, at all points, confine the arguments to female bodies because one of the ways in which anti-diets achieve success is to speak of weight control as a *human* problem. The falsely resistive character of anti-diets is highlighted in the second section to show that anti-diets are grounded consistently in historical conceptions of disease and its treatment. A posture of resistance is an integral part of oppressive practices. Dieting discourse functions within larger political and economic systems, which overlap and reinforce a general policing of women's bodies. The govern-ance of women's bodies, then, occurs through a multitude of politically-charged assumptions regarding the place of women in cultural practices. The weight reduction industry provides a vivid demonstration of the intersection of clinical, economic, and political structures that hold women in a permanent state of "disease."

*The Anti-Diet*

Weight loss formulas are grounded in a stance of resistance within the terrain of obesity as a disease. Arguments against dieting are especially evident in diet books because, here, the logic of the anti-diet is elaborately conceived and communicated within textual boundaries. Authors of diet books begin by informing readers that the text they are about to read does *not* promote a diet because diets are ineffective. In fact, only six percent of weight reduction attempts, according to medical estimates, result in permanent slenderness (Shephard and Shephard, 1985, p. 381). Harvey Diamond and Marilyn Diamond (1985), authors of the *Fit for Life* diet which boasts three million copies in print, for example, title their first chapter "Diets Don't Work." In the opening pages describing their approach, the Diamonds tell readers with considerable force that their approach "*is not a diet*" (p. 4). The Diamonds' condemnation of dieting is paralleled in every approach to weight loss I have encountered. Whether the method advocated receives credibility through training in medicine, psychology, sociology, athletics, an arena of media celebrities, or everyday experience, authorities in the domain of weight reduction agree on the futility of dieting. Each new author or entrepreneur presents her or himself as a *rebel* in the world of weight loss, as one whose keen vision sees that all diets ultimately fail.

Within the philosophy of anti-diets, weight loss efforts are seen to fail, perhaps most fundamentally and most often, because they are incompatible with human physiology. Weight reduction efforts forge a conflict between mind and body, in which the former struggles to control the latter. When the body is placed on a diet restricted to fruits or protein, for instance, bodily functions are impaired due to insufficient degrees of nutritional balance. Yet, the body is adept at self-preservation and regulation, often resisting mental attempts to alter body composition. Bayrd (1978) observes, "To achieve a consequential reduction in body weight, a dieter must do battle with his own body's remarkable capacity for maintaining body weight at a steady level" (p. 10). When body habits are interrupted with abrupt shifts in dietary patterns, the body protests through a reduction in metabolic rates, thereby preserving food intake as stored, rather than expended, energy. A. W. Pennington says of the body's propensity for preservation by way of dietary balance, "the appetite is balanced to the energy output with fine precision . . . Caloric evaluations cannot match, nor conscious willpower rival, the exactness and the persistence of this biological adjustment" (qtd. in Bayrd, p. 11). The less a dieter eats, in other words, the less a dieter is able to eat without gaining weight because the body adjusts "automatically" to alterations in dietary intake.

The body's triumph over dieting is demonstrated in the condition known as anorexia nervosa, a largely female disease of self-starvation. Anorexia is a weight reduction effort without end, even after the dieter has become emaciated. The anorexic demonstrates remarkable willpower by refusing all but minute quantities of food and thereby achieving triumph over physiological hunger. As Hilde Bruch (1979) observes, the anorexic attempts to master *all* dimensions of physiology, for example, "Swimming one more lap, running one more mile, doing ever more excruciating calisthenics, everything becomes a symbol of victory over the body" (p. 66). Eventually, however, the body wins the battle. As evidenced in the widely publicized death of singer Karen Carpenter, physiological realities override attempts to transcend bodily needs. The body demands nourishment for a continuation of life, regardless of the tight control mechanisms instituted by its inhabitant.

The source of anguish for the dieter, whether or not she develops an eating disorder, is a body at odds with mental strength, thereby revealing the relative impotence of reason and intellectual prowess. Mental powers are worthless without the body's willingness to perform in conjunction with them. In describing the relatively simple task of learning to tie shoelaces, Kim Chernin (1981) points to inevitable reliance on the body, which produces resentment towards the body's unwillingness to conform to mental demands:

> Somehow, in spite of the mind's clearly seeing how the shoe was tied, the fingers could not perform the task. Thus the body, stubborn or slow, requiring endless practice and repetition before it can even begin to approach the accomplishment of the simplest task, frustrates thought, calls into question the mind's sense of its own power, enrages the mind that cannot, for all its understanding, accomplish the tying of the shoe without the body. The body awakens in us a knowledge of our impotence, our inability to master the external world (p. 59).

As Chernin suggests, a disharmonious relation between body and mind results in the body's triumph and a subsequent confrontation with the impoverished quality of mental powers. Diets are self-defeating, in part, because they remind a dieter that she is not in control, that her desire to lose weight requires the body's willing participation; the body announces her powerlessness. The body is loathesome because it proclaims the relative impotence of the dieter's willpower.

To underscore the dieter's inability to exert control over her body, authors of diet books often recount their own experiences of discord between mind and body resulting from weight reduction attempts. In *Workout*, for example, Jane Fonda (1981) recounts innumerable personal attempts to gain control over her body through diets, which produced further disgust for her body (pp. 13-16). Consumption of tapeworm chewing gum, binge-purge behavior, an addiction to Dexedrine and diuretics, and pursuing countless "crash" diets led to further disgust for her body *because* they went against the body's natural needs and processes. Fonda's body resisted efforts to transform her appearance in an attempt to meet current demands for thinness within the worlds of modeling and cinema. An explicit link is established between the failure of diets and the resulting self-disgust as Fonda concludes, "If I had only understood twenty years ago the futility, the alienation, the self-denigration of trying to fit myself into a mold" (p. 16).

Along with a condemnation of unworkable attempts on the part of an individual to take control of the body, anti-diet proponents often point to the dieting industry as one which thrives on the exploitation of consumers. Persons who develop and distribute weight loss methods are implicated by dieting rebels for encouraging quick and often dangerous resolutions for obesity. The most outlandish methods often impair normal body functioning, and increase the efficiency of the body's mechanisms for preservation. Thus diet promoters encourage abnormal body functioning, subordinating the notion of overall health to quick results. Remar Sutton (1988) states, "There are no moral or legal restraints in the diet business. Anyone who can think up a new diet, and virtually any publishing house will publish it if it's radical or new-sounding enough" (p. 17). As Sutton's condemnation suggests, anti-diet proponents establish a clear distinction between themselves and "typical" diet peddlers. By implicating others, the dieting rebel is perceived as concerned with consumer welfare. The dieting industry, in effect, demonstrates questionable morality because cures proceed without regard for patient safety or a diet proponent's expertise.

In the dieting marketplace, lucrative profits override a concern with consumer success. When asked why there are so many diet books, for example, Sutton (1988) replies, "Because people like to make money" (p. 17). Promoters of diets are often presented by anti-diet proponents as persons who have negligible quantities of social conscience because they place financial gain over a concern for successful weight loss, and often over the damaging side-effects of unsafe diets. In *The Thin Game: Dietary Scams and Dietary Sense* (1978), Bayrd traces the history of profitable weight loss "scams" that have played on the desperation of obese persons. According to Bayrd's account, the dieting industry is highly lucrative and has few governmental controls, making it quite simple for a good businessperson to give the illusion of medical expertise without fear of social reprisal or sanction.

A notorious case of exploitation can be seen in John Andreadis' marketing of "Hollywood Beauty Cream" in 1948, which included circulars promising a "melting" away of fifteen pounds in thirty days (Bayrd, pp. 70–72). Although the U.S. Postal Service determined that Andreadis' scheme was fraudulent and barred mail order service of the product, Andreadis continued to earn sizeable profits by changing the labels on product packaging, developing new products, and changing his name to John Andre. Each time the Postal Service censored Andreadis, he developed a new product as a means by which to alleviate penalties and insure future business success. Eventually, with the development of a product called "Regimin," Andreadis succeeded in obtaining endorsements from medical and media figures. In 1958 the Federal Trade Commission filed a complaint against Andreadis for false claims in the marketing of Regimin. Six years later, after Americans had invested *$16 million* in the product, Andreadis was ordered to cease production and advertising.

A willingness to pursue desperate solutions to an overweight body is often associated culturally with women rather than men, thereby making women more susceptible to exploitation. Indeed, Shephard and Shephard (1985) observe, "In a society which stigmatizes being overweight, some women take great risks to follow fashion's dictate to look thin by going on crash diets or participating in the latest fad diet" (p. 381). Promoters of anti-diets often infiltrate the world of dieting on behalf of exploited female consumers. Weight conscious women are taught to be wary of diets, to become streetwise in their resistance to dieting scams. This condemnation of diets is a particularly effective strategy in the selling of weight reduction methods to women. Watson (1985), among others, notes that dieters are typically *seasoned;* they have tried numerous methods and failed. Women are likely to be in full agreement when authors report the futility of dieting because they have *lived* the impossible demands for thinness within culture, engaging, as Lois Banner (1983) has shown, in any number of activities to mold or reshape their bodies. At the same time, rigid standards for female attractiveness, combined with sanctions against women who are deemed physically unattractive, prevent most women from simply abandoning body concerns. In fact, repeated failure is likely to *heighten* a sense of desperation, a willingness to "try anything" in an effort to shed pounds. The dieting industry capitalizes on the experiential knowledge of women in order to cement an ongoing cycle of weight loss formulas, each of which generates enormous profits for the industry. By acknowledging the exploitation of female consumers, anti-diet promoters establish affinity with weight conscious women. A particular diet book author, for example, may be seen as one who understands women's experience, indeed, as one who *shares* women's experience. Understanding and shared experience establish a common ground on which to fight against the exploitive nature of dieting.

Because many women have tried countless weight loss methods, they are likely to exist in a relationship of permanent discord with their bodies. If diets fail, and culture abhors fat women, then a female dieter is potentially at odds with her body for the whole of her life. In Millman's (1981) investigation into the lives of obese women, the autobiographies of fat women point to life histories pervaded by body struggle and body disgust. Although some of Millman's respondents are less concerned about their fatness than others, all report ongoing sensations of displeasure when speaking of their bodies. Each woman struggles against physiological realities, but due to her body's regulatory mechanisms, she is unable to exhibit mind over matter. The prospect of a new diet produces anxiety because each successive approach will most likely result in yet another failure. Eda LeShan (1981) writes, when reflecting on her own history of dieting, that repeated failure means "each new diet is begun in a state of great ambivalence, which undermines our progress and dooms us to eventual failure" (p. 2). Dieting repetition produces ambivalence at the prospect of each new solution. Each new beginning involves an admission that the body has taken control, leaving the dieter in a state of precarious hopefulness regarding her ability to create lasting body changes. The body has a demonstrated history of resistance.

Anti-diets contain a resolution for the problematic relation between body and mind by promoting a truce, a reunion of body and mind. When overweight individuals stop dieting, they make peace with their bodies and exist in an experiential space characterized by harmony rather than battle. Proponents of slenderness stress repeatedly that *permanent* weight loss is contingent on seeing oneself as a non-dieter, as one who does not fight against the body. Authors and promoters themselves are often former diet fanatics for whom life-long slenderness transpired when dieting ceased. For example, the first chapter of Judy Mazel's (1982) successful *Beverly Hills Diet,* "The Transformation of a Food Junkie," contains a section entitled, "Fat, Fatter, Fattest: The Wretched Treadmill" (p. 9). Here, Mazel recounts years of crash dieting and negative experience with clinicians who encouraged her to consume thyroid pills, diuretics, and diet pills—all to no avail in achieving slenderness (p. 11). Not surprisingly, those who have resolved body problems, such as Mazel, who boasts a body weight of 102 pounds, are inordinately happy with their bodies, no longer struggling against body chemistry and/or the body's regulatory mechanisms. Readers are invited, along with the author, to stop fighting against the body and thereby resolve the "wretched treadmill" of dieting.

The treadmill of dieting is set in motion because although weight loss efforts often produce results, weight is easily regained when the individual stops dieting. When the diet ends, one is apt to resume familiar eating habits and regain lost pounds. Alternatively, slenderness may never be achieved due to eating binges brought about as a result of the restrictions characteristic of diets. For example, if a dieter thinks longingly about chocolate sundaes precisely because she cannot have them, a lapse in control is likely to occur. The Diamonds point out that when an individual is dieting, "you are usually thinking about what you're going to eat when the ordeal is over. How can you possibly succeed on your diet when all you are thinking about is food?" (p. 12). Consumers, like promoters of weight loss, must ultimately learn how *not* to diet if they hope to accomplish permanent slenderness and body-mind harmony.

The failure of dieting is located not only in exploitive practices and body regulation, but in dieter temperament. Frank Bruno (1972), for example, establishes an implicit connection between repeated diet attempts and personal failure when describing his approach in *Think Yourself Thin*. "This book prescribes no diets. If you are anything like the average overweight person, you have tried the high-protein diet, the low-carbohydrate diet, the Mayo Clinic diet, etc.... But you still can't lose weight. Why? Obviously, your problem is that you can't stick to a diet" (p. 4). Escape from the never-ending cycle of dieting requires the overweight individual to adopt a posture of resistance within the world of dieting. She must not fall prey to yet another promotion, gimic, or fad. Paradoxically, a dieter must cease dieting in order to diet successfully. In short, she must take up the sensibilities of the anti-diet promoter.

The dieter's stance of resistance entails a confrontation with her own tendency towards suffering. In the terrain of dieting discourse, the overweight person is one who suffers "voluntarily" through repeated deprivation. Because she does not have the willpower to diet successfully, and because suffering is unhealthy psychologically, the dieter must learn to satisfy her desires if she hopes to achieve permanent results. The Diamonds make an explicit connection between dieting failure and deprivation in observing, "Depriving yourself is *not* the answer to *healthy, permanent* weight loss" (p. 12). Similarly, in noting the impossibility of permanent deprivation, Sutton (1988) observes, "Diets for most people mean being *deprived,* and no one other than the occasional weird monk can deprive himself for all of his conscious life" (p. 16). In placing severe limits on consumption, the dieter is required to become a "weird monk," in Sutton's terms, by eliminating precisely those areas of existence that bring pleasure.

Anti-diets resolve suffering by shifting the temporal dimension of dieting. Specifically, proponents argue, life habits must be contiguous with eating; thus they recognize the self-defeating character of dieting which forces individuals to alter normal routines. Judy Mazel (1982) epitomizes the anti-diet philosophy in stating, "The Beverly Hills Diet does not represent an isolated space in time when we're either 'on a diet' or 'off a diet,' a mentality that equates losing weight with suffering" (p. xvii). If an approach to slenderness is equated with body persecution, the dieter becomes an unpraiseworthy martyr, the scarred embodiment of a set of principles that are doomed to failure *because* they are incompatible with the dieter. Often, the dieting martyr is viewed by others as masochistic because of the seemingly self-imposed suffering endemic to weight loss efforts, much as the choice to be a monk entails self-imposed restraints and deprivations. For instance, one who eats blandly prepared vegetables in the presence of others who are eating rich foods and desserts often calls attention to her willingness to *deprive* herself, to punish herself for former or potential indulgences.

The dichotomy of dieting and not dieting is problematical due to the guilt it produces for the dieter. Bodies of dieters signify past indulgences and thereby question the reality of deprivation. As an activity, dieting calls attention to past or hidden decadence, which is announced to others during periods of restriction. A complex dilemma involving guilt and suffering manifests itself during bouts of restraint. Susie Orbach (1979) argues that dieting *produces* an obsession with eating; a desire to indulge complements a desire for thinness. Implicitly, the ritual of dieting "carries with it an enormous amount of self-disgust, loathing and shame" because it points to an obsession with consuming more than one needs (p. 28). Dieting, then, announces indulgence rather than restraint or control. Guilt manifests through a recognition of one's capacity to consume in excess. Further, dieting underscores the hidden character of consumption, which the diet is designed to cure. Significantly, for example, eating for the dieting woman is often "done in secret or with friends" (Orbach, p. 28). Guilt is thus *produced* in the act of dieting, in trying to achieve an image of normalcy.

To promote a diet in which an author states directly that consumers will suffer or experience guilt constitutes a demonstration of abysmal business sense. Anti-diets promise an alleviation of the guilt and suffering contained in most diets. Initially, books such as Fonda's (1981) *Workout* appear to acknowledge the necessity of suffering for the sake of body satisfaction. Fonda describes a burning sensation in the muscles resulting from an accumulation of lactic acid, which "impedes muscle contraction" (p. 68). Rather than viewing the sensation as an indication of pain, however, Fonda adds, "I've come to look forward to it. It lets me know that I'm really working hard" (p. 68). Pain is here dissociated from suffering, and correlated with success, hard work, and strength. Moreover, in the opening chapter of *Workout,* entitled "A Body Abused," Fonda wholeheartedly condemns the suffering inherent in weight reduction schemes by chronicling a chain of past personal abuses. Implicitly, the suffering endemic to self-indulgence is contrasted to the positive "pain" of hard work and accomplishment.

A permanent reunion of body and mind, ending the horrors of dieting, involves changes in the life world of an individual, shifting the dieter's orientation from pain to pleasure. Dieters actualize pleasure by discovering a diet tailor-made to suit individual habits, thus requiring no alterations and no "diets." The discourse of weight reduction accomplishes a profound rhetorical feat in suggesting, simultaneously, that everything *and* nothing in a person's life must change in order to achieve the pleasure of slenderness. Specifically, diets fail because they are incompatible with the everyday eating habits of many people and ignore the diversity in individual lifestyles; success depends on finding an approach to slenderness that is consistent with the daily life of an individual. At the same time, the everyday habits of an individual have produced an undesirable body and prompted the overweight person to seek solutions. The irony in the combination of encompassing changes and minute alterations is epitomized in Mazel's book. In the introduction, Mazel boasts sales in the millions, recounting innumerable persons who have been "cured" by her approach; *and* she tells readers that her diet is not "a rigid regimen that insists on harsh, unbending conformity, that prescribes for all humanity as if it were a single eater. This is a diet for each individual" (p. xvii). Here, Mazel suggests, each consumer of her book becomes a unique individual in embracing her program, like the millions of other unique individuals who have done so.

Diets achieve mass appeal in the anti-diet philosophy by appealing to unique, choice making individuals. Bringing an end to dieting frees the individual from a troubled relationship with her body and from the exploitation of diet promoters. Freedom is manifested when the individual takes control of her body, instead of allowing the body, big business, or so-called medical "experts" to control her. For example, in describing the rewards of thinness, Robert Linn (1980) explains, "you can have the feeling of freedom from constraint, of being in control, and of not being at the mercy of anything or anyone . . ." (p. 97). Authors of anti-diet books, moreover, are for the most part slender and fit, displaying in a most empirical fashion the benefits of body control. They *embody* freedom; they seem to have undergone a transformation akin to rebirth, living comfortably in their bodies for the first time in their lives by virtue of being in control.

The anti-diet philosophy cancels the need for willpower through a curious construction of "natural" self-restraint. Taking control of the body in anti-diets requires a strength of will that is seemingly different from the willpower advocated in unsuccessful or exploitive diets. For example, many diet book authors grant readers permission to eat rich foods such as chocolate and pastry *in moderation*. Sutton (1988) explains, the key to a permanently svelte body is to "slightly modify your eating habits for the rest of your life" (p. 17). The dividing line between "fat" and "thin" sensibilities is an ability to judge the point at which the body is taking over, consuming more than it needs. The thin or physically fit person makes such judgments *naturally* and does not have to restrict intake consciously; strength of will is already in place. Thin persons are able to enjoy life's pleasures because control gives them freedom from *thinking* about food and diet.

An approach to dieting that condemns dieting for its repression of the individual is particularly well suited to the ideological structures in American culture. The sanctity of individuality, freedom of choice, and pleasure are historically grounded and communicated through countless cultural practices. Anti-diet approaches acquire political significance with the realization that power operations within a culture are effective only if they appear to preserve a commitment to individual choice making capacities. Michel Foucault (1980b) observes, "power would be a fragile thing if its only function were to repress, if it worked only through the mode of censorship, exclusion, blockage and repression . . . " (p. 59). The freedom in anti-diets is the liberty to invest one's own body with power it has been denied through dieting. In addressing the body and its investment with power, Foucault (1980b) suggests, "Mastery and awareness of one's own body can be acquired only through the effect of an investment of power in the body: gymnastics, exercises, muscle building, nudism, glorification of the body beautiful" (p. 56). Anti-diets promote a turn inward for the dieter, an opportunity to focus on the individual body and personal lifestyle. The strength of the individual is concomitant with the strength of the body.

Anti-diets work to locate sources of body "censorship" and, in the same move, reinstate a need for body control. Each new promise of body freedom demands yet another set of principles for life transformation, for an escape from principles imposed artificially. Invariably, anti-diets offer a program or technique for body transformation, juxtaposed with a condemnation of "cookbook" solutions. Such an orientation is epitomized in Mazel's (1982) approach because while dieters are promised freedom from a life of dieting rules, Mazel begins her book by stating, "If you read this book carefully and understand and internalize the rules and the commandments, my diet will work for you" (p. 1). The contradiction in Mazel's rhetoric expresses a central mechanism in strategies at work to further cycles of oppression by promising freedom. As Foucault (1980b) argues, "Power, after investing itself in the body, finds itself exposed to a counterattack in that same body" (p. 56). Once internalized, the "rules" of a diet are experienced *as* rules, as a "counterattack;" thus the diet fails, leading the dieter to yet another formula, another promise of freedom. The anti-diet escapes condemnation because it is the individual who must take control. After all, from the outset, the anti-diet promoter states in unqualified terms that diets do not work: one should not heed the wisdom of "experts."

### Clinical Roots: Heal Thyself

Responsibility for the body's appearance, within anti-diet philosophies, is complex. Many political, social, and personal practices converge to create a diffused sense of blame concerning the failure of diets. Clearly, the dieting industry is partly to blame for the repeated failure of weight loss efforts by devising "solutions" that are designed to generate profits rather than to cure obesity. Bayrd's (1978) account of an industry pervaded by dangerous and unworkable diets testifies to a history laden with abuses. Yet, such an industry could not thrive, as it has for decades, without a tacit endorsement from culture at large. In part, unsound weight loss methods are pervasive due to lax regulations from governmental agencies, as Sutton (1988) has noted above, and due to clever businessmen who understand how to work within existing governmental standards. Government and business, however, function within a larger set of cultural and institutional practices. Mass media, fashion and cosmetic industries, dating and marriage customs, among others, provide support for the weight loss industry. The marketing of bodies—indeed, the body is a *commodity* in American culture—represents an intersection of countless prescriptive voices, many of whom stand to profit from the promotion of slenderness.

The economic motivations within the diet industry are not restricted to popular or unsound weight loss promoters, but are locatable within a general framework of health and its institutionalization. Medical authorities exist in, and receive endorsement from, economic and political dimensions of the culture in which they operate. During eighteenth century practices, Michel Foucault (1980c) writes that a concern emerged with "the health and physical well-being of the population in general as one of the essential objectives of political power" (pp. 169-170). A merger of medicine and economics was in place by the nineteenth century, during which time a legislation of community health involved "the consideration of disease as a political and economic problem for social collectivities which they must seek to resolve as a matter of overall policy" (Foucault, 1980c, p. 166.) By virtue of its participation in community policy making activities, the field of medicine stood to gain much political power as an economic institution.

The professionalization of medicine, as an outgrowth of industrial society, helped to further the economic and political power of the health care field. Marilyn French (1985), among other analysts of medical practice, finds that the professionalization of medicine in Western industrial society altered conceptions of disease and its treatment (pp. 357-360). Prior to institutionalization, medical practitioners received little or no pay because healing others was viewed as an act of love and compassion and most often practiced by local women healers within communities. Undoubtedly, systems of economy and government contributed to conceptions of health during the period of pre-industrialization, but healers were not unified within a business or professional institution. The professionalization of medical practice "changed it into a commodity, something offered for money" (French, 1985, p. 357). In addition, professionalization consolidated the power of the medical establishment so that "lay" practitioners were gradually eliminated by being deemed noncredible in the professional hierarchy. Economic gain in medicine, then, like economic gain in industry within capitalist systems, is dependent on a narrowing of expertise in order to preserve an unequal distribution of wealth.

In point of fact, the fight against disease is financially profitable for the American medical establishment. Concerning the illness of obesity, many physicians condemn "quacks" and "frauds" who purport to having expertise for the sake of monetary gain, but many authors of popular diet books are themselves physicians. In addition, physicians have promoted diets every bit as dangerous as those offered by persons who do not possess medical credentials. Perhaps the most visible cases of blending monetary gain and untenable diets with medicine are seen in the widely distributed diets proposed by Dr. Irwin Stillman and Dr. Robert Atkins during the 1970s. Both authors enjoyed tremendous financial success, by, in effect, advising readers to produce a dangerous chemical imbalance within the body. The Stillman diet caused severe dehydration through a combination of low-carbohydrates and a copious intake of water, with no plan for replacing the salt lost through excessive urination (Bayrd, 1978, p. 57). Dr. Atkins' scheme eliminates all carbohydrates from one's diet, thereby encouraging *ketosis*. Ketosis, the result of a carbohydrate deficit which affects functioning of the brain and muscles, Bayrd (1978) observes, potentially results in "nausea, vomiting, weakness, apathy, dehydration, calcium depletion, kidney failure in susceptible individuals, cardiac irregularity, and a tendency to feel giddy or faint" (p. 57). Moreover, the diets proposed by Stillman and Atkins are ultimately ineffective in producing permanent weight loss because when a dieter resumes normal eating habits, sometimes as a result of becoming sick from the diet, she regains lost pounds. In Stillman and Atkins, then, we have a case of two physicians who proposed dangerous and temporary weight loss methods, and enjoyed enormous financial success by betting on the medical naiveté and desperation of consumers.[2]

Further, given the cost of American medical care, it can hardly be said that physicians are disinterested in the financial rewards accorded to those who exist at the top of the medical hierarchy. Physicians such as Stillman and Atkins are generally criticized by the medical community for the practice of crass and profit-seeking medicine, but the sanctimonious tone with which charges are leveled carries a note of hypocrisy when considering the astronomical cost of today's medical care. French (1985) points out that most uninsured patients are undesirable for physicians because, given the high price of medical services, uninsured patients may be unable to pay for treatment (p. 360). Patients who lack the luxury of health insurance are generally persons who are not gainfully employed, for example, members of minority groups and women, making it even more difficult to afford medical services. Thus it may be said, as French observes, "In capitalist countries, the distribution of ill health follows the distribution of income" (360). As a profit-based industry, American medicine is generally unavailable to persons whose income or insurance does not provide for it.

In the case of a "disease" such as obesity, the commodity orientation of medicine is supplemented by, or possibly grounded in, a curious disdain for overweight persons. Beginning in 1900, Millman (1981) observes, thinness became associated with wealth and high social standing (p. 101). The status of thinness, in turn, was linked to greater distance from animality and "base" human drives. Fatness, by contrast, indicated low status and low levels of self-control, cementing an association between body type, income, and morality. Although an association between income and body size is not readily acknowledged as a rationale for viewing obese persons negatively, the medical community does not have a history of kindness with respect to overweight patients. George Maddox and Veronica Liederman (1973) note that many physicians not only hold negative views of overweight patients, but that the quality of medical treatment may suffer as a result (pp. 84-91). Medical antagonism toward overweight patients and questionable treatment is highlighted as one of Millman's (1981) respondents describes her experience with two doctors:

> I had a cold, walked into his office, and he looked at me and said, "I'm not going to treat you unless you lose weight." I said, "I just want some cough medicine so I won't cough myself to death." He said, "Okay, I'll give you some cough medicine, but if you don't lose twenty pounds in two weeks, don't come back." [There was also] a woman gynecologist who didn't want to treat me unless I lost weight. I went to have my birth control pills extended, and she said, "I can't give you the pill because you have high blood pressure." I said, "How do you know? You haven't taken it." She said, "You're fat—you have high blood pressure" (pp. 16-17).

Physicians are not exempt from the stereotyping of patients according to cultural standards. Common societal views portray obesity as a sign of contemptable self-indulgence and decadence that would be remedied by a reduction in weight. The medical community, Hilde Bruch (1966) states, frequently shares this attitude: "obese patients' physicians are often handicapped by sharing the common cultural attitude of contempt for fat people and the assumption that all their problems would be solved if they lost weight" (p. 6).

Shared assumptions regarding obese persons by physicians and society are readily found, and are not restricted to isolated cases such as those described by Millman's (1981) respondent. Most often, discrimination appears in an implicit acceptance of stereotypes regarding the purportedly overindulgent character of fat people. Dr. Bayrd (1978), for all his labors in identifying exploitive practitioners within his own profession, notes that Atkins' approach "appeals to the weak-willed glutton that lurks in everyone who is overweight" (p. 56). Other physicians, such as Robert Linn (1980) make an effort to conceal *personal* prejudices by encouraging a dieter to see that "people" and "the world" see her in negative terms; it is "people" who view obesity as a form of criminal deviance: "when 'straight' people see people who are fat, they often unconsciously conjure up an image of how they got to be that way, of all the *gorging* those people must have done . . . the world tends to view them as the worst kind of gluttons" (p. 13). However, Linn cannot be faulted for a complete shifting of blame for prejudices against obesity; at times he speaks of views that "we" hold regarding fat people, implicating himself along with society. For example, he observes that when "we" see persons who are overweight, "we" construe their circumference as the outer proof of their inner lack of self-control" (p. 12).

Responses to obesity, and the consequent placing of blame for the illness, are further illuminated by examining the association of women and weight problems. Because obesity is viewed culturally as a predominantly female disease, possibilities for social and medical abuse are especially pronounced. Historically, femininity and pathology are intricately related within a political sphere of male-dominated health professionals who mirror their culture's views of women, despite proclamations of scientific objectivity. Defined in opposition to men, women are viewed, even in contemporary culture, as frail by nature and given to bouts of irrationality and emotion, predisposing them to illness. At the same time, determinations of female "health" are often contingent on a woman's conformity with cultural linkages between women and disease. For example, Ann Oakley (1981a) reports the results of a study conducted to obtain clinical perceptions of health, revealing, "Healthy women were more submissive, less aggressive, less competitive, more excitable, more easily hurt, more emotional, more conceited about their appearance and less objective than healthy men" (pp. 64-65). By making female health and female disease interchangeable, women become wholly and permanently diseased; indeed, within the community of health professionals and culture at large, "it is normal to be a man and abnormal to be a woman" (p. 64).

The equation between women and disease is longstanding and is traceable to cultural visions of feminine sexuality. Foucault's (1980d) investigation of sexuality reveals a threefold process during eighteenth century practices "whereby the feminine body was analyzed—qualified and disqualified—as being thoroughly saturated with sexuality, whereby it was integrated into the sphere of medical practices, by reason of a pathology intrinsic to it; whereby it was placed in organic communication with the social body" (p. 104). In this process, the diseased female body became *naturalized* within the medical community and the social body, with both domains providing support for female illness. As French (1985) observes, by the nineteenth century "it was generally believed that to be a woman was to be sick" because female reproductive functions "were seen as *inherently pathological*" (p. 358). Implicating women's reproductive functions as evidence for female pathology points to cultural and medical visions of feminine sexuality as diseased or disease-producing.

The androcentric correlation between disease and feminine sexuality is widely demonstrated within cultural practices, serving the power interests of dominant ideology. Mary Daly's (1978) analysis of gynecology reveals that the bodies of women have been physically mutilated, historically and cross-culturally, because they are seen partriarchally to be embued with dark and secretive sexual urges. Mutilation of the body is often used to "cure" women of a so-called natural propensity toward abnormal or "sick" behavior. The practice of clitoridechtomy, for example, carries with it an assumption that, if left to its own desires, the female sexual appetite will consume the body's inhabitant with self-directed pleasure. A woman who satisfies her own desires is a dangerous prospect for androcentrism because she threatens to expose a key element in the mythology upon which patriarchy is built: man is indispensable.[3] If she is given a label of disease, however, medical intervention underscores the legitimacy of women's natural propensity for disease.

Obesity as a female disease is often viewed as an expression of destructive rebelliousness, a defiance of the rigid standards for female appearance erected within culture. Linn (1980) points out, for example, that fat women are "down on men," fueling a cultural association between obese women and a resistance to the space allotted to women within patriarchy (p. 72). Regularly, obesity is paralleled with a chosen yet uncontrollable criminal behavior, much like cultural conceptions of feminine sexuality as both devious and out of control. In characteristic fashion, Linn, for example, explains eating compulsiveness to "repeat offender" dieters: "You know it's not rational. You know it doesn't make sense. You know it's wrong. But just like the habitual criminal, the overeater doesn't really understand his motives. You know you shouldn't do it, but you do it again and again. You are driven" (p. 98). Without too much difficulty, the word "overeater" could be substituted by any number of socially unacceptable female behaviors that are both mandated and punished within culture. For instance, in today's society women suffer from such "illnesses" as compulsive shopping, receiving abuse from men, and career anxiety.[4]

A bodily rebellion against cultural notions of female attractiveness, a seemingly willing violation of norms, is a particularly bold act when one considers that much of a woman's worth in society is determined by her external appearance, which is to say a woman's value exists in conjunction with her sexual attractiveness. Within the logic of dominant ideology, and certainly reproduced in weight reduction discourse, healthy women are attractive women. In reflecting on the horror of a friend's response to a fat woman, Millman (1981) writes, insightfully, "fat people seem to aggressively intrude themselves beyond proper boundaries . . . as characters who are disturbingly unresponsive to social control" (pp. 66-67). Obese women affront the sensibilities of masculine culture because patriarchal visions of femininity are not reflected in large women. Women who "aggressively intrude themselves beyond proper boundaries" defy associations between femininity and passivity, compliance, frailty, and nurturance. Rosalind Coward (1985) observes, "A large woman who is not apologizing for her size is certainly not a figure to invite the dominant meanings which our culture attaches to femininity. She is impressive in ways that our culture's notion of the feminine cannot tolerate" (p. 41). Obese women appear to take what they need, satisfying their own desires, without regard for male approval. It should come as no surprise, then, given the history of women and disease, that such women are seen as offensive because they occupy a space reserved for men.

The socio-medical perception of obesity as an irresolvable disease further complicates the placing of responsibility for the overweight body. Women are "naturally," hence unavoidably predisposed to fatness, thereby complicating the notions of volition, blame, and cure. Millman (1981) argues that due to the "dismal failure rate of diets obesity has lately come to be viewed as an 'incurable illness'" (p. 81). Defined as an incurable illness, obesity is a tragic condition and causes extraordinary pain throughout life. Through an analogy to alcoholism as a disease, Millman observes that in medical accounts, obesity "takes on the character of being beyond the simple volition of the individual" (p. 81). Compulsiveness in the consumption of alcohol or food moves beyond simple conceptions of will power, and into the terrain of involuntary physical addiction. An addiction is often accompanied by perceptions of self-disgust because the body has "overtaken" the individual, rendering her helpless in the face of food or drink.

Although a woman appears to be freed from responsibility for the disease of obesity when it is viewed as nonvolitional, she does not escape personal blame for either its development or its continuation. Even when a woman has been medically "predisposed" to obesity, given female biology, she is marked as one who has *permitted* a manifestation of excess poundage—much like the alcoholic who has "allowed" herself to drink excessively. As Millman sees, "viewing obesity as an illness still locates the cause of the problem and the solution within the individual" (p. 81). Obesity is "caused" by the individual, through her own tendency to consume more calories than her body expends, and continues as a disease because she cannot, presumably, control her eating habits. Because the individual "allows" herself to become diseased, she is also responsible for curing her illness.

Personal responsibility for disease is pervasive in the history of medicine, and is not restricted to illnesses in which a patient's lifestyle contains blatant body abuse. Cultural and medical responses to diseases such as alcoholism, obesity, and drug addiction, are merely cases within a web of connections between illness and individual character. Susan Sontag (1978) finds that during the nineteenth century, "the notion that the disease fits the patient's character, as the punishment fits the sinner, was replaced by the notion that it expresses character. Disease can be challenged by the will" (p. 42). Sontag traces the history of cancer as an illness to show the intricate ways in which a disease comes to be viewed as an expression of character, in turn, placing responsibility for the disease culturally and medically with the individual. In contemporary society, for example, seemingly *everything* related to personal or lifestyle choices causes cancer—smoking cigarettes, sunbathing, eating processed foods, receiving routine X-ray treatments, polluting the air with toxins through excessive reliance on motor vehicles, to name only a few. The disease of cancer is then thought to be avoidable if an individual avoids cancer-producing activities.

A lucid example of the association between willpower, disease, medicine, and culture, in the context of cancer, can be seen by examining responses to cigarette smoking. Clear connections between cigarette smoking and cancer were revealed in the U.S. Surgeon General's well-known report during the 1970s. Prior to medical confirmations of what had been considered speculative evidence for a cause-effect relationship between cigarettes and cancer, individuals were not held accountable for developing health complications resulting from smoking. Mass media, notably television and film, presented smokers as worldly, complex, and streetwise persons. Smoking provided access to a lifestyle associated with sophistication. After the Surgeon General's report, smoking was condemned as a personal activity. Cigarette companies could no longer advertise their products on American television because to do so, according to medical and governmental representatives, was tantamount to an endorsement of disease. Gradually, images of smokers in television and film reflected drastic changes in society's views of cigarettes. Today, smoking is indicative of an evil or deceptive disposition, of one who "lives for today," oblivious to the consequences of his or her actions. In fact, the lighting of a cigarette by a television actress or actor has become a cue to viewers that the character in question is evil and reckless. Alternatively, smoking a cigarette may point to a character's attempt to conceal nervousness or deception after committing a wrongful act. Smoking cigarettes signifies a flawed character because the smoker places little value on human life, establishing easy alliances, for example, between one who smokes cigarettes and one who murders or connives to take advantage of others.

In the final analysis, the smoker is responsible for the development of lung cancer, heart malfunctions, decreased effectiveness in the immune system, and numerous other health problems associated with cigarettes. The smoker, rather than the medical profession or other forms of cultural and political decadence, is held accountable for disease because, in the face of verified evidence for the dangers of cigarettes, she or he continues to smoke. A smoker *chooses* disease by refusing or being unable to quit. An inability to quit smoking, although cigarettes are recognized as a physical addiction, has come to be associated culturally with insufficient levels of willpower. Moreover, as cancer research progresses, other dimensions of the smoker's existence are linked to cigarettes; for example, recent evidence showing that smokers have poor dietary habits, making an indictment of the individual easier and more compelling. As the smoker is imbued with increasingly unhealthy and unappealing *voluntary* behaviors, she or he provides evidence to the whole of culture for pervasive character flaws.

Many parallels can be drawn between cancer and obesity as diseases within culture. The medical profession has had relatively dismal success in the treatment and cure of both diseases. Though cancer researchers today have certainly accumulated considerable knowledge pertaining to causes, contributing factors, and intervention techniques, cancer is still considered a fatal disease in countless instances. That members of society become filled with dread and sadness upon learning that a friend or family member has been diagnosed with cancer speaks to the frequency with which prognoses do not offer hopes of survival. Similarly, obesity is often considered fatal due to decreased heart functioning, among other health problems, and also as a disease that has frustrated medical attempts at treatment. Although the responses of friends and family to obesity may not be based in the inevitability of death, the eating habits of overweight individuals, like the habit of smoking, is viewed socially as a contributor to eventual physical demise. To continue smoking or overeating in the face of major health complications demonstrates foolishness on the part of an individual.

Obesity, like cancer, is comprehended culturally and medically by pointing to individual disposition and lifestyle, instead of pointing to the limitations of medical power. Shephard and Shephard (1985), for example, report that obesity in women is caused typically by psychological factors and ineffective weight loss methods, producing in women "an intensive negative sense of their own worth or [women] may feel hopelessly out of control in managing their weight" (p. 382). As representatives of the medical community, Shephard and Shephard conclude, "Although hypothyroidism (low thyroid) or other hormonal conditions occasionally account for obesity, most people gain weight simply because they take in more calories than they use up" (p. 382). Excessive weight loss, as epitomized in the predominantly female disease of *anorexia nervosa*, according to Shephard and Shephard, is also caused by individual rather than medical problems: "more often sudden weight loss results from a change in eating habits that, in turn, results from nervousness, anxiety, or depression" (p. 382). I mention weight *loss* because, in the space of one page, Shephard and Shephard excuse the medical community and a culture that makes absurd demands on women's bodies for a failure to find solutions to the problem of life-engendering body weight. Regardless of physical symptoms, an inappropriate body weight is found to be indicative of low self-worth, a lack of control, nervousness, anxiety, or depression. Personal qualities, not medical inadequacies, hold the individual within the confines of illness.

Sontag (1978) offers a compelling analysis of the role played by willpower in the diagnosis and treatment of disease, which holds particular relevance for the disease of obesity. Historically, there exists a connection between insufficient knowledge within the medical community and an attribution of causality to the individual. She writes, "Theories that diseases are caused by mental states and can be cured by willpower are always an index of how much is not understood about the physical terrain of the disease" (p. 54). The "expansion" of a particular illness, moving from medical communities to cultural practices and cementing the individual's responsibility for disease, takes place through the operation of two seemingly contradictory hypotheses. First, Sontag explains, "every form of social deviation can be considered an illness" (p. 55). For example, persons who steal the property of others unwittingly, which is a negatively sanctioned act, are suffering from the "disease" of kleptomania. As one who is under the spell of disease, the kleptomaniac cannot be held entirely accountable for acts of thievery; rather, she or he must be diagnosed and treated so that "health" can be reinstated. Health is indicated by a demonstration of socially acceptable behavior—an end to the practice of theft. Similarly, the body of an obese woman violates socially acceptable conventions pertaining to appearance; thus the patient signifies health—an erasure of disease— through a reduction in body size.

A correlation between disease and social norms is corroborated, Sontag argues, by a second hypotheses, which states, "every illness can be considered psychologically" (p. 55). Here, "people are encouraged to believe that they get sick because they (unconsciously) want to, and that they can cure themselves by the mobilization of the will" (Sontag, p. 55). The kleptomaniac, then, can be said to exhibit *psychological* rather than medical problems; there is an unconscious desire to steal, which only the individual can cure. Similarly, the obese individual is often viewed as one whose subconscious desires and impulses prevent weight reduction. Here, the individual is not only burdened with the label of "illness," implying sickness and malfunction, but is considered the cause of the disease for unclear reasons, lurking in the dark underside of conscious thought. Personal responsibility is alleviated and reinstated simultaneously. In combination, the two hypotheses function to complement one another, Sontag writes, because, "As the first seems to relieve guilt, the second reinstates it" (p. 55).

Proponents of anti-diets, within larger socio-political systems of "health," both embrace and condemn the notion of individual malady when discussing weight loss. Countless psychological theories are used as explanatory devices and as inroads to treating obesity, as cures for the deviance signified by the overweight body. Bruno's (1972) book, *Think Yourself Thin: How Psychology Can Help You Lose Weight,* epitomizes a genre of weight loss methods that are based in psychological principles. Many psychologists distinguish themselves from physicians in the treatment of obesity because the latter are seen only to treat physical manifestations of disease, while the former treat underlying psychological causes. While psychologists are often critical of the medical community's failure to consider the complexity of obesity, they corroborate medical principles by placing ultimate responsibility on the individual for the *existence* of disease. LeShan (1981), a family counselor and author of *Winning the Losing Battle: Why I Will Never be Fat Again,* highlights personal malady in the condition of obesity, stating, "No permanent weight loss can take place until there has been a profound change in one's attitudes and feelings about oneself" (p. 2). In LeShan's book, the patient initially "escapes" responsibility because her problem is not understood by the medical community. Yet, over-weight individuals must assume responsibility for illness since it is contained within them. If a dieter refuses treatment, whether medical of psychological, she invites a continuation of illness, and a continuation of deviance.

A combination of social deviance and individual impairments pervade the philosophy of the anti-diet, aligning anti-diets with highly traditional portraits of obesity as disease and perceptions of health within culture. The same double-edged sense of responsibility and resulting guilt is present in conservative *and* seemingly rebellious approaches to excess weight. When Fonda (1981) absolves women of blame for body abuse by pointing to oppressive beauty standards, and encourages individual control over the body through diet and exercise, she speaks a familiar irony. In the first section of *Workout,* women are told to resist cultural demands for thinness; in the second section, women are taught how to become fit and slender. Readers are led into the deep recesses of Fonda's life, which traces a history of deviance-illness. Today, Fonda's body is lauded socially—no longer diseased—because *she* took action to heal herself, rather than relying on so-called "experts." Fonda is an archetypal proponent of anti-diets due to the power she bestows on, and takes away from, the individual to control life circumstances.

A cultural and clinical propensity to demand of obese women evidence for self-control and a relinquishing of self-control is demonstrated effectively in the workings of an organization known as *Overeaters Anonymous* (OA). The group presents an intriguing analytic case because, patterned on the principles of *Alcoholics Anonymous,* it exists as a community of "diseased" individuals, predominantly women, who assist one another in overcoming addiction. Resocialization, from deviant to healthy (socially acceptable) eating habits, transpires through repeated acknowledgment of each individual's disease. Millman (1981) argues that OA represents an "increasingly popular view" of obesity wherein "obesity indicates deep psychological disturbances, that its cause and cure rest with the individual" (p. 29). Compulsive eating, seen as *chosen* behavior, can only be normalized through an acknowledgment of psychological disturbances. Rather than blaming forces outside themselves for obesity, OA members are "made to recognize that their suffering and shame have been created by their own compulsive eating" (Millman, p. 29). A realization of responsibility is concomitant with an awareness that the individual must cure herself; her membership in OA indicates a willingness to resolve her compulsiveness.

The curative powers of OA members are called into question by several factors. Because compulsive eating is not adequately understood by the one who is ill, the individual must relinquish control overtly, admitting powerlessness. Millman's (1981) analysis reveals a crucial principle in OA: "What is important is that the member surrenders her 'will' to a force beyond or larger than herself and acknowledges that she is not in control" (p. 33). A relinquishing of individual power is underscored in the ever-present "support" networks among OA members, which helps to police the actions of each member. Implicitly, the presence of support announces that the individual cannot, in fact, be relied upon to engage in self-cure. The support rituals characteristic of OA speak to an *absence* of individual power. For example, as Millman (1981) points out, a "new member, sometimes called a 'baby,' is asked to write down her daily eating plan and report it by telephone every morning to her group sponsor" (p. 31). An overriding premise in OA, then, is that individual members are both responsible for their disease and its cure, *and* that they are powerless to cure the problem of compulsive eating individually.

In many respects, OA practices consolidate to form a demonstration of the logic in contemporary weight loss discourse. Abnormal eating habits are contained within the individual. There exists hope and hopelessness regarding the prospect of permanent resolution. As women, members continue to be "sick" no matter what they do to correct the problem of compulsive eating. As in the case of Alcoholics Anonymous, members must continue to view themselves as diseased in order to become disease free. The repetition of going back to the group for further reinforcement is akin to the behavior of purchasing each and every new diet book, hoping to find a resolution, but sensing the impossibility of resolution. Members of OA, like other dieters, embrace cultural and clinical definitions of dietary acceptability and help to socialize and police other members so that they abide by such definitions. In addition, OA introduces a crucial component of dieting discourse—a demand on the individual for a recounting and recording of personal transgressions. As one who is diseased physically *and* morally, the obese woman is obliged culturally to "admit" to her sins and abnormalities. A continuous confession of wrongdoing, a meticulous and judgmental survey of behavior, grounds dieting behavior, and ultimately, preserves the disease of obesity.

# Chapter 2

## The Aesthetics of Women's Health: "Watching Yourself Until You're Sixty-Five"

*You have to watch yourself for your whole life if you want to stay healthy, I mean, if you want to be considered attractive. But sometimes that's not enough.*

*Sonja*

The self-scrutiny endemic to weight loss efforts is grounded in cultural conceptions of disease and its treatment. A personal goal of overall health, mandating lifelong changes in behaviors and thoughts, requires *ongoing* self-assessment, a stance of continual guardedness for the prevention of a consuming and degrading illness. Each new diet or product, promising freedom from self-scrutiny, works to cement an unending monitoring of the body. A dieter internalizes the prescriptions of particular weight loss formulas and the cultural structures that hold them in place. In this process she is divided against herself, placed in the role of "healer" with respect to her own body, made guardian of her own actions.

Existing as an onlooker to one's body is strongly tied to female socialization, wherein personal value and "health" are reflected in outward appearance. From earliest childhood, Nancy Henley (1977) has shown, women are encouraged to become adept at presenting the body to others for evaluation. Freshly polished shoes, ruffled dresses, ribbons and bows, intricately braided hair, and ladylike posturing, all work to elicit favorable attention from others. Onlookers take pleasure in the female child who, through body presentation, exhibits her finesse in understanding how others wish to see her. Male children, conversely, are praised if they pay little attention to physical appearance, and by implication, little concern for the pleasure of another's gaze. Presenting a male image of action—torn blue jeans, grass stained shirts, elbow scrapes, missing teeth, unkept hair—indicates that boys do not exist for the gazes of others. Rather, boys are given cultural license to gaze upon others. The societal approval resulting from an acceptable feminine or masculine appearance arises not only from the pleasure taken in looking at a pretty girl or an action-ready boy, but in the implicit messages contained in their overall comportment: she receives the gazes of others; he gazes upon others.

The dichotomy between one who gazes and one who is gazed upon is not paralleled solely with female/male gender positions. A woman's demonstration of skill in presenting an aesthetically pleasing body is accomplished within culture by training the female gaze to look inward, to become adept at gazing evaluatively on her body. Women learn the art of self-objectification for purposes of presumably impartial self-assessment. A primary component in female socialization, then, requires teaching women to make "objects" or spectacles of themselves. In learning to prepare herself for the active gazes of others, a woman becomes adept at seeing herself as others see her; she sees herself *as* an other. Accomplishing a position of transcendence with respect to the body entails division within the body, a dichotomy between spectator and spectacle, active seer and passive object. ⎯⎯

As a spectator with respect to her own body, a woman comes to evaluate herself *as spectacle*. John Berger (1972) writes, "A woman must continually watch herself. She is almost continually accompanied by her own image of herself . . . And so she comes to consider the *surveyor* and the *surveyed* within her as two constituent yet always distinct elements of her identity as a woman" (p. 46). Through no small amount of labor, women within dominant culture are given the task of watching themselves from a position that is both inside and outside the body. Because spectator and spectacle are within the body of woman, she appears to herself as an other who provides and receives external evaluations.

As spectacles, women spectators are obliged to present socially acceptable images of femininity to others. Appropriate body weight, as determined by clinical discourses, represents but one element in a normative system that combines feminine appearance, health, and behavior. Elements in the system overlap and reinforce one another to accomplish two goals. First, women expend substantial amounts of money on the "upkeep" of appearance/health, thereby helping to preserve capitalist economic structures. The female body is a commodity, a product, and requires the purchase of endless products to retain its value. Second, women assist in the strengthening of feminine imagery within culture by displaying, in a most *visible* fashion, continuous readiness for the gazes of others. For example, many authors of diet books point out that weight loss/health will "enable" the purchase of new and more fashionable clothing, improved attention to hair and make-up, reflecting a desire to be noticed by others.[1] Here, economic interests and visions of traditional femininity are perpetuated conjointly.

Women are socialized to view the ongoing surveillance of their bodies as a form of empowerment that arises from self-love. The newly slender woman purchases a new wardrobe, presumably, because she *likes herself* now that she is thin; when fat, she did not like herself and consequently did not give adequate attention to appearance. Significantly, an absence of self-love removes women from active participation in consumerism. Moreover, when fat, women are both marginalized and powerless, unable to receive admiration from self and others. A closer approximation to feminine imagery within culture points to greater appreciation for oneself, active consumerism, in turn indicating greater "health." Brownmiller (1984) addresses the ideological underpinnings of the link between femininity and self-love in stating, "To be insufficiently feminine is viewed as a failure in core sexual identity, or as a failure to care sufficiently about oneself. . ." (p. 15). When a woman's sexual attractiveness is clearly marked on the body, she exhibits health and self-love.

Love for oneself is written on the body as objectification so that, within dominant images of femininity, a woman who objectifies herself exhibits high degrees of individuality. She has taken charge, she has seen through the manipulation of society; her body points to a *singular* person. In addition, the distinctive woman has learned to control her body, rather than being usurped by cultural whims, bodily propensities, or desires. Her gazing powers set her apart from the masses of other women who follow the dictates of physiology and society, women devoid of individual strength. Self-love, within the rhetoric of femininity, is impossible for unattractive women not because unsightly physical features prohibit acceptance, but because they have failed to take control. They have not freed themselves from the majority of weak-willed, impressionable women who allow themselves to be controlled by others.

On a daily basis, women *live* the irony of femininity and health in exchange for false freedom. An important step in exposing the ideological dimensions of femininity involves listening carefully to the voices of women as they speak about the labor of tending to their bodies. Often, when women speak of beauty formulas or diets, their words are discounted androcentrically as mere trivia or attributed to narcissistic tendencies in women. However, I argue that the ease with which women's "body talk" is dismissed demonstrates yet another dimension of discourses wherein the goals of the dominant are preserved. If women are given a careful hearing, the paradoxes and discursive discontinuities in which they are trapped become quite visible. A combination of reverence for women's bodies and a condemnation of women's bodily concerns forms an experiential contradiction that works on behalf of dominant ideology.

The discourse of women's "health," as taken up by promoters of female slenderness and everyday women, represents a paradigm for the operations of power that govern women's bodies. In this discourse is contained training in body objectification, procedures designed to draw approving gazes from others, promises of body liberation that in fact speak to powerlessness, and a equation of health and culturally defined attractiveness.

I wish to examine in considerable detail three ideological facets of dieting discourse. I address them by turning to the voices of women who have lived the entrapment of feminine "health." First, women are bombarded with cultural imagery in which attractiveness is incorporated into an overall aesthetics of women's health. Although a concern with health is presented culturally as liberation from appearance constraints, women describe an opposite effect: health as the standard for attractiveness *heightens* a concern with outward appearance and mandates increased discipline. The activity of the internal spectator is expanded to include innumerable dimensions of body appearance. The politics of this conflict, secondly, are placed within a larger disciplinary framework. In particular, the bodies of women are supplanted with cultural gazes, working on behalf of prevailing ideology to police and monitor the actions of female bodies. Finally, cultural gazes are shown to be grounded in an equation between feminine sexuality and disease. Given the linkages between women and disease, the notion of female health is revealed as a paradox. In combination, an aesthetics of women's health and an internalization of critical gazes transforms women into evidence for an *absence* of female health, giving credence to the normalization efforts sustained by dominant culture.

### The Aesthetics of Women's Health

The illness represented by an overweight and unhealthy female body requires a merging of curative measures and disciplinary action. When a body shows a willingness to regulate actions, to resist temptation, the body is associated with an overall state of health. For example, as women report, thinness is less important in contemporary society than is being healthy: "It used to be that you had to be real skinny, but now health is more important;" "You have to look healthy—tanned and toned, not just thin anymore." At the same time, "health" is often manifested through a body devoid of excess flesh, which, in turn, testifies to discipline. Further, a demonstration of health requires attention to multiple dimensions of the body, unlike thinness, which has been traditionally demonstrated by low body weight. An aesthetics of health not only requires slenderness, then, but appropriate skin coloring, muscle conditioning, facial structure, and an absence of facial lines or "defective" features. Health, in Sonja's terms, "covers a lot more ground than just being skinny if you're talking about women's bodies."

An expansion of female body "problems" arises in the discourse of health, and is reflected in women's descriptions of the ideal female body in American culture. In turn, increased problems call for greater discipline or guardedness.

Although a shift to health concerns appears to alleviate a preoccupation with aesthetic deficiencies and promote greater tolerance for diversity in appearance, women observe, often implicitly, a focus on health mandates even greater restrictions on female bodies. Barbara's discussion of the ideal body, for example, is connected to a release from rigid standards; yet, her language choices and her "list" of requisites for attractiveness imply that women's "health" involves numerous restrictions.

> I guess there isn't one particular standard for attractiveness because there just doesn't have to be *one* anymore. I would say looking healthy is very important. [What do you mean?] Well, she dresses well. You don't have to be dressed very stylish; well, actually you do. You have to have a style about the way you appear. Your hair, your face, your clothes. You have to look healthy, and in looking healthy you can't be pale, you can't look tired, you can't look fat, you can't look flabby.

Barbara's description of female health, as viewed within society, is filled with imperatives centered on outward physical appearance. Simultaneously, she, like many women, defines health by identifying aesthetic concerns.

The domain of women's health/beauty also includes behavioral and attitudinal facets of female existence, extending further the list of societal prescriptions at work to expand links between women and illness. Laurie articulates the behavioral dimensions of feminine health: "You have to be healthy overall. There is the woman who is always fit, she has lots of time to do everything, she is really organized, she can budget her time." Exhibiting competence and attractiveness often points to admirable personality characteristics or "healthy attitudes" on the part of women. Many women, for example, connect health and beauty to high self-esteem, self-confidence, assertiveness, and sociability. As Marian observes, "a healthy woman has a good outlook on life [because] she shows other people that she values herself, she asserts herself, and that comes through in her looks."

In line with behavioral correlates of female health, many women point to an association between attractiveness and power. Healthy women achieve greater degrees of power than unhealthy women *because* the former engage in acceptable behaviors within the structures of dominant ideology: "If we do what we are told, we are recognized;" "Looking good gets your foot in the door because that's how people want to see women;" "Wearing a dress and high heels doesn't make me any more capable, but people make those connections in society." The power accrued to women who behave in socially acceptable ways combines conformity to general social values, for example, striving to be the top person in an organization, and conformity to standards for feminine appearance. To illustrate, Ellen observes a connection between physical attractiveness and power within hierarchically organized institutions and practices.

If you look at who is in power positions, who is high up in the administration both for women and girls, that is, who is head of the senate, who is head of the sorority, who is on the cheerleading squad, who has the administrative positions in terms of women, you do not see many women here that weigh two hundred pounds or who don't dress in a sophisticated way. You do not see many women or girls who are overweight, or who look like their hair isn't washed, or who have skin problems, or who don't dress in a sophisticated manner. You don't see those people in high up positions in the environment.

Achieving power, women suggest, is dependent on a combination of healthy behavior and a healthy appearance. In Ellen's description, the attractive women discussed are in "top" positions with hierarchical structures. Through a blending of beauty and power as traditionally defined, the women described reflect an acceptance of the values associated with hierarchy, competition, monetary success and power.

The difficulty of achieving power through physical, behavioral, and value criteria for women's health is further complicated by cultural depictions of female aging. Within culture at large, age is a factor in judgments of competence. For women, however, the component of age is particularly pronounced because beauty is generally associated with youth (Brownmiller, 1984, p. 131). In contemporary culture, the dynamics of female aging have become remarkably insidious as aging women are emerging as a newly appreciated social group. Regularly, contemporary mass media present "over forty" women who are considered beautiful and sexually appealing. Yet, the attractive older woman is news precisely because she is unlike most women, who are assumed culturally to become less attractive with age. Women over forty are recognized not because dominant culture has come to value female lines and full hips, but because the attractive older women who are held up to women as models do not *look* their age. They have taken remarkable steps to *prevent* physical signs of age. In reality, the appreciation for older women masks demands on women to regulate and restrict their bodies well beyond "youth." Lee suggests, for instance, that an appreciation for older women is connected to an aesthetics of health, producing an ongoing concern with physical attractiveness, "I think that being well fit and healthy is important now—working out, exercising, keeping in shape, and being toned until you're sixty-five."

Women express extraordinary ambivalence when speaking about the purported freedom implied by advanced age and cultural attractiveness. Although many women view icons such as Jane Fonda in hopeful terms, suggesting that women over forty can be considered attractive, they also fear the ongoing attention to appearance implied by an "appreciation" for older women. Although some women look forward to middle age *because* it allows less attention to appearance, others sense a demand for continuous body monitoring. Marian wonders, for example, "When will it end? I mean, you can just go on forever trying to be healthy, to be fit and in shape, because you see all these women in society who can do it." The demand for a perpetually youthful body, which utterly opposes the realities of human physiology, intensifies women's bodily concerns because the feminine "ideal" is modeled after an inexperienced, pre-sexual adolescent girl. Rosalind Coward (1985) argues that the "eulogies over Jane Fonda's body" are grounded in a cultural appreciation for unceasing female youthfulness; in Jane Fonda women are shown "a woman of nearly fifty with the fantastic body of a teenager" (p. 41).

A cultural demand for women's perpetual youth manifests itself in numerous dimensions of female appearance. An abundance of products and medical procedures are available to prevent signs of women's age on every conceivable part of the body. As cosmetic surgeon Paula Moynahan (1988) observes, in 1984 approximately five hundred thousand cosmetic surgeries were performed in the United States, and up to the present day, seventy-five percent of all consumers in the field of plastic surgery are female (pp. xii–3). Moreover, forty-three percent of all procedures are performed on women who are thirty-five years of age or younger (p. 3). Notably, each consumer good or service that offers youthfulness also promises enhanced self-worth *and* a capacity to break free from rigid beauty ideals. Moynahan (1988) combines youthfulness, self-worth, and individual freedom in describing the benefits of cosmetic surgery for women:

> Because so much of a woman's sexual identity is tied to her appearance, a marked defect or the inevitable lessening of youthful beauty caused by aging has special significance for the female psyche . . . cosmetic surgery has enabled many women to face the world more confidently by correcting defects that have made them self-conscious and by softening the harsh effects of aging. It allows you to be the best you can be for as long as you possibly can, to come as close as you can to your own beauty ideal (p. xiii).

Along with other promoters of women's "health," Moynahan offers a correction of physical "defects," leading to increased youthfulness and individuality. Concomitantly, Moynahan's description presents aging in the language of decline, slippage, harshness, decreased self-confidence, and increased self-consciousness. Readers of her book learn about the "secrets" of cosmetic surgery so that they, like millions of other women, can reconstruct an individual ideal, repairing the damage done by simply having lived.

Women express less optimism than Moynahan when discussing the implications of anti-aging cosmetic procedures. In part, women agree, taking steps to alleviate signs of age is important for women: "If you can afford to have surgery, then you ought to because you are at an advantage if you look good;" "Having something done to your body, like correcting a bulge or bump, can make you feel better about yourself;" "Having a face-lift or something like that can be good because it makes you look healthier and younger." At the same time, women are troubled by the underlying prescriptions suggested by what Margaret describes as "cosmetic surgery gone wild." Plastic surgery comprises part of an overall domain of femininity characterized by countless and visible signifiers of feminine "health." Sonja elaborates:

> It used to be that you could be thin and you were considered attractive. Now you have to also be in shape and you can't look the least bit old, even if you're fifty. You have to buy all kinds of things to stop the aging process, for your skin, your eyes, your nose, your ears, your thighs, you name it. And if none of that works, you go to your local plastic surgeon and he chops a bit off here and a bit off there. It really scares me.

Indeed, as Sonja observes, the so-called age of women's health and individuality, lauded by Moynahan, is "scary" when viewed as further entrapment in cultural discourses in which attention to overall outward appearance is both extended and intensified. The liberation promised by a reconstruction of youth, in effect, demands of all women confinement in a permanent state of adolescence.

An overall image of health, as women have already indicated, requires substantial attention to fashion in addition to body shape and conditioning, facial features, and valued personality characteristics. As Brownmiller (1984) notes, attention to dress has always been a critical element in the domain of feminine appearance, and has been characterized by restriction (pp. 77-102). Within the logic of fashion, though, a "healthy" woman is able to rise above the constraints of fashion, controlling her own body presentation. She is confident in her own value, not allowing a particular trend or designer to dictate her individual style. As in the parallel case of anti-diets, fashion promoters argue *against* conformity. Janet Wallach (1988), author of *Looks that Work*, announces, "The rules of fashion have disappeared. There are no longer the 'right' hemlines or hairstyles dictated by designers. Fashion is a free-for-all" (p. 16). Additionally, Wallach notes, "All too often we feel controlled by our clothes rather than the other way around" (p. 17). The contemporary woman displays health by taking a stance of resistance to prevailing fashion ideals; she "takes control" of her wardrobe and her self-presentation.

The current emphasis on health sometimes frees women from the constraints of fashions, such as corsets and push-up bras. Young women, in particular, are inclined to express some agreement with Wallach (1988): "I don't think it matters anymore what girls wear;" "I don't think you have to dress in one way to be acceptable in our society;" "Sure I might read about the newest Halston or whoever, but I think it's important to have your own style—it shouldn't be handed down from someone else." However, women are not convinced, generally, that resistance to the world of fashion, as depicted in a cultural aesthetics of women's health, is either possible or liberating. Rita notes, for instance, that the clothes indicative of health are often "necessary" and costly: "Clothes really seem to be a necessary part of this health business; the jogging outfits, the short skirts, the skimpy tops—they all say you're in shape, that you're healthy. It costs a lot of money to buy all those things." In addition to the expense of health fashions, women imply, a so-called liberation from fashion standards has little to do with their everyday experience: "My monthly credit card bills do not tell me that women don't have to worry about fashion anymore;" "You can see women who dress in a rebellious way, as if they don't have anyone to worry about but themselves, but most of us can't do that;" "Everyone keeps saying it doesn't matter anymore what women wear, but if that's true, why do I worry about it now more than ever?"

Fashion conformity in the lives of women is a complicated issue, because although women speak of a release from constraints in positive terms, the clothing displayed in the world of high fashion is often nonfunctional and restrictive. The images of fashion liberation held up to women, then, are difficult to process; indeed, outlandish attire is presented by fashion designers as nonconformist, but it also announces *heightened* fashion sense. Rita argues, "the models in magazines wear things you wouldn't be caught dead in because you just couldn't move or go anywhere looking like that. This is supposed to be the peak of fashion." The world of fashion is further restrictive insofar as the lives and interests signified by fashion models are elite—being in "the peak of fashion" is an unaffordable luxury for most women. And as Martha suggests, the elitism of fashion is not restricted to clothing, but represents an overall lifestyle:

> The women in magazines are just totally perfect. They don't have any flaws. It's not just that they're wearing something with a designer label, it's that they're also thin, with perfect hair and teeth and faces. They're always doing something exciting and they always have really posh surroundings. They have suntans and they never look old. Their lives are perfect. They're not real.

The "perfect" imagery surrounding fashion liberation points to an "exciting" and "posh" life that is ultimately "not real." In addition, in her general categorization of the women of fashion—"they're always," "they never"—Marsha suggests a low tolerance for deviation from narrowly defined criteria for female attractiveness in the world of fashion.

Coward's (1985) analysis of fashion ideology dispels the mythology of fashion liberation, and speaks more generally to the politics of women's "health." Although fashion freedom appears to acknowledge individuality, Coward argues, "One thing that fashion is quite categorically *not* is an expression of individuality. By definition, fashion implies a mode of dress, or overall style, which is accepted as representing up-to-dateness" (p. 30). A woman who "rises above" current and fleeting trends, as epitomized in the wearing of "timeless" or "classic" styles, is held within culture to exude greater elegance and chic, greater freedom from fashion rules. Her fashion sense is inscribed on her body precisely because she appears to denounce fashion. Thus, Coward observes, "even the fashion-designers whose living is made precisely through the construction of new standards perpetuate this mystique that some clothes and some designs are simply classically elegant, timelessly beautiful" (p. 31). And only the woman who is supremely confident, certain of her value, engages in the anti-fashion game of fashion.

The rhetoric of fashion points to a primary theme in women's descriptions of health. A tight regulation of body boundaries is made synonymous with freedom from regulative mechanisms. And here we have come full circle, back to the strategies of weight loss diets, who purport to free women, to permit an expression of individuality, by appealing to female health. As women have shown, placing women's bodies in the domain of health works to extend the labors of maintaining appearance. Rather than working to reduce one's body weight, a discourse of health requires a monitoring of weight, bulges, muscles, skin tone and texture, "defective" body parts, fashion, attitudes and behavior, to name only a few dimensions of female wellness. Innumerable aspects of women's bodies and women's lives are made both visible and problematic in the discourse of health. A *problematizing* of women's bodies mandates closer gazing and scrutiny, giving legitimacy to ever-greater discipline, to a consuming attention to appearance. In this process, the bodies and behaviors of women are held under a normalizing microscope which masks increasing control with a rhetoric of freedom.

### The Disciplinary Gaze

Control over women's bodies occurs through many institutions and practices. A coalescence of cultural voices works to illuminate the lives of women and to encourage self-correction. And because women's bodies are exposed by multiple sources, an original point of oppression is difficult to identify and to combat. As seen in the previous section, many institutional forces merge to both consolidate and disperse the responsibility for women's bodies. By implication, the unveiling of women's bodies gives legitimacy to ongoing discipline and regulation, to a penetrating cultural gaze. The ideological relations between the gaze and its capacity for normalization can be more fully understood by examining the power dynamics of compulsory visibility.

In his historical analysis of the relations between power and the institutionalization of punishment, Foucault (1979) locates an important shift in
disciplinary procedures which took place during seventeenth century practices. Corporeal forms of punishment, direct physical torture as the means by
which to underscore and make visible the power of government, was gradually
replaced by an "optics" of power. The primary task of power was no longer to
evidence its strength through physical brutality, but to establish, at countless
points and through innumerable mechanisms, the surveillance of all who
existed in its domain. The new mode of power is epitomized, Foucault suggests, in the architectural plans for the panopticon proposed by Jeremy Bentham (p. 200). Designed for use in prisons, the panopticon is a tower resting in
the center of multiple stories of cells arranged in a circular fashion. At the back
and front of each cell is a small window, allowing light to enter and illuminate
each individually housed prisoner. The tower contains windows corresponding
to cellular windows; due to the light entering from the back of each cell, guards
in the tower cannot be seen by prisoners, but inmates are completely visible to
guards. Each prisoner, Foucault writes, "is seen, but he does not see; he is the
object of information, never a subject in communication . . . this invisibility is
the guarantee of order" (p. 200).

The ever-present possibility of being seen, in Bentham's scheme, is precisely the mechanism that prevents disobedience and thereby guarantees order.
The presence of the tower, with its prospect of watchful eyes protected by invisibility, is in itself sufficient, theoretically, to retain complete order within the
prison. In a perfect exercise of power, guards are unnecessary because the
*threat* of their presence, utterly faceless and without form, forbids the luxury of
knowing precisely when one is being watched. The panopticon represents a
form of disciplinary power that is based on a principle of totalizing and
non-reciprocal visibility. Here, Foucault (1979) explains, power

> is exercised through its invisibility; at the same time it imposes on those
> whom it subjects a principle of compulsory visibility. In discipline, it is the
> subjects who have to be seen. Their visibility assures the hold of the power
> that is exercised over them. It is the fact of being constantly seen, of being
> able always to be seen, that maintains the disciplined individual in his subjec-
> tion (p. 187).

An optics of power, then, holds subjects "in a mechanism of objectification"
wherein "disciplinary power manifests its potency, essentially, by arranging
objects" within the space of domination (p. 187).

In contemporary culture, Foucault (1979) writes, the panoptic scheme
can be used whenever "one is dealing with a multiplicity of individuals on
whom a task or a particular form of behavior must be imposed" (p. 205). Power

in the form of surveillance makes a demand on the individual to monitor the actions of the self, subjecting behavior to ever-greater examination, making visible each transgression, and punishing oneself for wrongdoing. Optical power is placed within the body of each person over whom it presides so that the individual "assumes responsibility for the constraints of power; he makes them play spontaneously upon himself; he inscribes in himself the power relation in which he simultaneously plays both roles; he becomes the principle of his own subjection" (pp. 202–203). In the final analysis, the body of each person is governed not by a visible and openly repressive power source, but by those individuals who have become wholly exposed to the inspecting gaze of power.

Panoptic logic holds relevance for an analysis of female body aesthetics/ health. Women's bodies are desired for visual impact. Coward (1985) points out that while culture and history are "saturated with images of women's bodies and representations of women's sexuality," men's bodies "are characterized by the experience of strangeness, by a powerful sense of the unknown" (p. 227). A glorification of women as the "aesthetic" sex works insidiously to preserve the invisibility of men's bodies. Women are deserving of the gazes of others within this glorification because women's bodies are constructed as being more pleasing to the eye. As recipients of gazes which are housed in masculine images of women, the bodies of women become wholly visible and open to inspection in a manner extending far beyond the gaze of a particular male. The whole of culture watches women as a testament to feminine beauty, to the "inherently" aesthetic character of women's bodies. Coward explains that men's bodies, aligned with the controlling gaze, are not subjected to reciprocal scrutiny.

> Men's bodies and sexuality are taken for granted, exempted from scrutiny, whereas women's bodies are extensively defined and overexposed. Sexual and social meanings are imposed on *women's* bodies, not men's. Controlling the look, men have left themselves out of the picture because a body defined is a body controlled (p. 229).

As Coward suggests, the *invisibility* of men's bodies is needed for the control of women's bodies. Confined in a representational space characterized by compulsory visibility, women can be seen, watched, and judged within the boundaries of dominant ideology.

Cultural concerns with women's "health" provide a vivid demonstration of a non-reciprocal optics of power. Not only must women understand how they are viewed by others, but they must present their bodies in a manner that is consistent with the elaborate images of invisible tower guards. In order to be deemed "healthy," women are required to provide evidence for an internalization of panoptic logic; the eyes in the tower are supplanted in women. In

Foucaultian terms, a woman must identify herself as the principle of her own subjection, playing the roles of tower guard and prisoner simultaneously. She is spectator and spectacle, one who sees and is seen, because panopticism guarantees anonymity to institutional mechanisms. The act of policing the body is needed for freedom or a "release" from prison walls. The "healthy" woman, like the recently paroled convict, can roam freely once she has demonstrated a willingness to submit fully to the normalizing gaze of power.

Panoptic logic extends into numerous components of health aesthetics. The possibility of being seen and found deviant is ever-present, but locating the precise sources of evaluative vision is accomplished with tremendous difficulty. Women speak generally about cultural images which invade the body and work to produce negative body-consciousness. These images are not clearly defined and are not locatable within a single source; nor are they fully present or absent at specific points in time. They emanate from within and without the individual. Anita states, "All these body things can catch you off-guard." Women locate many persons, institutions and practices within culture at work to "oversee" the bodies of women, and encourage women to sense deficiencies.

An identification of specific or originary sources of evaluative gazing is further compounded by the constructed images of women presented within culture. Because beautiful women are given high visibility and are "made up," women report, the average woman compares herself to an illusion, never quite knowing, in Marian's terms, "what's underneath all the make-up and clothes." At the same time, made-up women are aligned with the "natural." Fabricated imagery, mistaken for the natural, complicates an identification of "real" women and a location of practices or institutions that give rise to illusory images. In Laurie's description of cultural standards for appearance, a pervasive yet "scattered" gaze is highlighted as she chains together many seemingly diverse images of women's bodies. Simultaneously, she calls into question the reality represented by the images described and concludes, "You just never know what you're really dealing with":

> It's funny because all the models have the natural look, the Christie Brinkley look. You know they have make-up on but it looks natural. It doesn't really make any sense. I guess we also get images of ourselves through movies and television, like in soap operas, where the characters always have their traumatic problems that keep the show going. Then, at the end of the show they list a lot of stores, so you can buy the clothes the characters wear. These people aren't real. Even their problems are made up, but they sort of set standards for us. It's as if they can manage their jobs and be home by 3:30, and their kids are home, and then I think, this doesn't make any sense because people work nine-to-five. It doesn't make any sense if you think about it. You just never know what you're really dealing with, or who thinks up this stuff.

Each time Laurie locates a source, she calls into question its validity by pointing to the illusory or contradictory character of the images presented to women.
Ultimately, the overseers of women's bodies retain invisibility, as suggested by
Laurie's assertion that one never knows "who thinks up this stuff." Marian also
addresses the pervasive and diffused character of feminine imagery, "It's just
everywhere, this stuff about women's beauty and fashion and make-up. You go
into the Seven Eleven at three o'clock in the morning to buy a pack of cigarettes
and there's Paulina, or whatever her name is, staring you in the face." Confrontation with a face indicative of acceptability, even if blatantly constructed for
effect, jars in women a sense of watchfulness, of judgment.

The diffused character of cultural surveillance is foregrounded when
women elaborate instances in which they experience a sudden and negative
awareness of the body. The experience is characterized by an abrupt shift in a
woman's relationship to her body. Prior to the shift, the body is not "thought
about" as something external to the person; after the shift, Lucy explains,
"you've got a big invisible bully who's picking on you and telling you you're an
ugly slob." Although some women describe the shift by identifying people or
situations, many struggle to locate clearly defined sources: "It's just something in me that snaps. I can be walking down the street just fine, and all of a
sudden I hate my body;" "Shopping can definitely do it because all these sales-
clerks check you out. But it's more than that. I can't really explain it;" "if I buy,
say, a *Vogue* and compare myself to those women, then go out feeling horrible
about my body, that's a kind of change in how I relate to my body. I don't know,
though, because there are a lot of other things going on."

An onset of negative body judgment, resulting from unclear causes, often
serves as the motivation to "shape up" or "do something" about the body.
Specifically, if the body is "improved," the judgmental gaze, covering many
aspects of women's lives, is diminished both in frequency and intensity. Indeed,
a central promise in weight loss discourse is ease in moving through the world,
an absence of negative evaluations by self and others. Frequently, women
describe body reduction as a means by which to undergo public scrutiny without fear of reprisals or self-condemnation. In discussing her desire to lose
weight before participating in a public performance, "where a lot of eyes will be
on me," Joan, a dance student, makes a clear connection between weight
reduction and an avoidance of public condemnation.

> In the classes I'm taking, I'm really self-conscious of my body because then
> I'm in a performance situation. We learn dances and routines, and my body is
> too heavy to execute the movements well. I can execute the movements, but
> my body pulls me down. I get tired and out of breath. I get really depressed
> about it. I mean, it *really* depresses me because I know people will see me and
> judge me. They will see me in public, and I don't want to feel like a cow. That's

why I've been trying really hard to diet lately. If I can just lose about twenty pounds I wouldn't feel so depressed because then I won't be judged in such an unflattering way, and I'll be able to feel better about myself. I just don't want to have to think about how I look in a performance situation because it throws everything off.

For Joan, a weight loss of twenty pounds will alleviate depression and negative body consciousness because she "won't be judged in such an unflattering way." Through weight reduction, *she* will feel better about being seen and judged by others.

As Joan illustrates, women often sense the presence of gazes and offer evidence for an internalization of panoptic logic. Through internalization, a woman becomes the source of her own restriction. Like the imprisoned convict, prior actions have led to a present monitoring of the body. In women's descriptions thus far it is clear that women relate body deviance to deficiencies in themselves. Joan, for instance, describes *herself* as a "cow" when she is overweight by social standards, which heightens her desire to take corrective action. Power mechanisms require women to be aesthetically pleasing, but are insured total invisibility once "defective" women have learned to act upon their own deficiencies, to see themselves as they are seen through the eyes of the collective and normalizing panoptic practices within culture.

A powerful undercurrent in weight loss discourse centers precisely on the element of illusory free choice, on a self-recognition of deficiency. Volition is exploited in panopticism because nonreciprocal visibility highlights the lives of prisoners; guards are impartial in exercising legal dictates. As a criminal decides to reform, dieting represents a "choice" to take disciplinary action against a deviant/unhealthy body. In fact, if a woman decides to diet for the sake of others—a husband or lover, for example—she is likely to fail in her efforts because she is said by "experts" to have no choice in the matter. Sonja explains: "You can't lose weight for someone else. I went out with a guy once who just watched every bite I took and that drove me nuts. It just made me eat more when he wasn't around. You have to do it for yourself and yourself only, or it'll never work." Unless the gaze of women's health is fully internalized, a woman is likely to transgress ("It just made me eat more when he wasn't around"), leading to failure in producing permanent health.

Many women reiterate the importance of reducing the body for the sake of self-improvement, not for the goal of pleasing others. Another link to the incarcerated individual materializes with the realization that others are often viewed as negative influences in the lives of criminals—as in a "bad crowd." That women reproduce their own oppression as self-improvement, in itself, points to an internalization of a political discourse in which outward appearance is combined with overall well-being. Joan points to the rationale of self-improvement with the implicit message in cultural images of women's bodies:

"Be the best person you can be. Be all that you can be."[2] Being "the best person you can be" comes into conflict with influence or manipulation by others. Lucy notes, for example, "You can't really make a change in the way you look if you're doing it for someone else. That has to come from inside. People can be very manipulative, but you have to kind of throw that off if you really want to improve yourself." Concomitant with coercive attempts to alter the body, Lucy suggests, is an acceptance of an other's or society's standards for appearance, which must be rejected or "thrown off" if one is to succeed in a reformation of the body characterized by self-improvement and freedom.

Self-improvement is dependent on a gaze which is at once critical and realistic: "You've got to see your body for what it is;" "liking yourself means stepping back, a lot of the time, and taking a good look at yourself;" "You have to break away from the models and magazines and work on accepting who you are." Seeing oneself clearly, apart from external images, permits impartial gazing and permanent body alterations. Paula's description evidences the two roles of the disciplined subject, one who sees and whom is seen, combined with choice: "You can't let other people's pictures of how you should be influence you. You have to see those things for yourself, and only when that happens can you change. You have to just stand back and form your own impressions."

When women underscore the necessity of objective body and self-assessment, the body is placed at a distance, evaluated as spectacle by the spectator/judge/woman. In a lengthy description of her first experience away from home and familiar friends, Monica posits the necessity of a self-directed gaze, in her words, to "get a handle on what I was going through" in the midst of a difficult transition. She indicates, as do many women, that body control or well being is dependent on personal objectivity.

> I moved away from home and out of state when I first graduated from high school. That was a lot for a young girl to bear. Nothing was familiar to me; the way these people lived seemed so different. I started to feel really fat and ugly. I didn't have any friends and, of course, I attributed that to my body. But I don't know what made me feel that way. There was just such a consciousness about it or something, everywhere I went. I felt like everyone was looking at me and that made me think there must be something really wrong with me. I can't tell you how awful it really was. I finally decided I had to do something to make this situation better or I just might do something drastic. I decided I had to see myself realistically, and I was overweight. I went on a diet and really watched everything I ate. I lost twenty pounds in two months and felt great. I could wear clothes that other women were wearing, and I just started giving a better picture of myself to society. It could never have worked if I hadn't decided on my own to lose the weight. It's true what they say about being able to do anything you want. If you want to look like a model or a beautiful woman, you can do it, but you have to do it for yourself and it takes a lot of hard work.

Monica's story is filled with evidence for a contradictory logic in an optics of women's "health." Her description endorses familiar cultural images of feminine beauty as the grounding for her new confidence and, simultaneously, she stresses the necessity of breaking free from those images. An inordinate amount of hard work is required if one hopes to attain beauty, enabling the gift of a "better picture" to society. Yet the labor is oddly dissociated from society, self-focused. Through her own determination, Monica sees the "objective" truth about herself and chooses to make changes in her body, changes that bring her closer to cultural images of female attractiveness, and ironically, strengthen her individuality.

An ability to see oneself from an objective vantage point for purposes of becoming more attractive/healthy depends on coherence between spectacle and spectator. If the spectacle does not receive a favorable assessment from the spectator, the division between spectacle and spectator is widened. Many women report, for example, that losing weight or in other ways coming closer to beauty ideals represented within culture, enables them to feel less objectified *by themselves*. Laura expresses a correlation between a lessening of self-objectification, self-judgment and weight loss in stating, "If I lose weight I feel like I have a better relationship with my body. It's not something I have to think about or worry about. I don't have to constantly tell myself how terrible I look." Indeed, a lack of harmony between spectator and spectacle, for women, produces a conscious mode of unpleasant objectification. Having a "better relationship with my body," for Laura, means less thought and worry about the body. And, perhaps most importantly, "constant" self-reprimanding comes to a halt: "I don't have to constantly tell myself how terrible I look."

A condemnation of the unsightly body, which is required for a demonstration of keen surveillance, produces alienation from, *and* better knowledge of, the body. When women do not conform to cultural standards for appearance, Marcia Millman (1981) points out, the body is often "disowned" by its inhabitant; "The body is regarded as an unwanted appendage of the head-self; the head tries to distance and dissociate itself from the body as much as possible" (p. 180). Here, the body is viewed as disconnected from the self, as something that cannot be integrated seamlessly into an overall sphere of personal existence. To illustrate, many women speak of waiting to purchase fashionable attire until they become thin. Here, the present body is disavowed and ignored, disconnected from the person. A dissociation of self and body, in itself, is grounded in knowledge of the body's unacceptability in the domain of cultural gazes. Body alienation evidences a total internalization of external gazes. That is, disowning the body on aesthetic grounds emerges from a clear understanding and acceptance of cultural standards for attractiveness.

The promise in weight loss/health discourse of a reunion of body and mind, a lessening of self-consciousness through a merging of spectator and spectacle, is confounded with the realization that improved knowledge of the body, for women, is often experientially synonymous with body alienation. Seeing oneself more clearly is strongly linked to a rejection of the body. Louise makes this point effectively in observing, "The more you get to know about beauty tips and diets and all those things, the more of you there is not to like." Although endless varieties of beauty products and diets are sold to women in the name of self-knowledge and improved self-esteem, women suggest an opposite effect: greater *dislike* for the body due to an expansion of the territory covered by women's health.[3]

The concept of body-consciousness is very complex in the context of body alteration and the internalization of the gaze. Authors of diet and health books often distinguish between negative body consciousness, associated with being overweight, and positive body consciousness, which is the outcome of slenderness. Whereas being fat produces a tendency to disown the body and fear the gazes of self and others, thinness allows a woman to welcome the prospect of being seen. For example, Robert Linn (1980) indicates, thinness leads to pride in the body; thus one will more readily expose and flaunt her body to others (pp. 87-97). To be sure, feeling as though she looks attractive, given cultural images and the priority of the visual in assessing women, can do much to bolster a woman's overall confidence. Yet, for women, the experience of being "exposed" to the gazes of self and others, whether a woman is fat or thin, attractive or unattractive, is often unpleasant: "Sometimes it's not worth it to present yourself well appearance-wise because it's as if you're on stage;" "You can get dressed up and know you look really good, but then people look at you, and that just makes you even more aware of your body;" "Everybody looks at a pretty girl who walks into a room. I admit that at times when that happens, I'm envious, but at other times I think, I'm glad I'm not being stared at."

A closer approximation to feminine ideals can work to *intensify* the experience of objectification because, frequently, the body undergoes greater public and private scrutiny. Numerous women report that when they are considered unattractive by cultural standards, others "will not give me the time of day," which is often pleasant because a degree of privacy and invisibility is retained. Additionally, women indicate a chaining effect in their fixation on consumer goods and services when attractive by social standards. Georgia explains, "The more time and money I spend trying to look good, the more time and money I spend trying to look good." The woman who "makes heads turn" invites inspection by others, and is seen, culturally, to spend much time inspecting herself. Being admired by self and others introduces the possibility of increased judgment and objectification, and may be informed by self-objectification. Placed at a distance from others or "standing out" for one's aesthetic appeal is seen by women to increase the discord between spectator and spectacle.

Within the field of the gaze, women are placed in a position characterized by compulsory visibility and objectification regardless of physical/aesthetic conformity. If she is attractive, a woman is watched; if she is unattractive, she is watched. Either state of physical presence can bring societal disapproval and mandate discipline. Aesthetically pleasing women, Berger (1972) notes, are often depicted as persons who are imbued with vanity and narcissism (p. 51). And within cultural practices, one must be wary of vain women because their "beauty" is superficial, masking a greedy and underhanded interior. Beautiful women are seen to use the body as a form of currency, access to elite social circles, among other profits. A central requirement for women's health is evidence for participation in consumer markets, yet the same evidence reveals women as crass opportunists.

Thus, beautiful or "healthy" women, like women who are considered unattractive by cultural standards, pay a price for their deviance. The beautiful woman retains her value by presenting herself as a spectacle, yet her value is undermined through a reduction to the status of a strangely volitional object. By being both valued and condemned as an object capable of deception, beautiful women are trapped in a precarious situation because signs of labor in the domain of feminine health—attention to appearance, conformity to cultural beauty standards—are the signs of female capacities for deviance, for masking "true" character. Beverley summarizes the dilemma: "Our society has us in a real mess. If you're a girl you're supposed to look pretty, but if you're too pretty or beautiful, it's bad too. Not bad in all situations, but I think beautiful girls are thought of as conniving, they're well, just not what you think." Thus, for example, Brownmiller (1975) points out that beautiful or sexually provocative rape victims are often held accountable for "inviting" an attack because they are said to weaken the defenses of their attackers. Attack is justifiable punishment for one who has deceived, who is not what she appears to be.

An undercurrent of deviant feminine sexuality flows through women's body experience, registering uneasiness at the prospect of physical conformity *or* physical deviation. Either set of physical features, acceptable or unacceptable, signifies the "hidden" quality of feminine deviance, giving credence to ongoing surveillance, continuous efforts to "expose" the bodies of women. Joan describes in considerable detail a "thin and getting fatter protective film going on" over her body, resulting from a positive acknowledgment of her weight loss. Her description points to conflicting elements which open her to greater inspection and threat as a result of becoming thin. Although she initially enjoys an increased level of attractiveness, she soon becomes frightened as others shift their responses to her, as others begin to treat her more sexually.

When I lose weight, I feel real good about it. I dress nicer, and I wear clothes that are more flattering and more revealing, and I think I behave with more confidence, particularly with men. I'm not self-conscious in a destructive way. But then I have a tendency to gain the weight back based on not being comfortable with that image of myself, and the consequences of the shifts in behavior. People compliment me and friends grab my ass and make funny, friendly overtures. On the surface they appear to be nonthreatening. But I walk a lot when I get thin and, particularly in a city, there are always men who whistle, and look, and make obscene remarks. And then I experience a real struggle over wanting to gain weight back. I'm not even conscious of it as far as my eating habits. But suddenly I notice a thin and getting fatter protective film going on all over my entire body. It's one way of dealing with some of the hassles of being real attractive and getting all the attention that goes with it.

As Joan becomes more confident in, and content with, her body, becoming more *connected* to her body, and men begin to treat her *more* like an object, she regains weight to avoid objectification. In transforming herself into an unpleasant spectacle, she returns to an experiential place, wherein she is rendered nonsexual *and* unhealthy, but still objectified. Whether fat or thin, Joan demonstrates the internalization of a gaze that finds women's bodies to be untrustworthy.

### Feminine Sexuality and the Impossibility of Women's "Health"

The multi-faceted relation between spectator and spectacle, combined with an internalization of this relation, is confounded by a more general division in the domain of feminine sexuality. As seen in chapter 1, women are often depicted culturally as "inherently" diseased or unhealthy due to sexual functioning, but the ideological threads of an association between women and disease are comprehended only when the moral backdrop of feminine sexuality is foregrounded.

Historically, the bodies of women are aligned with nature, with earth, and are thus imbued with uncontrollable urges and baseness. The bodies of men, conversely, are aligned with culture, order, and reason. Marilyn French (1985) argues that within sexual divisions, women are placed in opposition to male transcendence and volition, and come to signify elements of being which man cannot incorporate into his identity, "Women, associated with necessity (non-volition), with nature, flesh, emotion, were emblems of what had to be rejected in order to create a transcendent world" (p. 103). By projecting onto women all those qualities that he cannot exhibit, without foregoing his transcendence, man fills a dual function in the service of domination. He establishes woman's flesh as the enemy and legitimizes efforts to control the "wildness" of woman. Success in demonstrating a capacity to "tame" women underscores male power.

The culture-nature dichotomy is likely to be prominent "in societies in which control is seen as a high good; if women are not identified with nature, the reason is that men have 'tamed' them, and usurped their powers of the wild" (p. 109). Constructing women as creatures in need of taming accomplishes two goals. The wildness of women is first exaggerated, establishing a clear difference from men. Second, masculine powers to subdue, to bring under control, are simultaneously underscored. A masculinist vision of the feminine difference works only if women also exhibit a propensity for wildness. Women's bodies are caught in a duality of culture and nature, as "mediator between humanness and the wild" (p. 109). Images of feminine sexuality, working in the service of male power and control, are supplanted within the bodies of woman as an opposition between goodness and evil, the virtuous and the profane.

Mutually exclusive female capacities for goodness and evil lurk in the background when women behave and receive judgment. Goodness and evil are represented, respectively, by self-sacrifice and over-indulgence. Elizabeth Janeway (1980) points out, "In one the female symbolizes chastity; in the other she embodies insatiate, nymphomanic greed . . . " (p. 5). Within western cultural imagery, the polarity of feminine capabilities is epitomized in the Biblical division between the virgin Mary and Eve. Not only is Mary a "good" woman, but she has accomplished bodily transcendence to the point of producing a child without being made unclean by sexual activity. She is a wholly *inactive* body, a "picture" of chastity, and herein lies her goodness. Mary is pure and only an object of vision. Eve, by contrast, is ascribed to the realm of "bad" women because she acts, she participates in the world, she has experience: she is *bodily*. A propensity for livelihood, Eve's legacy, must be continually checked by Mary, brought back into a motionless state. Yet, Eve's capacity for trickery is always at work to outwit Mary's goodness. Janeway observes that when an impossible combination of sacred Mary and profane Eve is supplanted in the body of each woman, "a state of civil war become endemic" (p. 7).

The "eyes" with which women engage in self-judgment, struggling for mastery over the profane/living/body, are housed in masculine constructions of femininity because men are afforded the power of naming within culture. Through an internalization of male gazes and male values, women evaluate themselves as they are evaluated by men. Thus Berger writes, "The surveyor of woman in herself is male: the surveyed female" (p. 47). Women *become* men in the process of self-assessment, demanding that the body make a spectacle of itself. As Sandra Bartky (1982) points out, women's self-objectification "is not just the splitting of a person into mind and body but the splitting of the self into a number of *personae,* some who witness and others who are witnessed" (qtd. in Martin, 1987, p. 21). The masculine *personae* in woman bears witness to images of women as untrustworthy, open to temptation, prone to manipulation and deception, with a strong propensity for evil. It is the capacity for *goodness* in woman-as-represented that is male, the capacity to transcend baseness and the flesh. Male eyes of judgment in women work to insure feminine virtue, and importantly, highlight the possibility of transgression. A lapse in surveillance is likely to prompt slippage into feminine "badness," resulting in destructive consequences for men.

The impossibility of living two bodies results in female paralysis. It is not merely the image of woman as motionless that paralyzes female bodies, but also the vision of woman as active/bad. The *combination* of the two images produces human beings whose footing is always shaky, forever unstable and unsure. Female attempts to demonstrate goodness, for example, often underscore badness. When women monitor actions to display body control, the body's propensity for wildness is underscored. Only an out of control body, like a convict's body, must be tightly regulated and policed. A demonstration of body control works as its own version of deviance. The "good woman," who unfailingly gives a nonthreatening image of woman to patriarchal overseers, can be seen merely as one who has mastered the art of masking female wildness; hence, she is as dangerous, seemingly by her own admission, as her openly defiant counterparts.

A classic case of good women who conceal badness is seen in countless depictions of demurely dressed women, wearing eyeglasses and matronly hairstyles, who suddenly and without much effort transform into bad women by unbuttoning blouses, removing glasses, and letting hair fall to the shoulders. Here, evidence for woman as innocuous is evidence for woman as dangerous. The good woman masquerades as someone "other" than herself. In a lucid description of the impossible body dilemma characteristic of femininity, Evelyn observes, "You just can't win. You're trapped. If you meet the standards in society, make an effort to look attractive, then you're being fake. If you don't do anything to make yourself look acceptable, then you're considered ugly and no one will have anything to do with you." Forever "trapped" in a web of contradictions, women can either present an image of "fake" goodness or "ugliness." In either case, Evelyn sees, "You just can't win."

The unhealthy or "excessive" female body, as constructed within American culture, provides a paradigm for a division between the sacred and the profane, and the resulting "civil war" endemic to women's body experience. Unhealthy women are viewed as persons who, by way of self-indulgence, have lost control over their bodies and their sexuality. For example, prolonged and frequent sunbathing, alcohol consumption, and cigarette smoking lead to accelerated aging of the skin, placing the woman with facial lines or sagging eyelids at a disadvantage in the pursuit of sexual pleasure. There is "too much" experience written on her body; she is morally suspect because she is bodily. Erasing evidence for self-indulgence requires a "correction" of the skin—a facelift perhaps. That is, the good woman intervenes to clear away the signs of body excesses, of indulgence.

The good woman and the bad woman become interchangeable in the battles fought within the body. In rendering herself morally upright by erasing body history, the good woman increases her sexual desirability, placing her back in the company of bad women.

The moral transgressions of good and bad women are tied directly to violations in feminine behavior. Many women report, for example, that when their bodies are physically substantial, they experience a sense of power because they are not treated like child-women. Further, as Joan suggests above, a woman is in control of her sexuality—in particular, she controls the sexual responses from others—when she does not present her body in a manner that conforms to standards of female attractiveness. At the same time, Millman (1981) points out, women in general are associated with a "forbidden, excessive, degraded, or distorted sexuality" (p. 157). In reflecting on differences in the treatment she receives from others when she is fat rather than thin, Lynn describes the "positive aspects" of being overweight, but at the same time, she confirms the images of secrecy and deviance associated with "excessive" women:

> If there is something to your body besides skin and bones, you can command people's attention. They can't treat you like you're stupid and have nothing intelligent to say. Those are the positive aspects of being big. I've gone from being fat to thin many, many times, and it's really hard for me to say, honestly, that being fat is better. But sometimes it seems like I'd rather be fat because then you don't have to deal with people thinking you're mindless and helpless. People don't just see you as someone to look at, as a non-person. But then again, if you're fat you're also kind of a non-person. People just see you as this big blob that sits in her bedroom and eats doughnuts all day long.

In Lynn's description, it becomes difficult to distinguish the actions of a good woman from the actions of a bad woman. Fatness or thinness places one in the realm of "non-personhood," which bespeaks "inhuman" and "deviant" sensibilities.

If patriarchal imagery is functioning effectively, women identify with the contradictory and bipolar logic of dominant ideology in which women both gain and renounce personhood by becoming objects or *only* bodies. The purported reward for a demonstration of goodness/health is objectification, placing women squarely in the company of their bad/unhealthy counterparts. Robert Linn (1980), for example warns overweight women that because they cannot be viewed as the objects of male gazes, they cannot be treated as human beings:

> Who's going to stare at you or undress you with his eyes? Nobody. Who's going to ask you out for a drink, hoping to take you off to bed, not caring a fig about who you are or what you have to say? Nobody. In fact, no one's going to look at you as a purely physical object. And, in the process, many people will probably also never bother to learn about that beautiful soul of yours. Should someone ask you for that drink, you know automatically that's *all* he wants (p. 72).

The woman who worries about rape or "being sexually evaluated or even accosted by the groping hands and rude looks of strangers," according to Linn, is suffering from "sexual paranoia" (p. 72). The "cure" for sexual paranoia involves transforming oneself into an object of male sexuality. Objectification here becomes liberation *and* imprisonment.

Evidence for the so-called badness of feminine sexuality, in Linn's (1980) logic, is also evidence for feminine goodness. Within cultural practices, it is only "bad" women who readily engage in sexual activities upon meeting a man in a bar; yet it is also bad/unattractive women who cannot elicit male sexual interest.

The interchangeability of women is crucial to a maintenance of domination. It should not be surprising, then, that an insidious politics of women's health emerges at a time when women are working toward empowerment. As women strive to gain the recognition typically reserved for men, representations of women connote ever-increasing concerns with the "defects" of women's bodies. Everywhere in institutions and practices, from products to combat excess flesh, facial lines, and fashion ignorance, to a cultural obsession with premenstrual syndrome, all members of society are reminded, in this era of female empowerment, that women's bodies are subjected to compulsory visibility because they are diseased and in need of repair/reconstruction.

# Chapter 3

## Speaking Transgressions:
## "Making a Believer of Me"

*You've got to believe there's a stage beyond the point when you're depriving yourself. You have to keep telling yourself that.*

*Marian*

The compulsory visibility required for a demonstration of the interchangeability of women's "health" and "disease" is intricately tied to systems of representation. Women's bodies are written in the language of deviance, inscribed within the boundaries of morality as understood culturally. That is, women's bodies are represented within cultural practices, held up for public and personal scrutiny, bearing witness to the "diseased" nature of woman. Through demands for a display of health, women replicate one another as a testament to feminine illness, representing "woman" to and for dominant culture. A display of woman is grounded in and reproduces the representational schemes constructed for the maintenance of masculine order within culture. Regardless of differences or idiosyncracies among women, *all* women must be coded and categorized in the realm of deviance/illness if men, marked as opposition, are to retain their alignment with health, reason, transcendence, and invisibility.

An internalization of masculine linguistic codes and structures guarantees the preservation of dominant ideology because, through internalization, women think and behave according to categorizing schemes designed to marginalize women. Governance in the domain of language provides the power to place boundaries on the experiences of cultural members; insofar as individuals think within the limits of language, governance extends to all dimensions of existence that can be perceived, experienced, and reflected upon. In the language of the dominant, masculine existence provides the reference point—the dispersed center—within which social members are apprehended and named. As Lana Rakow (1986) points out, "men have been in a position to 'structure the structures,' to make their use of metaphors and metonyms count, to construct a symbolic system which fits and explains their experiences, creating a gendered world within which we take our gendered places" (pp. 22-23). Masculine categorizing schemes position women within a place characterized by disease, and it is the power to position others that provides masculinity with its greatest tactical strength. When those whom are named within dominant codes can be counted on to reproduce their positions in culture, offering evidence for the so-called natural differences between women and men, ideological threads retain invisibility. And women, as others, speak on behalf of female disease.

A reproduction of women's health/disease depends not only on body visibility and an internalization of representational schemes, but on a speaking of transgressions. The woman who is marked, and marks herself, in the language of excess is required to both see and declare her deviance, to stand before self and others, *confessing* her excesses. Theological undercurrents inform the experience of speaking transgressions, both in structure and content, providing evidence for the "sinful" character of woman. Confession proceeds from a recognition of sin, a desire to obtain forgiveness, to become clean again, by way of recounting one's deviation from scripture. In the act of confession, woman is the spokesperson for her deviance and seeks forgiveness from an omnipotent, silent, inspecting other.

The dual-identity of Eve and Mary, supplanted in each woman, both grounds and mandates a continuous confession of wrongdoing. In Christian doctrine, Elizabeth Janeway (1980) writes, Eve's needs "were declared to be excessive and disgusting," while Mary "offered the only accepted role in which sexual activity could be undertaken by women at all" (pp. 7-9). Mary must extract from Eve an admission of transgressions in order to realign the body with a vision of feminine sexuality that renounces pleasure. Acceptable sexuality, if Mary is the model, is in fact a nonexistent, dormant sexuality. Mary is untouched, untouchable, existing as a non-body. And because women have bodies, rendering impossible the key criterion for a demonstration of goodness, confessions take place with tremendous frequency. Mary plays the role of confessor, recognizing and listening to the atrocities of Eve, whose confession proceeds through an experience of the body.

The experience of body reduction as talked about by women draws from representations of female sexuality that must be renounced and embraced in the act of speaking. Women code their own experience in the language of the dominant; women define their bodies as excessive, deviant, untrustworthy, and in need of surveillance and control. At the same time, women's speech points to gaps and discontinuities within representations of women. Though trapped in codes that reproduce disease by promising health in exchange for confession, women disrupt the continuity of dominant markers by complicating straightforward images of female bodies and experiences.

I wish to examine women's merging with, and breaking from, dominant codes first, by considering the ideological dimensions of confessional discourse. Here, confession is seen to indict innumerable female experiences, requiring women to "reduce" themselves—to erase the body—in the name of feminine "health." In the context of confession, I examine the representational dynamics of body reduction discourse by highlighting the metaphorical structures that infuse women's bodily excesses and women's expressions. Women's speech is found to both reproduce and dismantle dominant culture codes and categorical schemes.

## Confessing Excess

A blending of domination and confession extends beyond, yet includes, the boundaries of female excesses. Confession proceeds by way of an implicit comprehension and acceptance of law or scripture. A recounting of wrongs, in other words, assumes knowledge of correct or morally acceptable thoughts and behaviors. Moral imperatives ground the confession, and in fact, the confession is lauded precisely because, in being self-referential, it signifies an internalization of "truth" as represented in scripture. As in panoptic power, the confession forces one to see the "truth" about oneself through continuous self-inspection, accepting with humility and graciousness absolution from those who legislate the "truth."

Michel Foucault (1980d) argues that the self-referential character of confession works in the service of domination, of truth-as-represented. Within the parameters of the confessional relationship, the individual is both absolved of wrongdoing and identified as a wrongdoer. Two opposing personages, one aligned with truth/law and the other with transgression, are housed within a body that is reunited with the truth about oneself only by admitting a failure to see the truth about oneself. The one who confesses is promised salvation *because* she reveals, to a confessor who represents truth/law, a body deserving of condemnation. As a "ritual of discourse in which the speaking subject is also the subject of the statement," Foucault writes, the confession

> is also a ritual that unfolds within a power relationship, for one does not confess without the presence (or virtual presence) of a partner who is not simply the interlocutor but the authority who requires the confession, prescribes and appreciates it, and intervenes in order to judge, punish, forgive, console, and reconcile; a ritual in which the truth is corroborated by the obstacles and resistances it has had to surmount in order to be formulated; and finally, a

ritual in which the expression alone, independently of its external consequences, produces intrinsic modifications in the person who articulates it; it
exonerates, redeems, and purifies him; it unburdens him of his wrongs, liber-
ates him, and promises him salvation (pp. 61-62).

The individual is internally divided in the confessional relationship, with the
side of truth and law presiding over the one who speaks her own sins.

Telling the truth about oneself, to oneself, is a pervasive cultural activity,
legislating morality and working to "normalize" individuals who transgress
the laws governing numerous institutions and practices. As a means by which
to insure control and order, Foucault (1980d) observes, the confession "plays a
part in justice, medicine, education, family relationships, and love relations,
the most ordinary affairs of everyday life, and in the most solemn rites; one
confesses one's sins, one's thoughts and desires, one's illnesses and troubles;
one goes on telling, with the greatest precision, whatever is most difficult to
tell" (p. 59). Speaking the truth about oneself, to physicians, clergymen,
lovers, teachers, among others, underscores the power of normative bases of
judgment, for implicit in the act of confession is a promise to realign thoughts
and actions with predominant social values.

If confession articulates acts of wrongdoing for purposes of insuring salva-
tion/social order, persons who are defined as deviant within the boundaries of
prevailing ideology are expected to confess with greater frequency and urgency
than persons who exist on the side of dominant culture. Apprehended as
deviant, persons who are marginalized within dominant culture are seen to
engage in numerous forbidden acts and are therefore deserving of punishment.
Indeed, as shown by Thomas Young, Charles LePlante, and Webster Robbins
(1987), "deviation from the dominant cultural value system constitutes crime,
sexual deviance, social problems, and other forms of social wrongs subject to
sanctions and penalties imposed by the dominant group or power elite" (p. 60).[1]
The acceptance of an "outsider" within the dominant order requires an endorsement, an internalization, of the very laws that have found her to be
deviant. An outsider is promised integration, demarginalization, through acts
of confession. Although an outsider may admit to varying unacceptable deeds
or thoughts, it is the *fact* of the confession that provides the possibility and
impossibility of inclusion and salvation. Self-incriminating utterances announce a tension between the forces of goodness and evil within the body of
the speaking subject, tension underscored and compounded by the speech act.

The ideological dimensions of confession are unrecognized, and social
order insured, by framing confessional discourse in the language of liberation
and self-knowledge. An inability to inspect one's own thoughts and actions, to
see and confront one's problems or deficiencies, is associated culturally with
an ignorance of the self, with a refusal or inability to know oneself. Admitting
to problems and exploring their intricate workings is a necessary step in freeing

the individual from those aspects of herself at work to undermine morally upright or "normal" sensibilities. In recognizing and correcting her own wrongs, bearing witness to them and expunging them from herself, the confessor endorses truths that have escaped and marginalized her.

The confessional relationship, due to its division between wrongdoer and judge, not only preserves ideology with a blanket of "truth," but through a nonreciprocity of disclosures. Again, similar to the optics of power, the person who provides intricate details of transgressions does so before a judge who does not, in return, offer a recounting of personal sins, but listens silently and ultimately renders a judgment. The sinner's desires, thoughts, and actions become wholly visible to the one that sits in the domain of truth and salvation. Thus, Foucault (1980d) writes, although confession is understood culturally as a means by which to free or liberate a sinner from the confines of immorality,

> the agency of domination does not reside in the one who speaks (for it is he who is constrained), but in the one who listens and says nothing; not in the one who knows and answers, but in the one who questions and is not supposed to know. And this discourse of truth finally takes its effect, not in the one who receives it, but in the one from whom it is wrested (p. 62).

When power has achieved optimal effects, the opposing personages of wrongdoer and judge embody the sinner so that, like prisoners of panopticism, the processes of truth-telling and judgment take place within the individual. Panoptic power is maximized when tower guards are unnecessary for the preservation of order, when the mere *possibility* of their presence prevents transgression. The keepers of the scripture or law are no longer required for a legislation of "truth" when their wrath is fully embodied in their subjects.

The confessional relationship and its operations have considerable relevance for an understanding of women's body experience. As outsiders to dominant culture, women are represented as deviant and as persons who are held accountable for their wrongs, who must "display" their imperfections. Women are often expected to testify openly to deficiencies or "sins." Further, women are promised greater self-knowledge through confessional behavior. And indeed, there is much evidence to suggest that women engage, or are seen to engage, in an abundance of confessional behavior for the sake of self-knowledge. In her analysis of advice columns for women, Rosalind Coward (1985) indicates, for example, women are given information so they might achieve greater self-understanding by seeing their defects and "improving" themselves for the sake of harmony in relationships with marital or romantic partners. Further, as Coward notes, "Advice columns are built on acts of public confession, of making your innermost thoughts known by telling the columnist what is happening to you" (p. 136). Through a speaking of one's deepest thoughts to a relational partner, a woman becomes wholly visible and known to herself and to the social body.

Encouragement for female confession is proportional to women's resistance toward traditional depictions of femininity. Specifically, the more women resist dominant visions of femininity, the more they are encouraged to confess misguidedness and inadequacy, to show that they are overwhelmed when they take on "too much," when they are in excess. The misguided woman is in excess of the markers ascribed to her within dominant culture; she exceeds the boundaries of her prescribed place. Arguably, confessions are demanded of women with greatest urgency precisely when women are most actively involved in a questioning of, and potential resistance to, dominant representations. Confession reestablishes the order of the dominant by extracting from women nonreciprocal and self-referential disclosures which, in the same move, reprimand women for stepping outside the parameters of femininity and endorse prevailing images of women.

The representation of "women's issues" in recent decades is pervaded by confessional dynamics. Not coincidentally, during this time we have witnessed an expansion in the opportunities afforded to women. Contemporary women are taught that power is in the offing for those who fill the contradictory demands of being female and rejecting all things female.[2] Barbara Ehrenreich, Elizabeth Hess, and Gloria Jacobs (1986) trace the past two decades of women's sexuality as depicted in American culture, revealing that in the 1980s women are portrayed as persons who have been impoverished and confused by increased opportunities for women (pp. 161-191). A wealth of concerned psychologists, sociologists, physicians, media reporters and programmers, among others, conduct countless studies to bring scientific validity to arguments for a return to traditionally feminine roles, while appearing to sympathize with the ambitions of women. By way of scientific "proof" women are given "evidence" for their limitations, and encouraged to announce their weaknesses in the name of improved self-knowledge. Ehrenreich, Hess, and Jacobs describe a 1984 episode of "NBC Reports," for instance, in which "a long parade of academic experts" depicted sadness and futility on the parts of ambitious and seemingly successful women:

> The program showed attractive, educated women with good jobs who seemed hopelessly lost at singles gatherings; others were working out every day—not for pleasure but for vanity, in the hope of simulating the body of a teenager. Then there were women mooning over other people's babies, proof positive to the viewer that they needed a man and a family (p. 173).

Notably, here it is *women* who speak to the limitations of women, the price paid for attempting to exceed the boundaries of femininity. The testimony of women who are overwhelmed in traditionally male domains, by their own admission, assist women in achieving greater knowledge about who they "really" are.

Confessional dynamics are particularly visible in a genre of recent bestselling books designed to assist women in confronting incorrect or ineffective relational behaviors. Unsuccessful relationships are viewed as a direct result of female growth and ambition. In *Smart Women, Foolish Choices,* for example, clinical psychologists Connell Cowan and Melvyn Kinder (1985) identify the consumers of their work:

> Who is the "smart woman" to whom we address this book? She is career-oriented and actively involved in her personal development. She strives for a strong identity as a woman and as a person. She has assumed responsibility for the direction in her life. She is confident and values her self-esteem. She is curious about and involved in the changing nature of male/female relationships. Yet she is likely to feel that her love relationships with men are disappointing, frustrating, and very confusing. She senses that her choices may be foolish (pp. xv-xvi).

In conversations wherein countless female patients have confessed to the confusion described by Cowan and Kinder, the authors state their position: *"the more intelligent and sophisticated the woman, the more self-defeating and foolish her choices and her patterns of behavior with romantic partners"* (p. 6). What causes women to make foolish choices? Cowan and Kinder turn to the argument of excess, noting "women's expectations regarding relationships have been exaggerated by the belief that they can 'have it all'" (p. 7). Smart women, by contrast, are those who own up to their limitations, make few demands on relational partners, and love themselves for doing so.[3] Wise women are liberated from confession and unhappiness through confinement within femininity as represented.

The invisibility afforded to men in the social economy of confession reinforces the self-referential character of women's illnesses. In representing the opposite of disease, male sensibilities and actions need not be examined or "confessed" because men are aligned with normalcy. To illustrate, Steven Carter and Julia Sokol (1987), in *Men Who Can't Love,* suggest that men are not accountable, and should not be penalized, for failure in love relationships because they "can't" love. If men are *unable* to love, they are under no obligation to acknowledge deficiencies because they are not making choices with regard to thoughts or actions; they are behaving "naturally." Although men are not held entirely blameless according to Carter and Sokol, the authors make women responsible for recognizing and correcting his "inability" to make a commitment in stating, "in order to do something about the commitment problem *you* must understand exactly what is going on inside his head... Then, and only then, will you be capable of having the kind of love you need and deserve" (p. xii). Thus, although an inability to love may certainly be comprehended as a serious masculine malfunction in need of correction, ultimately, it is women who hold unrealistic expectations and demand too much from men. Receiving the love that women "need and deserve" requires a woman to acknowledge *his* inability to love as her problem.

Perhaps nowhere are confessional dynamics more apparent in women's lives than in issues pertaining to body appearance/health. On an everyday basis, most women are bombarded with images designed to call attention to the defectiveness of women's bodies and to offer an escape from perceived flaws. The "ideal" woman, as Laurie suggests, "is not real," but it is precisely her dissociation from the body that renders her healthy. Like Mary in Christian doctrine, the fashion model on the glossy pages of a magazine is "untouchable" both literally and figuratively. Both women represent unattainable levels of bodily transcendence. In the domain of women's health and beauty, it is the untouchable woman who exists in the body as judge and who prompts confessions of female deviance. If a woman keeps a watchful eye for imperfections and works to fix them on an ongoing basis, she demonstrates self-knowledge and health. Although she recognizes perfection or a complete absence of sin as an impossibility, for in this domain of the female body she represents imperfection and immorality, she must believe in the possibility of approximating the ideal, which endorses womanhood through an erasure of the female body.

For women, a demonstration of health and a concurrent avoidance of condemnation is in no way separate from slenderness. In fact, slenderness is often viewed as a core requirement for a resolution to innumerable personal and physical problems because a thin body offers visible evidence for confinement in woman's socially sanctioned place. The thin body is ethereal, transcendent and delicate, exhibiting a monitoring of the body's actions. A theological link between thinness and women's place within dominant representations is made explicitly in Rudolph Bell's (1985) work, *Holy Anorexia,* where the author traces the incidence of starvation among female saints. Bell suggests that a perception of power and a relinquishing of individual power is characteristic of past and present "saintly" bodies, "The suppression of physical urges and basic feelings—fatigue, sexual drive, hunger, pain—frees the body to achieve heroic feats and the soul to commune with God" (p. 13). A central distinction between male and female saints which fuels confessional obligations in women, Bell observes, is that for women "evil was internal and the Devil a domestic parasitic force, whereas for men sin was an impure response to an external stimulus, one that left the body inviolate" (p. 16). Thus, demonic forces are struggling against godly forces *within* the body of woman; communion with God demands a sacrificing of bodily needs, a breaking free from alignment with the Devil.

A contemporary version of female thinness and sacrifice is promoted by Francis Hunter (1976) in *God's Answer to Fat... Loøse It.*[4] Hunter indicates that too often overweight individuals are plagued with concerns over how much they can consume, rather than how little. She advises her readers to adopt her motto, "Jesus, how little can I get by with—not how much can I eat!" (p. 45). Consuming more than her body needs violates the rules of God, mandating an avoidance of excesses, a deadening of bodily desires. In a chapter titled "Learn the Law," Hunter states that when she was overweight, "the one who really convicted me was the Holy Spirit, but his convicting power became strong when I learned the law on food and discovered how outright sinful certain foods are!" (p. 85). By confessing to excesses of the flesh, Hunter loses weight for God and releases herself from the grips of the Devil inside herself. Quoting from the sixth chapter of Romans, Hunter advises readers to follow in her footsteps, choosing their own masters, choosing obedience over sin, and through an attendant release from bondage, God "will take you and be your master, and you will be his slave" (p. 85). Enslavement to God, for Hunter, is the precondition to liberation and freedom.[5]

To accomplish the transcendence signified by thinness, many women engage in frequent or *continuous* dieting which is underpinned by a confession of unchecked desires. Marsha states, "For me life is like a diet. Either I'm breaking it or sticking to it." The letter of the law is "broken" and reestablished throughout Marsha's life as a dieter. Although dieting is placed in a context of health, the attendant confessional dynamics of self and body condemnation remain. For illustration, Sandra notes, women who are "perfect in their appearance" always "look together and healthy." A short time later, however, she grounds a perfect, healthy appearance in thinness as mandated by others, "Everyone tells you to diet. Thin is in. Be skinny. I get very upset, I wish I was thin. I try and I'm beginning to face [the fact] that I'm not going to be the skinniest person. I want to go on a diet because I'll be happier if I'm thinner." Though Sandra realizes that she cannot be "the skinniest person," or one who is "perfect" in appearance, she wishes to diet "because I'll be happier if I'm thinner." By coming closer to images of perfection, she may prevent the implicit condemnation of "everyone" who "tells you to diet." Further, in suggesting a correlation between happiness and thinness, Sandra embraces cultural scripture which links the enslavement of women to freedom from constraints.

As a confessional discourse, strategies and strategists contrast the horrors of a woman's current existence to a blissful afterlife. The "heaven" of slenderness is envisaged as the reward for a good life in which a woman does not take more than her share, and in so doing, displays respect for powers greater than herself. A common advertising technique for the promotion of weight loss methods, for example, involves the presentation of "before" and "after" photographs of a particular consumer.[6] Prior to body salvation/slenderness, the consumer is a vision of excess—overweight, unfashionable, slovenly, lazy, self-indulgent; after, she is thin, draped in fashionable clothes, exhibiting keen attention to hair and cosmetics, and appearing energetic. Such imagery is powerful not only because it suggests that "real" women can be saved through weight loss, but because every facet of a woman's appearance is indicted within the boundaries of a bipolar vision of "heaven" and "hell." Notably, for instance, numerous products marketed for women, from mental health facilities to hair care products, are promoted through contrasts in social conceptions of physical beauty and physical ugliness.

Every woman who embarks on an attempt to lose weight, if she wishes to be a fastidious dieter, must embrace a picture of an afterlife. An image of "what you'll be like when it's over," Ruth observes, "has to be there from the start or you won't be able to lose weight." Visions of fantasy and physical perfection pervade the afterlife, and provide a contrast to the impoverished state of present existence. To illustrate, Judy Wardell (1985) ends *Thin Within* by contrasting former confinement with an escape sanctioned by God, "You have been given all the keys to release yourself forever from that chicken coop. If you are ever tempted to go back to the safe, plump-chicken mentality, return instead to this book. It will remind you that you are free to fly . . . always remember who you are: an eagle . . . God bless you on your journey" (pp. 283–284). Along with a reduction in body size will come overall improvements in appearance, personal relationships, employment opportunities, ambition, to name only a few. In describing the future transformation envisaged as a result of her present diet, Paula associates slenderness with "lots more opportunities in life":

> I've been on a new diet for the past month and already I've lost twelve pounds. I'm doing it, sort of, because I want to change jobs and I think I can get a better job if I lose weight. But there are other reasons, too. If you're thin, you have lots more opportunities in life. You can wear nicer clothes, better quality clothes, and you just take better care of yourself. I mean, you'd do your hair in a nice way and wear good make-up because you'd like yourself more. And all that will help you to seem more confident in yourself, and that right there will get your foot into many doors.

For Paula, along with many women, it is the vision of afterlife that sustains dieting vigilance. To succeed, she opposes the lives of fat women and thin women and resolves to make the transition from fat to thin.

Images of afterlife characterized by overall spiritual and social health demand a repeated condemnation of a woman's *present* body and present life. Although, as seen in chapter 1, authors of anti-diet books denounce a condemnation of the body, the call for overall health as the solution to dieting often intensifies a woman's castigation of her body and further binds her to the "scripture" of weight loss discourse. She must remind herself that she is unattractive *and* unhealthy, bound to an impoverished life, if she reatins her current body. Reminders often occur through behaviors such as the purchase of scales and full-length mirrors, or the pasting of pictures of pigs and cows to the refrigerator door. In denouncing her body, a woman's present existence is viewed not only as undesirable, but as temporary. Marcia Millman (1981) observes, in the logic of before/after imagery, a woman's present life becomes unreal as she struggles to achieve slenderness. Here, a woman "turns all her thoughts and attentions to the future when she shall be slender. Her present self and her present life circumstances are discounted as temporary, preparatory, not the real thing. Real life, she reasons, will start after she loses weight" (p. 193).

The dichotomy between women's current/earthly existence and her future/transcendent life is underscored in many everyday experiences in the lives of women. Many women, for instance, report that they own "fat" versus "thin" wardrobes. Marsha states, "I have a fat wardrobe and a skinny wardrobe. There's a two size difference in the clothes." "Fat" wardrobes are designed to cover or "hide" the body from self and others, enabling women, temporarily, to "forget" or erase current body boundaries. Marsha observes that if she "streamlines" her clothing, she looks thinner than if she wears "funky flares and super tights," which highlight the shape of her body. "Thin" or fitted wardrobes are permissible when the body shows an ability to transcend bodily necessities. The body can be displayed to self and others if it has been "saved" from a woman's capacity for excess.

Marsha's experience is echoed in numerous conversations with women. Though women may not distinguish explicitly between two wardrobes, many speak of the necessity of "hiding" the body from self and others when it exceeds acceptable boundaries: "If you've got a weight problem, you should never, never wear real fitted clothes;" "When I'm feeling fat, I never dress or act in ways that draw attention to myself;" "When you see fat women on television programs, they're always wearing baggy clothes so you can't see the shape of their bodies. That says a lot, like maybe they should hide their bodies." As Sonja indicates, however, hiding the body ultimately fails to create an illusion of thinness because the markers which erase body boundaries serve to remind the body's inhabitant that she is still restricted by present body dimensions; she has not transcended her body:

> You can cover up a lot of problems with the right clothes. If I gain a lot of weight I tend to wear bigger things and darker colors. I don't like this bit with, what is it they say, *slenderizing* fashions? If you have to wear those things, you must have a weight problem. But I do it anyway because it's better than looking like a fool. I mean, who wants to see rolls of fat? But you're really not kidding anyone when you wear those things that are supposed to make you look skinny.

So-called "slenderizing" fashions, in women's experience, work as another version of confession because they are coded culturally as evidence for a *failure* to transcend the body. Linn (1980) describes one of his patients, for example, by noting, she "thinks she has solved her problem by wearing caftans all the time . . . She has them all made for her by a dressmaker, and the fabrics are beautiful and the detail exquisite. Even so, she invariably looks like an elephant dressed by Omar the Tentmaker, and she's really fooling no one" (p. 93). Hiding the body becomes a futile task because self and others read efforts to erase body boundaries as evidence of excess. Women suggest that there are multiple ways in which they are reminded of the body's unacceptability when overweight, despite efforts to hide the body. Marsha describes the responses of store clerks, for example, when she wears her "fat wardrobe" to shop for bathing suits:

> I needed a bathing suit to go to a beach party. So I walked in [to the store] and they are grabbing all the largest bathing suits that they could find . . . Oh God, what would you do if someone really bad off came in here, I thought. How would you treat them? . . . So I try on a thousand of them because I'm really hard to fit anyway. When you get off the scale that morning and you're wearing clothes from your fat wardrobe, you know this is not going to be the most exciting thing in your life. And now you're sorry that they are measuring you and checking out your rear end. It gets old . . . And they would never say to someone who is very thin, 'Oh, that's so slimming.' No one ever says to you, 'Oh, that dress is so slimming' because then you'll know not to buy it because it means that you're really fat and you need to be slimmed down.

Although store clerks may be unable to determine the precise measurements of Marsha's body on sight, her "fat wardrobe" communicates unacceptibility; she is considered overweight by personal and cultural standards. The actions of self and others produce a *remembrance* of the body in the very efforts to forget the body. If a woman is thin, as Marsha indicates, store clerks do not laud the "slimming" benefits of particular styles. Only fat women are reminded of body excesses.[7]

Moving into the afterlife of thinness, women report, entails a constant recollection of the body's unacceptability. In many respects, the body is supplanted with an all-seeing, all-knowing other who guarantees the need for ongoing confession through remembrance.[8] The other is a compilation of persons, situations, and experiences that represent desirable female body dimensions; a judge who is incorporated into the bodies and lives of women. The other monitors food intake, body presentation, exercise, interactions with others, and weight. Women who exhibit guardedness concerning body proportions are not lauded for beauty or slenderness, per se, because as history has shown, standards for attractiveness undergo dramatic variation. Rather, guarded women are revered for their willingness to embrace confinement as the hallmark of liberation.

A transcendence of the body signifies the power of the will to moblize the body. Moving from a "before" to an "after" picture of oneself is contingent on an association between present existence and an absence of willpower. Mental resolve and discipline are required to bring a woman closer to a culturally acceptable body. As suggested by Kim Chernin (1981) in her description of social responses to anorexic girls, an emaciated female body signifies willpower: "when we gaze with envy as she passes us in the theater, proudly swishing her narrow hips, it is the triumph of her will we are admiring" (p. 48). The emaciated woman is a vision of sacrifice, much like the female saints described by Bell (1985). She has managed to erase the body and underscore the body's existence in the process of confession.

## Disciplinary Metaphors

The experience of dieting as confession entails an internalization of the dual personages of savior and sinner. The extent to which women internalize this relationship, and reproduce a continuous condemnation of the body through a struggle between personages, can be revealed by examining women's descriptions of dieting as experienced. In particular, the language used to communicate the experience of body reduction underscores the power of dieting "scripture" in women's attempts to break free from the restrictions and penalties of dieting. The following discussion takes up the confessional underpinnings of female body reduction as represented by women. The metaphors of dieting coalesce to form a condemnation from which the dieter must, but cannot, escape. Each attempt to attain salvation is grounded in metaphors of damnation. The language of dieting, then, becomes primary in understanding the impossibility of women's salvation.

Language choices emerge from particular modes of experience that are directly relevant or meaningful for individual language users; one's experiential history provides a backdrop for the relation between perception and linguistic choices. The metaphorical concepts used in everyday language both draw from, and point to, the experiences of cultural members. Metaphors bring together two or more domains of experience and allow individuals to live an event, place, person, and so forth, in terms of other domains of experience. To illustrate, in a study of the metaphorical structures in television news, Dennis Mumby and Carole Spitzack (1983) find that the representation of American politics is pervaded by a "politics is war" metaphor. The domains of "war" and "politics" are brought together through metaphorical structuring, and reflected, for example, in references to discussions between world leaders as "battles" in which participants bring "heavy artillery" so that an "opponent" can be "conquered." Politics as experienced within American culture entails victories and defeats, weakness and strength, violence, and competition.

The concepts used in giving coherence to the world, George Lakoff and Mark Johnson (1980) argue, are metaphorical in nature; thus they are not aligned solely with matters of intellect, but "also govern our everyday functioning, down to the most mundane details. Our concepts structure what we perceive, how we get around in the world, and how we relate to other people. Our conceptual system thus plays a central role in defining our everyday lives" (p. 3). Conceptual systems are highly interrelated so that experience as represented draws from other domains of thought and behavior. The metaphors used to characterize an experience provide significant insight into the ways in which the experience is lived by an individual. Concomitantly, metaphors and their entailments are drawn from cultural and ideological conditions, impacting on, and becoming enmeshed with, the experience of an individual.

Drawing from the work of Lakoff and Johnson, Emily Martin (1987) examines the metaphors used by clinicians to characterize women's bodies and body functions. Here, many cultural images and assumptions about women coalesce to formulate "scientific" accounts of women's bodies. Martin points out that nineteenth century medicine presents the body as an information-processing system, with input, output, energy expenditure; as a "factory" for the production of useful goods and services, a maximization of profits with minimal waste and losses (pp. 42–45). Consistent with interests in science and industry during the nineteenth century, images of the body suggest mechanization; the body is both producer and product.

Within metaphorical structures centered on production, female biology is couched in terminology pertaining to insufficient output, wasted energy, slowdowns in production, or worse, in the case of menopause, as "the disused factory, the failed business, the idle machine" (p. 45). Similarly, the menstruation of pre-menopausal women connotes "a productive system gone awry, making products of no use, not to specification, unusable, wasted, scrap" (p. 46). Women who are not engaged in the "production" of children are subjected to the life of a business owner gone bankrupt. Signifying poor managerial sense, wasted resources, unrealistic expectations, and a paucity of "output," nonproductive women endure impoverished and shameful lives.

The healthy female body as represented culturally is decidedly heterosexual in character. Much of a woman's value as machine is contingent on the production of children and an investment in male pleasure, not on an ability to pursue individual goals or to form relationships with women. Cultural visions of women alone or lesbian couples are not objectionable on sentimental or aesthetic grounds, but because the bodies in question are squandered on women. In the staple pornographic scene of women lovers, for example, female bodies are useful because they give pleasure to an implied male voyeur. Thus, images of women together are not alarming in principle; rather, despair centers on the possibility of nonproductive bodies, bodies inpervious to mechanization. Wasteful women can regain the respect of fellow associates by admitting to misguidedness and flawed business sense, vowing not to repeat mistakes. Gaining credibility with colleagues may well involve a detailed recounting of precisely what went wrong, plans for improved performance in future ventures, and a request for reentry into the sexual marketplace.

In the world of women's health, the attractive heterosexual body is viewed as an "asset" because it holds economic value.[9] The body is only an asset, and only "healthy," however, when it conforms to standards for feminine appearance and behavior within dominant images. A curious paradox comes to the fore when female production/reproductive capacities confront prescriptions for feminine appearance. Specifically, as Susan Brownmiller (1984) points out, "Reproductive maturation gives a young woman her figure, the somatic emblem of her sexual essence" (p. 27); thus, a woman is desirable because she signals reproductive fertility.[10] She is a valued commodity in the heterosexual mating game for her body suggests an abundant capacity for production/labor. At the same time, the physiological changes that occur as women reach reproductive maturation—fatty tissue deposits, broadening of the hips—are precisely those elements of female bodies that must be erased if women are to be considered valuable and healthy.

Caught in a double-bind with respect to value and production, women embark on countless efforts to signify womanhood *and* an absence of womanhood. The fresh, "unspoiled" body of a youthful virgin is highly valued in patriarchal culture, in part, because her body does not signify womanhood; yet her value rests in an eventual willingness to be made "unclean," to be made a woman. The experience of body reduction as described metaphorically highlights the impossibility of representing the female body in an acceptable manner. Because the resolution of double-binds is both urgent and impossible, reducing the body involves constant scrutiny and labor, a willingness to "work" on the body, to both display and conceal signs of a male-centered womanhood.

The metaphors of body reduction frame women's experience in a complex cluster of images and concepts. Since women must display production value *and* purity if they are to be considered attractive, but cannot display both simultaneously, speech about the body is often filled with irony and contradiction. For example, many women discuss the importance of presenting an attractive body to society *and* suggest that women should not waste time on such superficialities. Alternatively, the "pure" body and the "reproductive" body are often viewed within dominant culture as interchangeable; they are both commodities whose value hinges on sexual labor, performance, and production. Having internalized a difference between pure and reproductive women that is actually *not* a difference in everyday experience, women's speech calls attention to the artificiality of the difference, its removal from their everyday lives. Paula makes this point concisely in stating, "You always see women who look like mothers and dress like mothers, and then you see girls who are supposed to be appealing, sexually that is. And you have to somehow wrap those two up into one and you've got an appealing female. It's so unreal. Women don't live like that."

The unreality of female images is countered by false promises of a real acquisition of physical perfection. And here we return to the theme of confession. If women work hard enough and with great powers of inspection, their continuous confessions of excess/deviation are insured. Women's confessions of excess take place within larger cultural institutions and practices, where women's bodies are represented in the language of impossible dualities such as deficiency/excess, sacred/profane, obedient/defiant, giving/self-centered, gentle/wicked, healthy/sick. By internalizing the representations of dominant culture, women come to experience their bodies as deviant and worthy of damnation, but also as salvageable. Attempts to save the body are corroborated by metaphors which frame dieting experience in the language of damnation.

In the remainder of this section, I trace the predominant metaphorical structures in women's descriptions of dieting. Here, women are shown to take up the language of weight loss discourse and to live their bodies through the metaphors of marginality. Escape entails further experiential sedimentation within the precarious, and ultimately unresolvable, dualities characteristic of women's bodies as represented/reproduced within dominant culture. I draw from the voices of women to describe four predominant metaphors, each of which mandates and reproduces a continuous confession of wrongdoing: temptation, accountability, deviance, and masochism.

Consistent with the promoters of anti-diets, women report that they have often been led astray by faulty or ineffective weight loss methods. Of the many women who describe weight loss efforts, each delineates numerous diets. Diets often fail, women point out, due to many unworkable diet plans, leading to an inability to produce "true" resolutions for an overweight body: "A lot of diets are just stupid. There is no way you can really keep weight off if you follow what they say;" "There was a diet when I was in high school where you only ate bananas. Lots of that kind of thing is floating around, which never really solve a weight problem;" "There are liquid diets now and a lot of people are on them, but to me, they just give you a false and short sense of security."

False and unworkable doctrines are tempting because they offer expedient results, but make women susceptible to countless forms of blasphemy—fad diets, drug-induced weight loss, exploitive physicians and businessmen—none of which has a woman's permanent salvation in mind. Rose explains, "It's sometimes tempting to look for a fast solution, but you have to tell yourself that the people who sell that junk are just out to make a profit; they don't care about you." Permanent salvation, then, is dependent on a diet which enables a woman to rise above or transcend the power interests of those who wish to exploit her problems. She must see for herself the sources of her problem, but doing so is complicated by others who attempt to lead her astray with false promises, evidenced by her repetitive failure. Joan, like many women, expresses the "muddle" created by the combination of repetitive dieting and the necessity of rising above diets so that she can produce a change that will "work and last":

> The thing that has worked for me in the past twice, with big weight changes, was to go on a thousand calorie a day diet, write down what I ate, count the calories, and get a little more exercise, and discipline myself. That worked both times. I took off twenty-five pounds one time and twenty the next. But I've gained them back both times, and since then, or rather, since then, around, and in between, I feel like I've read everything there is to read about changing things behaviorally, changing things psychologically. You know, change your thinking and this will happen, change your habits and that will happen. I'm kind of right now just in a muddle over it. Change your exercise and that makes a difference. I've done all that at varying times and to varying degrees. I'm at the point where I really feel like something has to happen. There has to be a complete change in the way I am about food, or my habits have to change and everything has to change in order for it to work and last. I don't want to diet anymore. I'm sick of dieting.

Finding something that will "work and last" is contingent on locating a solution that will change "everything." At the same time, Joan has "tried everything" without success.

A metaphor of *temptation* infuses the experience of body management as portrayed in weight loss discourse. The body is experienced in terms of a desire for the forbidden, a sense of being overpowered, the presence of sanctions for "giving in" to temptation. In describing the availability of food in American culture, Linn (1980) writes, "Temptation lurks in every aisle. And those who try to escape find the streets outside lined with fast food emporia, offering instant gratification to the hit-and-run eater" (p. 9). Linn's description highlights the dark and underhanded character of temptation, as something that "lurks" and from which one must "escape." In a similar fashion, Hunter (1976) asks overweight readers, "how many times do we pass by a store that has some real super goodies in it, and we discover that we have fallen into temptation, because we are irresistibly drawn in to buy some of whatever that little goodie is in there" (p. 87). Implicitly, both authors characterize temptation as pleasure-filled yet dangerous, as something that takes a person by surprise and attempts to undermine individual resolve.

In the world of dieting, temptation is often provided by external and internal sources. Regardless of the kind of temptation, however, the dieter is held ultimately responsible for her lapses in vigilance. When a dessert tray is placed before a person who is dieting, the desserts and the person holding the tray are seen by the dieter to provide the sources of temptation. Yet, only those individuals who are weak-willed and easily led into transgression lack the capacity for overriding the desire for delectable foods. Weak persons are likely to be distracted from the task at hand—body mastery—and relinquish control in the face of forbidden pleasures. Overweight individuals are often portrayed in weight loss discourse as persons who succumb to many forms of indulgence. Richard Stuart (1983) observes, for example, "the overweight tend to be more distractable than those of normal weight," and consequently they are apt to stray from the path of a diet (p. 75). Although forbidden desires "lurk in every aisle," only thin individuals are able to resist acquiesence to the distractions presented in everyday living. In fact, their bodies *signify* an ability, in Paula's terms, to "stick to your path and not let things get to you."

Temptation is viewed by women as something that is thrust upon an individual *and* as something that can be conquered. Additionally, temptation is seen to be abundant, but dangerous due to the fleeting character of forbidden pleasure. Women point to distractions in dieting and connect resisting tempta- tion to strength of will and determination: "My roommates are always saying, 'Oh, let's go out for a pizza, let's go out for Häagen-Dazs, let's go out for pastry,' and that can really tempt a person. I mean it's just hard to resist that kind of pressure sometimes. But you just have to make up your mind. You don't *have* to go;" "When you see [the] girls who can just eat anything and you're sitting there with your plain lettuce you sometimes think, what's the point? Why should I suffer? But those are the times, when you're really tempted to chuck the diet in the garbage can, that it's most important to fight off the urge to eat because you know you'll regret it later;" "My mother is [a] great cook and she's always trying to force food on people. It's really hard to say no to her homemade fudge, for instance, but you just have to." Although women point to external sources of pressure (roommates, thin women, mother), they place ultimate responsibility with the individual to "fight off the urge to eat." Giving in to temptation is *chosen* by an individual, and something to be avoided by her.

Acquiescence in the face of temptation is aligned with a metaphor of *sin*. A diet is envisaged by women as a doctrine from which one must not transgress. Straying from doctrine constitutes sinful behavior. A link between temptation, sin, and dieting appears, for example, in a recent television commercial for low calorie ice cream. A woman is being tempted with ice cream, and with consider- able frenzy she tries to resist by saying, "It's so sinful, I can't." Upon learning that the ice cream is reduced in calories and thereby not sinful, she accepts the dessert and a halo appears above her head, signifying goodness. Regularly, women place eating behavior in a polarity of good and bad, suggesting that giving in to temptation is bad or sinful: "I can be really good for a long time, and then I slip and start eating all kinds of bad foods;" "You know there are certain things that are bad to eat, and you try to be good, but it's hard sometimes;" "There are these totally sinful cookies that I love . . . and it's hard to say no to them."

Weight loss discourse depicts dieters as persons who are easily led into sin due to moral instability and disingenuous beliefs in scriptural truths. Women who pursue one diet after another, hoping to find salvation, are continually reconverted to the religion of dieting, provided they are "good" women. Roland Barthes (1985) draws an analogy between conversion and scripture by characterizing dieting as a religious phenomenon; "Going on a diet has all the characteristics of a conversion. With all the same problems of lapsing, and then returning to the conversion" (p. 33). That many diet book authors present readers as persons who have "tried everything" indicates an assumption of the reader's history of weakness in the presence of temptation; each new weight loss program promises a true and final salvation, a true *conversion* to goodness. Moreover, the promoters of weight loss formulas rely both on lapsing and reconversion. They know that readers will invariably return to the flock, attempting goodness once again. The price paid for living outside the scripture is permanent damnation.

When women speak about dieting, a dichotomy between salvation and condemnation appears, but the division is far less simplistic than weight loss discourse would have us think. The lines separating adherence to scripture from lapses in control become blurred as women live the restrictions and moral judgments associated with *both* goodness and badness. Recall, for example, Joan's effort to rid herself of objectification by self and others through a transformation from fat to thin, only to discover that she is equally objectified when thin. Moreover, women indicate, supposedly sinful behavior is associated experientially with goodness and self-respect. Marian observes, "When I've done a really good job at work, or I've gotten through a crisis at home, I feel like being good to myself and treating myself. I'm proud of myself and figure I owe myself a reward, so I'll eat foods I enjoy and not worry about them being fattening." Further, as Sonja implies, along with many women, a *violation* of scripture signals health and salvation: "Don't get fat, exercise, be healthy, be beautiful, be nice. All of that stuff turns us into neurotics and it usually doesn't work anyway." Insightfully, women realize, a demonstration of so-called feminine virtue, signified through fidelity to body discourse, is conducive to neurosis/illness and thereby stands in opposition to health and salvation.

The metaphoric structure of temptation is often accompanied by a metaphor of *accountability* from the person who suffers lapses in control and risks her salvation. Perhaps epitomized in the practice of confession, a sinner is required to "list" instances in which she has given herself over to temptation.

The sinner must reckon with her behavior by explaining it to self and an other. Similarly, body reduction discourse often promotes a recording of consumption and its effects, for example, in detailed diet plans, weight charts, scales, mirrors. Lapses in vigilance or insufficient adherence to doctrine must be explained and justified. The dieter must "settle accounts" and realign herself with scripture by explaining her misguided actions.

Primary in weight loss discourse is a demand on the individual to recognize herself as a choice-making creature, and thus she is overweight due to her own faulty choices, much like the sinner is unclean because she "chooses" to violate religious doctrine. Although her motives may be unconscious and not readily apparent at a conscious level, the overweight woman must accept responsibility for actions. Linn suggests that fatness is a *chosen* body condition in stating, "It is something you subconsciously chose to do, and you worked damned hard at your goal by eating continually" (p. 70). Linn encourages readers to acknowledge sins by reckoning with bad choices. Accounting for sins raises unconscious motives to a conscious level and enables a woman to see the error of her ways. Diet book authors such as Judy Wardell (1985) endorse a call for accountability by providing readers with multiple charts and logs on which to record consumption, psychological states, and reasons for deviance.[11] In turn, by making her hidden desires and motives conscious, a woman is able to choose her behavior, and gain control over her body.

Women describe dieting as an experience that is pervaded by accountability. Many women speak about the necessity of "keeping track" of eating and exercise habits, and explaining deviation from scripture. Angela observes that "a diet can only work if you're really, really careful about what you eat; you have to keep track of it. And if you go off your diet you have to look at the reasons why." Many women echo Angela's sentiments, and those of Linn and Wardell, by emphasizing the importance of understanding why overeating occurs: "A lot of the time I just eat mindlessly and don't really know why I'm doing it. I need to figure that out;" "People do a lot of things that are bad for them and those things can really affect you. It's so important to step back and think about those things, like eating too much or drinking too much, or you'll just keep doing them;" "You'll never stick to a diet unless you know why you overeat." Importantly, women are ultimately encouraged to look to themselves, their own character defects, when resolving body deviance.

The accountability metaphor is complicated, for women, with the realization that dieting *produces,* rather than resolves, a demand for accountability. Specifically, many women suggest, by informing others of their weight loss efforts, dieters are expected to confess and explain their sins. As Andrea points out, "I never tell people when I go on a diet because then everytime I eat potato chips or have some pizza, they say, 'I thought you were on a diet'." Numerous women report similar experiences and state that they feel *more* watched and judged, more accountable, when engaged in dieting behavior. In addition to scrutiny from others, women indicate, they watch themselves closely and judgmentally in the process of dieting; thus dieting increases instances in which women must confess to transgressions: "If I'm not on a diet, I just don't think to say, 'Oh, you shouldn't eat this, you shouldn't eat that.' But when I'm dieting I constantly do that;" "I spend the most time criticizing myself and looking at myself when I'm on a diet, and it sucks;" "Silly things get very exaggerated in importance when you're on a diet. You watch everything and get orgasmic when you get clothes that are one size smaller. And if you don't go down by that one size, you're practically suicidal because you blew it."

The confessional language of dieting connects a metaphor of social deviance to metaphors of temptation and accountability. Weight loss texts often describe obese persons by using terminology associated with criminal acts, which carry an implicit assumption of social deviance. To illustrate, the failure of many individuals to retain weight loss is often described as "recidivism." Moreover, like the criminal, an avoidance of repeat offenses in the world of body reduction is contingent on "discipline" and "guardedness" with respect to the body. "Cheating" on one's diet or covering up one's crimes of excessive consumption exhibits a failure to maintain discipline and testifies to deviance. Linn highlights an association between deviant behavior and secrecy in describing the actions of overeaters, "just as people slink off by themselves to indulge in other acts that make them feel guilty—masturbation, reading pornography, whatever—bingers slink off alone to indulge their insatiable craving for food" (p. 107).

A metaphor of deviance also entails guilt if the offender hopes to resolve her immoral cravings. Guilt functions as evidence for an acknowledgement of deviance; and in the case of weight reduction, as an acceptance of prevailing cultural standards for attractiveness. Were eating not connected to female deviance within culture, women would not feel the need to express guilt regarding food consumption. And were there not a demand on women to be thin, eating would not be associated with deviance. Thus, the guilt experienced as a result of overeating is grounded in a sense of remorse for a failure to present a desirable body to self and others. Guilt is an admission that one ought to conform to the prescriptions of beauty ideals, but has difficulty in doing so. Lucy explains, for example, that when her boyfriend calls negative attention to her food consumption, "I kind of blow up and say, 'Hey, I'm really sorry, I'm not perfect.' I always end up feeling guilty when he implies that I can't even live up to a set of basic rules, like saying I won't eat chocolate anymore."

The experience of weight consciousness is often expressed through the language of deviance, guilt, and punishment. Women often speak of their bodies as "prisons" from which they must escape, as forms of incarceration resulting from deviance that produces numerous forms of social and personal constraint. In reflecting on her body, Jane Fonda (1981) notes, "As a child, I was your basic klutz—awkward, plump and self-conscious . . . I could hardly get across a room without bumping into something. I resented my body. I felt that a different, more interesting me had been imprisoned in the wrong body" (p. 13). Here, the *body* is a prison which condemns its inhabitant to a life of torture, the actions of the individual have imprisoned the body. Feeling personal guilt over her imprisonment is a socially expected response because she has, in effect, punished herself by failing to present an attractive body. It is the *body*, rather than unrealistic standards for attractiveness, that constraints the individual, that makes her, in Fonda's case, feel "klutzy" and "awkward."

Careful monitoring of actions alleviates guilt and positions the dieter in a space characterized by obedience rather than deviance. Although an "escape" or "release" from body imprisonment is linked in weight reduction discourse to liberation, freedom from a deviant life, a newly liberated body often feels equally incarcerated. In a lengthy description of responses to her weight loss from self and others, Rita incorporates numerous deviance and incarceration metaphors in her so-called "freedom":

> I decided a couple of years ago to stop doing everything wrong when it came to my body. I started exercising, ate the right foods, just generally I decided to take better care of my body. I wanted to feel happier and freer in the sense that I wouldn't worry all the time about these things. But it's funny because doing the whole health and beauty bit gets you deeper into thought about it. I spent a lot of time asking myself if I was exercising enough or eating too much, and then I started thinking, oh my God, now I'm really trapped. I've made a commitment to these things and there's no way out. I was locked into these rituals as if my life depended on them. If you just throw up your hands and decide to stop, then you're going to feel bad about yourself. And I did feel better for looking good. It's just that sometimes I'd realize how much time went into it all and felt like I couldn't stop: I didn't like that part of it because it made me feel so restricted.

Although Rita stopped being "bad" in an effort to feel "happier" and "freer," her actions produce feelings of entrapment. She is "trapped," "locked in," and "restricted," with "no way out."

As in the case of accountability metaphors, many women report that they feel less deviant when they are not dieting. In the absence of a weight reduction or "beauty" program, the body is not policed continuously and forced repeatedly to recount transgressions of deviations from scripture. A release from constraint based on choosing not to police the body makes sense, given that images of feminine health/beauty within dominant culture are invariably tied to constraint. In the name of attractiveness, women's bodies have been restrained by bone-shattering corsets, bound feet, starvation diets, to name only a few. That women do not feel "privileged" or "free" for having to endure such tortures constitutes an infinitely rational, healthy response.

Women who recognize both the necessity and the constraint of dieting are characterized through a complex metaphor of *masochism*. Within dominant ideological frameworks, women must be made to feel as though they are diseased *because* they engage voluntarily in ongoing attention to physical features; and diseased if they do not exhibit preoccupation with appearance. Distinctions between attractive and unattractive women collapse when both are characterized by seemingly self-imposed suffering. The unattractive woman suffers because she is coded ideologically as someone who does not like herself; her body points to self-hate. She has "gone downhill," declined into hell/bodiliness, in physicality and self-respect. The attractive woman is equally masochistic because she suffers through countless "beauty" treatments and programs—restrictive fashions, high-heeled shoes, starvation diets, bleaches, dyes—torturing her body in the name of attractiveness.

As one who actively seeks and enjoys pain and suffering, the masochist is defined socio-culturally as an abnormal individual. By implication, characterizations of masochism assume that the natural state of human functioning entails a pursuit of pleasure, or at any rate, an avoidance of pain. Historically, the label of masochist is more often applied to women than to men, and validated through countless images of women who appear to enjoy suffering (Caplan, 1985, pp. 1-16).

Self-loathing in the world of an overweight woman is multi-faceted because her body is seen within culture to reflect insufficient degrees of self-love *and* excessive self-indulgence. Consuming more than her share is seen culturally to damage a woman's body and her psychological well-being, pointing to a "willingness" to abuse herself. When women describe their bodies as overweight, their language reveals a connection between self-imposed abuse and disdain for the body: "Whenever I eat something I know I shouldn't have, like a candy bar or a milkshake, I really start to hate myself;" "You have to see that you bring on your own pain if you just pig out all the time when you're supposed to be on a diet;" "The worst part about gaining weight is that you know you caused it; you've brought on this misery for yourself." As women suggest, the price paid for over-consumption is self-loathing; hating oneself results from an acceptance of personal responsibility for wrongdoing.

Self-loathing, however, is not a straightforward experience in the lives of women. As women reported in chapter 2, an onset of negative body consciousness is often sudden and inexplicable. When many women speak about the experience of being on a diet, they do not do so in the language of self-love, but of suffering and dislike for oneself. The suffering about which women speak is not entirely synonymous with the depiction of suffering contained in anti-diet orientations. Rather, as Rita observes, "If you really thought you were okay, you know, happy with yourself, you wouldn't put your body through all these diets." Rita indicates that weight reduction efforts signify unhappiness with oneself; a willingness to suffer results from feeling unacceptable. Sonja posits a similar view, noting, "it's sad sometimes to be around a woman, or especially around a real young girl, who is ordering plain lettuce and a teeny piece of broiled fish when everyone else is eating great food. They really suffer for the sake of looking thin. Don't get me wrong, I wouldn't mind being that thin, but not if I have to do what they do to themselves."

In addition to the suffering associated with dieting, efforts to "maintain" or "keep up" physical attractiveness entails frequent sacrifice and punishment. Contrary to cultural images which equate attractiveness with pleasure, many women argue that pain is often an accompaniment to physical beauty. In recalling her memories of watching her older sister, for example, Martha points to numerous links between pain and attractiveness. Being female, she explains, is "scary" from the perspective of a small child:

> I remember it was kind of scary to be a girl when I was little. I have an older sister and I remember that she'd just spend forever doing things to her body that were hard for me to understand. She was always dieting, so she'd never eat sweets, and I thought, why doesn't she want something that's so good? I have a vivid memory of going into the bathroom one day and she was there, with little bits of cotton stuck to her legs because she was bleeding from shaving. And pulling out hairs from her eyebrows, I thought, no thanks, that's not for me. When I think back to that time it's hard to believe I do those things now because it looked so painful and I couldn't figure out why she would do those things.

Martha's story, filled with images of pain and sacrifice, is shared by many women. Importantly, women exhibit keen awareness regarding the suffering endemic to *all* female experience in the domain of physical appearance.

The confessional methaphors of temptation, accountability, deviance, and masochism, as evidenced in women's speech, highlight an adoption of the damning scriptures within dominant culture. Yet, the same metaphors are incorporated as women describe bodies that are supposedly saved from damnation. Regardless of a woman's particular physical qualities, then, women are encouraged, through confession, to remind themselves of frail morality, to explain their behavior and seek forgiveness, to embrace an identity characterized by deviance, and to suffer. As demonstrated, however, women are extraordinarily insightful in matters of appearance. Women's speech indeed bears the marks of beauty/health discourse, but provides a rich critique of cultural representations by pointing to the interchangeability of feminine health and disease. Confessing excesses and inadequacies to oneself, women see implicitly, locks them further into the damning scriptures of patriarchal ideology.

# Part II

## Others in Relation to Bodies

---

# Chapter 4

## Family Relationships:
## "Mother Criticizes, Father Compliments"

*The hardest thing you can do is to raise a daughter.*

Joan

A confessional gaze accomplishes the legislation of female morality through an expansion of the personal territory opened to scrutiny and condemnation. Contemporary images of women's health promise a release from the promoters of beauty and their products, and encompass freedom from all forms of unhealthy attachment within culture. Healthy women are those who, like purveyors of anti-diets, retain a posture of rebellion when confronted with restraints in any dimension of personal existence. Central to women's health, given the priority afforded to human involvements in female socialization, is a scrutiny of relationships. Discourses on women's excesses encourage a critical examination of relational ties, a *breaking* of ties if necessary, in order to achieve a body free of disease. Strength and independence coalesce in beautiful women to signify a mastery of person and body, a complete transcendence of earthly entanglements.

A primary source of relational oppression in the lives of unhealthy individuals centers on family life. The family constitutes a particularly binding form of constraint not only because earliest socialization regarding identity is based in familial interaction, but because patterns in daily life are learned in the family and come to pervade adult experience. In anti-diets, the poor dietary habits of adults, for example, are often traced to childhood and family life. Regulatory mechanisms within the family, R.D. Laing (1972) has shown, are often difficult to challenge because, through sedimentation, they become invisible to family members. In fact, seamless functioning is dependent on collective concealment of the limits of familial membership.[1] Further, regardless of family patterns and their adherence to cultural images of family life, a family comes to

experience its own operations as "normal." For example, in the recent
attention given to the sexual abuse of children by family members, the abused
child invariably reports an initial inability to know that sexual relations within
the family are abnormal or atypical. Aberrant family behaviors, if unchallenged,
lead to unhealthy practices and relationships in adulthood. The abnormal
adult, then, must turn a critical lens on family life, analyzing the ways in which
she has been positioned in an unhealthy system.

Discourses on body reduction combine unhealthy family patterns with a
pronounced blindness regarding an individual's ability to combat family
disease. Unhealthy women are those who have neither identified nor challenged the control mechanisms in family life; they are enmeshed uncritically in
disabling family systems. Robert Linn (1980) traces many of his own clinical
cases to show that overweight persons cannot separate themselves from familial demands and expectations. Here, family members, like purveyors of diets,
are seen to have a vested interest in manipulating others through false information. Linn asks readers, for example, "did your mother tell you that you were
beautiful—when you were really badly overweight?" (p. 105). Similarly, in a
discussion which parallels eating disorders with alcoholism, Barbara McFarland and Tyesis Baker-Baumann (1988) identify dysfunctional families as those
in which an establishment of individual identity boundaries is difficult. The
authors state, "Eating disorder families have difficulty finding a balance
between the individual 'I's' and the collective family 'we's.' This 'we' makes it
difficult for members to identify their individual needs, strengths, and abilities"
(p. 36). Freedom for the individual is rendered impossible because unhealthy
familial operations promote blindness, ignorance, and dependency.

Entrapment by the family is resolved through a careful examination of the
practices and imagery indicative of confinement. A general tendency to present
family life and family members in perfect mental and physical harmony is often
identified by dieting rebels as destructive to individual independence. Unhealthy families are those whose functioning reflects exaggerated concern with
the gazes and judgments of others. McFarland and Baker-Baumann (1988)
address the problem in their identification of the "perfect" family, in which
importance is placed on "appearances, the family's reputation, the family's
identity, and achievement. They are overly concerned with how they are seen
by the community" (p. 35).[2] An exploration of the constraints found in perfect
families is often pervasive in celebrity authored health and beauty books,
where the stage-like character of family life is seen to produce an obsession
with appearance and approval. Cherry Boone-O'Neill's (1982) account of her
struggle with bulimarexia is pervaded by images of an overly visible family life;
a family given to constant inspection by society, which prompts continuous
inspection *within* the family. Alternatively, the public attention given to the

death of singer Karen Carpenter presents images of a family in which a heightened concern with public perceptions is linked directly to Carpenter's eating disorders and subsequent death.

Equally problematical is the family in which apparent permissiveness masks rigid controls. Here, the operations of oppression are more insidious than in overtly constraining families because members are led to believe, falsely, that controls do not exist. In the recent attention given to anorexia and bulimarexia, for example, a consistent and overriding theme centers on daughters who are positioned in the family as bright, independent, and responsible members. Hilde Bruch (1979) examines the parental shock resulting from a daughter's anorexia, noting, "Many parents will state without hesitation that this child had been superior to her siblings, had given more satisfaction, and had made them feel secure in their capacities as parents" (p. 40). A good daughter does not require controls because she does not misbehave or otherwise disappoint her parents. Yet in significant ways, a daughter's anorexia points to extreme insecurity in the family system, a pronounced fear of losing family approval. The anorexic, Bruch writes, "experienced childhood as full of anxiety and stress, constantly concerned with being found wanting, not being good enough, not living up to 'expectations,' in danger of losing their parents' love and consideration" (p. 41). Thus, a seeming absence of constraint is experienced as powerfully restricting, promoting an inability to establish independence from the family. Because they are unable to free themselves from familial expectations, anorexic girls "grow up confused in their concepts about the body and its functions and deficient in their sense of identity, autonomy, and control" (Bruch, p. 41).

A parallel manifestation of the family dynamics in anorexic families can be seen in families wherein members are encouraged to overeat. Membership is dependent on an excessive consumption of nutritionally unbalanced, unhealthy, fattening foods. In the family described by Linn (1980), for instance, doting mothers and grandmothers establish dependence by leading an overweight child to believe, wrongly, that she is beautiful. Alternatively, Judy Wardell (1985) warns of a parental tendency to corrupt children through sweets and junk food, which skews a child's ability to understand proper diet and leads to weight problems. Indulgent families are constraining because while they appear to offer freedom, they mandate pronounced dependence on the family for favorable evaluation. Children from such families are readied for a painful existence because rejection or ridicule by non-family members occurs with great frequency, demanding a return to the family for acceptance. Insofar as children are highly bound to the family for affirmation, the indulgent family provides only an *illusion* of independence. Members are in fact doubly constrained through a lack of social acceptability and an excessive reliance on the family.

Women are at a particular disadvantage in overcoming the effects of disease-producing families because the direct care and preservation of family life is established culturally as a female responsibility. Michele Hoffnung (1984) locates the emergence of contemporary family life in nineteenth century industrialization, which generated sharp divisions, for example, separating "work from play, production from reproduction, adulthood from childhood" (p. 125). Prior to industrialization, "the bearing and rearing of children was integrated into the other work women did and was not their most important work" (p. 125). By centering female identity in the private domain, women are aligned with home and children due to the capacity for reproduction, and seen to be "naturally" immersed in the personal and nonproductive business of raising children. Haunani-Kay Trask (1986) observes, "the 'naturalness' of childbirth gives rise to the 'naturalness' of child-care, which in turn gives rise to the 'naturalness' of belonging in the domestic realm" (p. 17). By centering women in the domain of family life and giving primacy to child-care, the contemporary family is dependent on woman's *inability* to rise above familial dynamics, on her "natural" enmeshment in the family system.

A woman's blindness regarding the family system is exacerbated by her association with children. Women are constructed culturally as persons who, like children, exist subjectively by nature, as impossibly connected to everyday surroundings. If a childlike state is the "natural" condition of women, then "normal" women behave in ways that run contrary to independence and maturity. In summarizing clinical and cultural perceptions of women, Ann Oakley (1981a) points out, "For a woman to be considered mature and healthy, she must behave in ways that are socially undesirable and immature for a competent adult" (p. 65). An escape from her association with children is required by dieting rebels if a woman hopes to achieve body liberation and health; she must prove herself to be fully functioning and capable of objective assessment. She rejects the views of experts. Her willingness to examine her life through the lens of anti-diet rebellion is a step in the right direction because, in the act of examination, she demonstrates a critical transcendence of her relational life.

The liberation afforded by women's separation from children is complicated by the realization that visions of deviant feminine sexuality and morality ground the association between women and children. Michel Foucault's (1980d) study of sexuality parallels the eighteenth century emergence of the "nervous women," epitomized in the mother, with obsessive concern over the deviant sexuality of children (pp. 103-104). Although childhood may be associated with innocence, it is also aligned with a defiant refusal to obey rules and an indifference to the perceptions of others which is itself disease-producing. If women wish to become free from the constraints of others, they may well wish to retain the childlike capacity to rebel when behavioral or attitudinal prescriptions are imposed by others. The internal conflict for women, which mirrors an ideological conflict in the domain of sexual difference, entails a battle between the virtue of control in the form of transcendence and the desire for rebellion: self-restraint and unchecked consumption. Given the virgin/whore dichotomy supplanted in woman, a defiance of boundaries may lead to transgressive action, in turn calling for punishment and further restraint. In describing the tendency to succumb to desires for food, Linn (1980) points out, failed dieters are unable to balance temporary satisfaction with consequences: "The pleasure of the food in your mouth lasted only a few minutes. The guilt and self-reproach lasted for hours, sometimes even days. And the weight itself remained for months" (p.113). A strong and liberated woman must give up the pleasures of defiance because she sees, in the larger scheme of her life, that indulgence produces much greater confinement.

A complicated polarity of good women and bad women frames the experience of body reduction in the context of family relationships. Women's voices display the tensions wrought by the anti-diet rhetoric of independence and the cultural place reserved for morally upright, "guarded" women. The boundaries separating good and bad women are blurred as women differentiate between and collapse both sets of imagery. Overwhelmingly, women identify the mother figure in families as the principal influence on body experience and acceptance. Fathers are relatively absent from women's descriptions, which is telling when thinking about women's cultural connectedness to home life, and linkages between female disease and feminine sexuality/morality. The relative absence of father becomes a powerful presence in the lives of women because, in his otherness to the world of the feminine, he sidesteps involvement, moral evaluation, accountability, and confession.

## Mother-Daughter Relationships

The mother-daughter bond has long been viewed as primary in the formation of female identity. In recent years, feminist writers have afforded particular attention to mother-daughter relationships in the context of psychological and social development. Male and female children undergo differing modes of ego development, translating into dissimilar relational experiences. Nancy Chodorow's (1978) examination of motherhood reveals that basic elements of family structures "entail varied modes of differentiation for the ego and its internalized object relations and lead to the different relational capacities for boys and girls" (p. 92). In a re-reading of Freud, Chodorow utilizes object-relations theory to suggest that during the Oedipal period, male children are forced abruptly to "separate" from mother, shifting identity allegiance to a father figure. Female children, conversely, retain a seamless connection to their mothers, and thus never experience the violence of separation, the abrupt break in identification with mother. Because girls have not been "forced" developmentally to erase identification with the primary caretaker and nurturer, who is most often mother, they have no early psychological basis upon which to fear connectedness to others.

Carol Gilligan's (1982) work presents a particularly compelling argument by suggesting, through a critical reworking of developmental theories, that women are socialized to embrace a sense of connectedness to the world around them. Traditional developmental theories have disparaged the mother-daughter bond by taking the process of masculine ego emergence as the norm, wherein the male learns that he must separate from others as he has separated from mother. In a re-examination of Kholberg's models of moral development, however, Gilligan argues, women's so-called inability to reach the level of moral development achieved by men, according to Kholberg's scheme, is based in a tacit privileging of masculine transcendence which points back to Oedipal fears of separation from mother. Similarly, Gilligan points out, Freudian accounts of women's attachments to their mothers assume female deficiency in the domain of ego development: "He considered this difference in women's development to be responsible for what he saw as women's developmental failure" (p. 7). By dismantling accounts of impoverished views of female development, Gilligan opens avenues for alternative readings of women's relationships.

The mother-daughter relationship is potentially enriched when understood as a multi-faceted connectedness between two bodies. Sustained and uninterrupted identification between daughter and mother, coupled with the reality of genetically and sexually similar bodies, establishes a complex body relationship between daughter and mother. Yet, caution is also needed when positing a seamless connection between mother and child due to the ways in which female attachments are viewed within culture. In anti-diets, woman's "inability" to separate from others is the source of her disease. Because women are enmeshed in cultural practices which equate morality with transcendence, and establish woman as a barrier to the accomplishment of both, mothers and daughters are likely to experience great ambivalence regarding their attachments. Further, as Oakley (1981a) indicates, healthy women are viewed as those who embody an opposition to the world of masculinity. Jane reflects on her own mothering skills, for example, to indicate conflict between her desires for connection and separation, both of which seem healthy and unhealthy:

> I am heavily involved in much of what [my daughter] does. I know I'm supposed to be involved, but it feels unhealthy so much of the time. It's hard for women because you are supposed to be right there for your kids all the time, but you are not supposed to smother them. There's a fine line between those two things, and I haven't worked out the difference yet. I want to be

there and support her, and I want to believe we share a lot, but in other ways I don't want to be there. I want us to be able to be different. There's always this thing I have about pushing closer to her and pushing her away at the same time.

The tension in Jane's relationship with her daughter reflects the duality of women's position within culture, the division between a woman engaged in efforts to sustain and sever connection.

A tension between woman's capacities for connection and separation is required for the legislation of women's morality. In women's body experience as described, connectedness is apparent and challenged; mother or daughter is "self," but she is also "other." Susie Orbach (1979) observes that issues concerning body and identity in mother-daughter relationships are locatable within a constant vacillation between desires for similarity and for difference, movement toward and away from one another's bodies (pp. 16–19). Mother's body represents goodness within culture, but also signifies powerlessness; daughter's body must be readied for independence from mother, but simultaneously prepared for a life of sacrifice and dependence. Marie captures the slipperiness of mother's position in a daughter's experience:

> I am so distant with my mom sometimes that I just can't believe it. It is really as if we are in two different worlds, as if we're not related at all. We look different, we act different, we are just so *unlike* each other. But we are also the same, just absolutely the same. I know I'm contradicting myself, and maybe it's because I don't want to think we're alike, but, well, all I can say is that it's not a contradiction for me to say we're totally alike and on the same wavelength, and totally different. I can't see myself making the same choices she has made. I want more in my life than kids and a husband, but that's a hard thing to talk about because I love my mom a whole lot. I respect her.

The tenuous character of attachment in relationships between mothers and daughters makes sense, given the positioning of women in family life, and more generally, in culture. Women are aligned with the bodily, the subjective, the childlike; yet, women are also called upon to enculturate family members almost single-handedly. Oakley (1981a) points out, for example, that in John Bowlby's bestselling book of the 1950s, *Childcare and the Growth of Love*, "mothers' more or less continual presence was essential to their childrens' mental health" (pp. 214–215). Mother embodies conflicting elements because children constitute physical evidence for her unity with the natural *and* for her capacity to transcend the desire for self-directed pleasure. Further, a good mother spends the majority of her time in the company of children, yet a mother's alignment with children indicts her on the grounds of disease and moral suspicion.

The governance of women within culture is dependent on evidence of a constant battle between childlike and adult sensibilities. In patriarchy, Trask (1986) argues, "women come to occupy an *intermediate position* between nature and culture: more conscious and purposeful than animals, but less creative and transcendent than men" (p. 16). Mother is a figure whose identity is conditional on a *division* between culture and nature within the space of her body; she mediates both but does not rest comfortably in either. The "nervousness" of the eighteenth century women/mother is grounded in a recognition of displacement, of embodiment of an incompatible duality.

The capability to be a healthy mother who produces healthy children is undermined repeatedly by women's intermediate position. Children are often dependent on mother for the fulfillment of physical and cultural needs, neither of which can be completely filled by mother because she is required to both recognize and dissociate from the needs of children. To illustrate, Orbach (1979) points out that from the time children are born, a mother is reminded of deficiencies in her "natural" capacity to feed her children: "After the birth of each baby, breasts or bottle becomes a major issue. The mother is often made to feel insecure about her adequacy to perform her fundamental job. In the hospital the baby is weighed after each feeding to see if the mother's breasts have enough milk" (p. 10). Mother is imperfectly natural or she would not require assistance from culture in producing milk, but the cultural preoccupation with her body's capacity to produce milk, in itself, connects mother with nature. Jane describes a typical scene at the family dinner table, for example, in which mother is both an "expert" on food and "helpless" in understanding healthy eating habits:

> We all sit down to eat dinner, and right away my mom starts telling everyone about the vitamins in this, and the protein in that. She's an expert when it comes to everything connected to food and eating. That's why it makes me so mad when she acts like she doesn't know anything sometimes. If my dad says something like, "broccoli does not have fiber," she will say, "oh, you're probably right," even though she is the one who knows all these things. Or sometimes she acts helpless, as if she doesn't know anything at all, as if she has never cooked a meal in her life. It reminds me of those commercials where a wife is busy cooking her dinner, and then some giant or he-man bursts through the window and says, "oh no, lady, that's not the way to do it," and suddenly she starts acting stupid about something she has done for years.

As Jane suggests, mother's expertise in family matters can be undermined easily. Acknowledgment of limitations in mothering is not simply a matter of acquiesence to male dominance, but is mandated socio-culturally for a demonstration of mother's intermediacy.

An inability to perform competently in domains which have been deemed central to mother's identity prompts a monitoring of behavior. To avoid negative judgment from others, morally upright women must learn to exhibit finesse in surveillance of the self, to confess deficiencies with ease. As women describe good mothering, metaphors of discipline, surveillance, and confession emerge with consistency: "Being a mother means [that] you're always on guard, always watching to make sure nothing bad happens;" "I know I don't have enough control over my kids, I mean, I'm bad in that respect because I want to have control, but I don't always want to be the bad guy;" "You just have to admit when you've messed up, I mean, if you're a mother. You can only do so much and then you have to say, 'Okay, I can't handle this anymore'." In the case of Jane's mother, a preoccupation with family dietary habits demonstrates a monitoring of family behavior and a monitoring of her position as mother within the family. Mother gains respectability within culture by governing the actions of family members not due to the power represented by a capacity to direct the lives of others, but because mother's surveillance of others signifies governance of herself.

The self and other interchangeability of mother's gaze is addressed as women suggest that morally questionable mothering is connected to a failure to control children. In each case, disobedient children signify maternal deviance: "You sometimes see mothers who let their kids run around like maniacs. They can be in a public place, screaming and carrying on, and the mother will just sit there and let them;" "Children have to be disciplined or they get spoiled. I hate to see a mother who lets her children get away with murder; you know they'll be the kinds of people you can't stand as grown-ups. I think that tells you something about the mother;" "I went to the doctor last week and there was a little girl and her mom, waiting in the waiting room. The girl was so obnoxious and her mom didn't do anything about it." Marsha provides an insightful synopsis of mother's complex visibility, gazing powers, and responsibility for children:

> When you see a kid being bad, or being rude, it's almost natural to blame the mother because she is usually with the kid. I don't see very many fathers in grocery stores with a trail of screaming little ones in tow. So then it's easy to say, "Oh, what's wrong with that mother?" She's pretty much there with them all the time, so you expect her to watch over her kids and make sure they have proper discipline. I don't think a lot of people realize the stress of being in charge of kids. Everything is blamed on the mother, mostly because she's just there, with these kids morning, noon, and night.

Mother's disciplinary gaze must be particularly keen when the object of her vision is a daughter's body. Cultural assumptions of affinity between mother and daughter, due largely to shared sexual and gender identity, establish greater urgency in monitoring efforts. Indeed, Orbach's (1979) study is pervaded by images of watchful mothers whose cultural credibility depends on a monitoring of daughters and selves. On shaky moral ground themselves, mothers are seen culturally as persons who socialize daughters by encouraging acceptable modes of feminine behavior and disposition, but also as persons who must recognize deficiencies in their capacities to do so. Mothers who permit excess in the bodies of daughters, for example, signify excellence in the task of feeding others; at the same time, the excellence points to inability to control personal desires. Gabrielle recalls an experience in which she witnesses a mother and daughter eating in a restaurant, expressing revulsion toward the mother for exhibiting a lack of control in the eating habits of her daughter and herself:

> I am almost sure these two were mother and daughter. They looked alike and had the same body shape—big fat stomachs and broad shoulders. Anyway, they were eating like pigs. I couldn't believe that woman would let her daughter get to be the same way she was. Their clothes were dirty and didn't fit very well. They just looked like real disreputable people. I know I'm sounding mean when I talk like this, but there was something about this scene that stuck with me. I didn't like the way that woman just let her daughter pig-out, and you could see that the girl would grow up to have no self-control; she'd be just like her mother.

Gabrielle's story indicts the mother for overindulgence, filth, and a lack of self-control. Taken together, mother *and* daughter are "disreputable" due to the mother's seeming indifference to the dietary habits and general appearance of herself and her daughter.

A good mother watches over her daughter and reprimands excesses in order to avoid personal and social condemnation. Orbach (1978) writes, "The mother may see her child as a product, a possession or an extension of herself. Thus, the mother has an interest in retaining control over how much, what, and how her child eats. She needs to encourage this initial dependency for her own social survival" (pp. 18–19). As Orbach suggests, mother retains a position of moral acceptability by signifying her willingness to nurture others without self-interest. A good mother's monitoring, however, also functions as a confession. Watching and reprimanding the actions of one who is constructed as an extension of the self announces mother's own capacity for excess. A failure to govern is equally worthy of condemnation because a daughter's appearance points directly to a mother's capacity for self-governance.

An avoidance of social and personal condemnation is dependent on body governance, but a mother who closely monitors the actions of her children is equally criticized. Anti-diet images of maternal love are focused generally on the "overbearing" mother, the mother whose gaze instills fear and forced compliance in others. For example, Linn (1980) describes a "slender Park Avenue mother" who abhors her son's habit of eating junk food (p. 76). To "punish his mother for her interference in his activities," the son rebels and becomes, in the mother's words, " 'vulgarly fat' " (p. 76). The overbearing mother's attempts to legislate control are seen by Linn to backfire, promoting disease in others. Significantly, the mother is characterized as an elitist, self-centered intrusive woman. In addition to her Park Avenue status, Linn notes that she "engineered" her son's marriage to an acceptable partner, and that she refers to her son's diet as " 'plebian food' " (p. 76). Although her body and behavior signify an ability to transcend bodily desires and to exert tremendous control—signs of feminine health in anti-diets—she is condemned and "punished" for the same reasons.

Mothers who are seen by women to be overbearing or self-centered are viewed in highly negative terms. In many respects, women reproduce cultural views of acceptable mothers as persons devoted to unending sacrifice and a selfless involvement with children, but also as persons whose involvement with children is problematical. An unacceptable mother, though she may be considered physically attractive by social standards, might well be perceived as morally suspect. As Linn's (1980) illustration suggests, elitist mothers pose moral jeopardy because they represent a capacity to weaken others, to both encourage and condemn a loss of control: the elitist mother is Eve. In her description of pretty mothers, for example, Nicole links many unacceptable female behaviors to self-centered women, which suggest faulty mothering:

> I knew lots of mothers who were really pretty. I thought they were really pretty, and they just hung around in their bathrobes and slippers, smoked cigarettes, and really gossiped. They were really uptight about how many kids played in their houses, who slept over—really private. I used to think they were really unattractive to be around, regardless of how pretty they were technically.

The mothers described by Nicole violate cultural images of mothering. Hanging around in bathrobes and slippers, smoking cigarettes, and gossiping are all indicators of indulgence, or a refusal to be bound by daily schedules and prescriptions for ladylike or motherly behavior.

Women also condemn the mothers of friends in cases where mothers are seen to hurt their daughters through insensitive treatment. Insensitivity is typically manifested as intense and judgmental surveillance. In many respects, the problematical mothers described by women typify those seen in the McFarland and Baker-Baumann (1988) description of "perfect" families, wherein the image of family life presented to society overrides a concern with the welfare of children. A desire for perfection, cultural evidence for effective mothering, is in itself indicative of maternal self-centeredness. Several women describe image-conscious mothers by using metaphors that point to inappropriate and thereby sick maternal actions—"bitchy," "ruthless," "obsessive," "cold," "nuts," and "crazy." Marsha provides a detailed account of the pressure and embarassment suffered by a friend due to "sick" behavior on the part of her friend's mother:

> I've seen families, like my friend's, and the things her mother does to her are sick. My friend will call home, three hundred miles away. She is short so every pound shows. If she is fifteen pounds over where her mother thinks she should be, her mother says, "So, how's your diet?" My friend will tell her mother, "I'm not on a diet." Her mother says, "Well, what do you mean? You're not going to have any friends. How do you expect people to talk to you if you're so obese?" Her mother's behavior is sick, and it makes my friend cry. That is not going to help anybody lose weight. You don't need someone constantly pounding it into your mind that you look gross and ugly.

Marsha continues by describing the impact of the mother's behavior on the daughter. As in her initial description, Marsha judges her friends mother, but adds an assessment of her friend's inability to meet mother's demand for thinness:

> Deep down inside, she knows she is a fat person. Everytime she goes shopping she buys a bigger size. She'll see an outfit on a model and say, "Oh, that's gorgeous, but I could never wear it." Her mom is telling her she's disgusting and gross. But to my friend who sees the models, it's as if she'll probably never be like one of them, no matter what she does. And then there is her mom, saying "Nobody is going to talk to you, you're not going to have any friends." It's as if everything in life revolves around how much she weighs, which isn't true. I just hurt for her when her mom does this, when she implies to her own daughter that she's some kind of leper.

Marsha condemns the behavior of her friend's mother, and questions the validity of the mother's tendency to give body weight top priority. Perhaps most importantly, the efforts of the overbearing mother invariably *perpetuate* disease. Mother's sickness, a desire for social approval in her ability to exert control over her children, is responsible for generating sickness in her daughter.

Many women who criticize the mothers of their friends suggest that being in the presence of exceedingly weight-conscious mothers is uncomfortable and annoying. Frequently, self-consciousness is experienced by women in the presence of a mother who is seen to be overly judgmental and critical of a daughter's body. In reflecting on days at the beach with her friend's family, Diane recalls, "Her mom never said anything to me such as, 'Oh, you should lose ten pounds.' But she harassed my friend continually and we weighed about the same. So I just knew for certain that her mom was looking at me and thinking, what a fat little slob. It made me feel so self-conscious." Even when women do not fear negative judgment from a friend's mother, they express irritation when the mother offers compliments or praise because these behaviors, like implied criticisms, announce excessive attention to body weight. Laurie explains:

> I have a good friend whose mother is on her back constantly. Her mother is real skinny, you can see all of her bones, and she just drives my friend crazy. So we'd go out and eat a lot, just out of spite, to get away from her X-ray eyes. I couldn't stand to be around her mother because she'd always say, "Wow, you look so good. You look like you've lost weight."

From Laurie's perspective, the mother's compliment is unpleasant because it is issued by someone who possesses "X-ray eyes" and uses them to scrutinize the body weights of others.

Women's descriptions of bad mothers point to a central power dynamic in mother-daughter relationships. A strict monitoring female actions is required of, and castigated by, healthy *and* unhealthy mothers. In supplanting the theological polarity of Mary and Eve within the bodies of daughters, mothers reproduce their own discursive positions. Because daughters learn, as women, that mothers are untrustworthy, maternal actions are in need of surveillance. Daughters become one element in a panoptic legislation of maternity, and because they are also female, daughters reveal their own need for surveillance.

A daughter's inspecting gaze is complicated by the fact that she is expected culturally to become her mother, taking up mother's battle between resistance and constraint. Paradoxically, a daughter must transcend mother in order to achieve health, but must also align herself with mother in order to achieve feminine health as defined culturally. The impossibility of a daughter's position of surveillance is foregrounded in Kim Chernin's (1985) analysis of female and male identity in the context of parenting. Chernin notes that male development carries an implicit goal of surpassing the father, "to face the father at the crossroads and symbolically to kill him and take his place in the world" (p. 51). By contrast, female development requires a preoccupation with mother's life, a taking up of mother's world as if it is the daughter's own life and as if it represents something alien, something other than the daughter's life. Chernin writes:

> A girl must brood upon her mother's life. Everything she comes to think about the mother and the act of mothering, everything she knows and senses about the institution of mothering and the particular experience of it her own mother has known bears an immediate and urgent relevance to herself . . . The

contrast for most women between their life of possibility and their mother's life of limitations continues to haunt them through every stage of growth and development, making separation a perilous matter... (pp. 56-58).

Freedom from the disease-producing character of mother is often culturally mandated and attempted, significantly, through a rejection of mother's body. A pervasive theme in studies of anorexic girls, for example, centers on a rejection of the body precisely at the point when childbearing becomes possible (Palmer, 1980, pp. 50-57). Associations with mother are announced bodily, Chernin (1985) suggests, and produce "the anguish of a person confronted by the fact of being fundamentally and irrevocably female" (p. 53). Yet, complete rejection is often difficult because the same mothers who represent bodily excesses are those who signify goodness, a willingness to govern and restrain themselves. Women indicate, for example, that overweight mothers often diet incessantly. Emily clarifies the impossible task of emulating mother's behavior as a means by which to reject mother's body:

> My mom is continually, and I mean continually, on one kind of diet or another. She tries everything and she's still fat. She says to me, "Don't eat that chocolate or you'll be just like me, always having to diet." One time she grabbed a candy bar right out of my hand. She just took it from me, and I guess she was probably right. Candy is bad for you. It's hard, though, to have someone who is fat telling you not to eat when you're not really fat, at least not as fat as she is. You get a mixed message because she is saying, "Do what I tell you to do," but obviously, whatever it is she's doing is not working.

Equally problematic in a daughter's rejection of femaleness is the mother who has given up her efforts to monitor consumption. According to anti-diet logic, women who abandon cultural restrictions exhibit independence (Fonda, 1981; Mazel, 1982; Wardell, 1985). The mother who transcends constraining imagery, then, should present an inviting picture of liberation. However, the liberated mother becomes synonymous with the elitist mother because both exhibit tendencies toward narcissistic excess, both are aligned with disease, and both are deserving of punishment. Striking parallels to elitist mothers emerge when women describe mothers who, in April's words, have "given up" on dieting: "You have to watch out for that kind of woman who just doesn't care anymore, she just lets herself go and doesn't really care about anybody else;" "A lot of women let everything fall apart once they're married—they just don't care anymore;" "I know it gets harder when you get older to stay in shape. I think it's hormonal, but I still think you should try to control yourself."

The tension between images of good and bad mothers is recognized acutely by daughters who are themselves mothers. In *Perfect Women,* Colette Dowling (1988) traces her daughter's history of eating disorders to reveal the complexities of mothering in an appearance-obsessive culture. A daughter's body and life represent a youthful and valued version of mother, but a daughter, ultimately, will suffer the same physical and psychic deterioration. Because mothers are acutely aware of the benefits of attractiveness, and of the ease with which beauty is seen socially to disappear through aging, they may be inclined to emphasize and minimize appearance as a priority. Moreover, mothers may wish for "good" daughters as a validation of personal identity, but they realize, at least implicitly, that goodness and attractiveness are often construed as culturally incompatible, yet somehow established as a goal for women. With tremendous consistency, women speak the contradictions of mothering, the moral and experiential dilemmas that inform maternal success: "You love your daughter more than anything else in the world, and of course you want her to be happy. But there's a struggle there too because you don't want her to be unattractive, but you don't want it to be so that that's all she cares about;" "I want my daughter to succeed in life and to find a good husband one day. Those two things don't always mix;" "It makes me happy when my daughter comes to me for advice, but I also want to say, 'Oh no, don't listen to me because look at my life'." Joan addresses the complexities of maternal contradictions as she describes her relationship with her daughter:

> The hardest thing you can do is to raise a daughter. You want good things for her, you want her to be happy, and you want to picture her singing her way through the world. Now here attractiveness gets to be a real bind. You don't want her to get so wrapped up in beauty, weight, etc. but here you are, having to do it yourself. I feel like a hypocrite sometimes because [my daughter] is sitting on the bed while I'm getting dressed, and I'm telling her to stand up for herself and be strong, that how she is as a person is most important, and I'm putting on my support hose and mascara. She's getting such mixed messages and I worry about the effect it will have on her.

Liberation from mother is ultimately an impossible task. Mother's slippery position in the economy of sexual difference prepares a daughter for the life deemed culturally appropriate for women. Nicole describes the mother's role in the context of the daughter's appearance: "We have to be desirable for men to want us, and I think mothers instill that in daughters. A big precedence is placed on being attractive from the beginning because we are being prepared for our roles, which are wife, mother, and all those things." Tendencies toward female excess must be checked, repeatedly, by a normalizing gaze. Heterosexual desirability is dependent on evidence for women's self-monitoring because, governance announces disease, a propensity for deviance. The efforts of women to escape mother, to become someone other and in control, are themselves forms of confession because they announce a female wish to be something other than a woman.

Women recognize themselves in descriptions of their own mothers. Over-whelmingly, however, they possess the wisdom to see that cultural characteri-zations of healthy and sick mothers are fraught with paradoxical imagery. Women suggest an association between maternal strength and an ability to survive within a culture that both lauds and condemns mothering: "A mother has to be a very strong person. She has to listen to everyone else's shit, and then she's called smothering;" "I have a lot of respect for women who survive raising a family. I don't think men could take the stress of always looking out for other people;" "Being a mother means that you have to make yourself out to be a total flake, even though you know you're not. You know you're smarter than most people, but you can't show it, which is why men don't have the guts it takes to be mothers;" "If you're a mother, you have to keep yourself up appearance wise, but then again, you can't be gorgeous or people think you're not a proper type of mother. There are just so many things you can do as a mother, but nothing is ever quite the way it's supposed to be. I think that's why people think a mother is not an important person, but you know in your gut that you couldn't live without her."

## Father-Daughter Relationships

Relationships between fathers and daughters have been given far less his-torical attention than those between mothers and daughters. Traditionally, father-daughter bonds are often simply less involved than those of mother and daughter for two reasons. First, mothers are typically the primary nurturing presence in the home, with fathers moving from home to public domain each day while a daughter is growing and developing under the guidance of her mother. Second, due to a shared female identity, daughters and mothers are assumed culturally to interact in ways that are deeper and more intimate than fathers and daughters. A mother serves traditionally as a model for a daughter, as someone to emulate; father represents an opposition to the world of femininity. Insofar as fathers and daughters are ascribed opposing identities within culture, combined with father's general absence from home life, women's explorations of the connectedness between fathers and daughters are almost nonexistent.

Father's perceived otherness to the world of femininity occupies a com-plicated position in discourses of women's health. In anti-diets, oppressive fathers are rarely mentioned, and even less frequently explored in any detail. For example, Linn's (1980) chapter, "How Your Compulsive Eating Began," includes only one explicit reference to fathers in the development of unhealthy eating habits, and significantly, the reference is parenthetical. By contrast, numerous descriptions of maternal figures are offered, including the "Italian grandmother," the "Jewish grandmother," the old-fashioned mother, the Park Avenue mother, and the "grandma-temptress" (pp. 98–106). By implication, particularly given the visibility afforded mothers, father does not constitute a pronounced obstacle to women's health. When fathers are mentioned by dieting rebels, it is typically done, as work by McFarland and Baker-Baumann (1988) suggests, within the framework of a diseased family system. If father is diseased or disease-producing, his illness is traceable to a constraining or otherwise domineering female, rather than to an inherently male propensity for disease. Susan describes the punishment endured by her father when her mother attempted to exert control over his eating habits:

> When my mom got mad at my dad I used to get scared. All he did was eat something and I didn't see why that was so terrible. I didn't want her to get mad at me, so I'd watch what my dad ate and not eat whatever it was that made my mom so mad. She was really down on sweets, and my dad had a sweet tooth, so I knew not to eat sweets. I can't explain why, but I used to feel sorry for my dad because my mom got mad at him. Sometimes she wouldn't even talk to him, just for eating Oreo cookies.

Implicitly, Susan suggests unreasonable behavior on the part of her mother; her father is a victim of maternal irrationality and anger.

The power of mother's gaze is often foregrounded as women describe fathers. In countless stories, mothers are depicted as persons who criticize and legislate fathers' eating habits: "His hand goes into the bread basket and it gets slapped;" "My mom runs the kitchen like the gestapo;" "She watches him like a hawk, waiting for him to screw up, so she can correct him." Yet, father's power to govern the family is often enhanced by mother's blatant monitoring of family life. Returning to Foucault's (1979) discussion of the panopticon, the invisibility of tower guards is essential to an exercise of power. Mother's exercise of power is overt, visible, identifiable, and scrutinized within culture ad nauseam. In his invisibility as a source of power, father's capacity to govern is accentuated. Judith provides a story about her mother and father, for example, in which father's panoptic power is underscored:

> I always know where my mother is coming from. I mean, she's just out with everything, so you're not left guessing. Get me alone with my father and I don't know how to act or what to say. I never know how he's seeing me, or *if* he's paying any attention at all. Sure, I get some clues, but he's not the type to tell you what he's thinking. I guess he's sort of like that strong and silent type you hear about in movies.

As Judith suggests, an identification of acceptable behavior is rendered difficult with one who has the power to see and hear, but is not required to reveal his judgments.

The panoptic power of father's presence is often underscored as women speak about adherence to fraternal rules, even in father's absence. When father's absent presence is combined with minimal expressivity, a daughter's guardedness with respect to her own actions is often exacerbated. Evelyn elaborates:

> I think most people have had that feeling of, wait until your dad gets home. It's like he's there in the house whether or not he's there physically. You kind of know the things that will upset him, but you're not real sure because, at least with my dad, he doesn't say much. My mom was the one to tell him what I did wrong, and sometimes he'd get mad, and sometimes he'd act like she was being ridiculous. So you go about your business at home, not knowing how he's going to react until he reacts. It's this fear of him, but you don't know why because he's not really there, and you're a lot of the time left guessing about how he's going to deal with what you're doing.

Father's gaze plays an important part in the lives of daughters precisely because it is seen to be ambiguous and sporadic. His ability to retain distance from the world of femininity, to gaze as a present-absent outsider, serves two political functions. First, father is often perceived by daughters to be accepting and unconcerned with the trivial issue of appearance: "Oh he was really great about it, never criticized me;" "Dad is always sensitive and never tells me when I've gained weight;" "My dad had too many important things on his mind to get wound up about my body weight." And second, father is seen as healthy because he does not become smothering or overly attached to the lives of his children. The state of health described by dieting rebels is epitomized in fathers, whose priorities are acceptable, and whose standards are not imposed overtly on others.

Father's inexpressivity often masks very rigid assumptions concerning acceptable feminine behavior and appearance. Lenore Weitzman (1984) argues that "fathers are more concerned with sex-typed distinctions than mothers," and promote stronger sex typing in their children than mothers (p. 164).[3] Further, in a study by Judith Langlois and Chris Downs (1980), Weitzman explains, it was found that "fathers provided the most vigorous and consistent pressure for sex-typed behaviors" (p. 164). Thus while fathers appear to be absent from the home and to exert little influence in the socialization of daughters, father figures take active steps to insure sex-appropriate behavior.

Preparing a daughter for her identity as a woman is coupled with the implicit sexual undercurrents of female/male involvement. A female child's body is approached by a father with love, admiration, and respect. Feelings of fraternal uneasiness regarding a daughter's body often surface when the female child approaches puberty; that is, when the girl signifies a capacity for child-bearing. William Appleton (1981) points out that prior to an emergence of a daughter's sexuality, father and daughter exist in "a sexless, romantic, almost religious love . . . " (p. 39). Romantic images of daughters are possible because traditionally, fathers are uninvolved in tending to the "dirty" physiological needs of children, such as changing diapers, cleaning bloodied wounds, or bathing a child infected with disease. As a daughter's body begins to change, the purity of love between father and daughter is more difficult to retain. In addition to material signs of maturation, daughters begin to focus their energies increasingly on boys. In turn, a heightened female interest in physical and sexual attractiveness is imperative in the world of heterosexual love. In theological terms, father begins to see Mary transform into Eve.

The transformation from nonsexual to sexual love complicates a father's responses to a daughter's body. In one respect, an emergence of sexuality should please father because it is evidence for a daughter's ability to become a "good" woman, a productive body, a mother. At the same time, Trask (1986) points out, culturally, menstruation signifies filth and baseness (p. 22). As women describe fraternal comments on appearance, metaphors relating to cleanliness, "tameness," and goodness appear with extraordinary frequency. Father works to suppress his own response to a daughter's sexuality as bad or unclean by projecting his perception onto her. Barbara states: "My dad always thought it was very important to be well-groomed. Not to have wild hair or look unclean, to take showers every day; just to look neat. He didn't think you should be trendy in the way you dress." If women violate father's expectations, Laurie observes, there is often a negative response to the daughter: "My father would always buzz out when I would wear my favorite ripped up shirt. He'd say, 'You are not going anywhere with me in that shirt.' My father's concern was with looking real good."

A "good" daughter does not encourage sexual advances from outsiders to the family, and thus retains her nonsexual character, enabling father to more readily deny her sexuality. Within the dichotomy of good and evil women, the good daughter is virtuous because she does not attempt to usurp male power. Virtue in women is incompatible with power, thus a daughter's purity suggests a willingness to exist passively, without propensities for revenge or defiance. A denial of a daughter's sexuality, then, functions to preserve fraternal power. At the same time, denial or suppression of female sexuality carries an implicit, perhaps unconscious, recognition of the evil and dirty character of women's bodies. Thus, father views daughter as one who embodies propensities for good and evil.

If a daughter is viewed as one who contains the duality of good and evil, father is obliged to offer support for goodness and attempt to prevent badness. Typically, women indicate, fathers avoid making references to the body or to body parts, instead providing an overall, and often moralistic, evaluation. Marsha illustrates:

When my parents, say, pick me up at the train station, and I haven't seen
them for a long time, we all hug each other. They will both say, "Honey, you
look nice," or "You look good." But when we walk to the car, my mom will put
her arm around me, stroke my hair, touch me. I think I'd drop over if my dad
stroked my hair. I'd be really shocked because he never does anything like
that. And he'd never, like my mother [will do], say, "Your eyes are so pretty
when you wear that blouse," or "Your hair is so shiny and beautiful." I mean,
I've never really thought about this before, but the only things he says are
really general. They are usually positive, but always really general.

In Marsha's description, father promotes acceptable morality by applying the
labels of "nice" and "good" to his daughter's appearance. Mother, perhaps
because she is already aligned with goodness and evil by virtue of her status as a
woman, offers moral assessments *and* responds positively to body parts.

Fraternal uneasiness regarding feminine sexuality is also apparent when
considering that responses to a daughter's body, typically, place responsibility
for response with the daughter. Father, then, does not comment directly on *his*
orientation to the daughter's body, but on hers. The father may refuse to be
seen with the daughter if she does not appear in ways that are acceptable to
him, but as Susan implies, he is likely to shift the issue from his preferences to
her flawed sensibilities: "I loved a pair of Levi jeans I'd just gotten. At the time
they were the coolest thing you could possibly wear. I was going with him to
pick up some groceries. He saw me in those jeans and said, 'Don't you have any
respect for yourself?' " In questioning Susan's self-respect, her father avoids a
direct expression of his own objections, retains unilateral gazing power, and
avoids direct commentary on her body.

An avoidance of direct indications of fraternal disapproval with a daughter's *body* is generally pervasive in my conversations with women. While
mothers are perceived to offer numerous assessments of specific aspects of a
daughter's body, fathers are seen to comment on the overall personality characteristics implied by a daughter's appearance. Even when offering positive
feedback on a daughter's attractiveness, fathers still speak in generalities or
take note of things that have been added to the body. Among the positive
remarks given by fathrs are, "That looks like a new dress; it's pretty," "You look
nice," and "You look like such a lady with your hair curled."

Fathers are seen by women to be far less concerned and far less judgmental
than mothers in matters of appearance. Many women, as indicated earlier,
report that fathers compliment appearance far more than they criticize.
Although this tendency may serve to indict mothers for being overly critical,
compliments are a powerful normalizing agent. Langlois and Downs (1980),
for example, find that fathers encourage appropriate gender behavior in
daughters through positive feedback, while sons are given negative feedback
and punishment for a violation of sex-role expectations (cited in Weitzman

1984, p. 164). In addition, compliments inform the recipient as to the priorities and demands of the issuer. To illustrate, if a daughter is responded to positively when she wears dresses, but receives a minimal or nonexistent response when she wins a scholastic award, the father indicates that, according to his views, a feminine appearance takes precedence over academic achievement.

Fathers *do* offer explicit criticisms of appearance, women explain, but tend to do so in a nonserious manner. Most often, negative fraternal judgments are relayed by fathers and understood by daughters as "jokes" or "teasing." Through joking or teasing, a person is able to communicate personal perceptions and judgments, without being held accountable for them. The structure of these acts helps to retain the invisibility of father's judgmental gaze. If the recipient of a joking remark becomes upset or angry, it is she who appears unreasonable or ill humored. Angela recalls, for example, that her father "used to say jokingly, 'Oh, how's my little fat girl?'; then if I said, 'That's not funny,' he'd say, 'Can't you take a joke?'" As in the case of father ascribing moral characteristics to a daughter based on appearance, joking shifts responsibility from the person who jokes to the recipient.

In the relationship between father and daughter, joking and teasing are often seen by women to dismiss father's criticisms. That is, if he is perceived to be nonserious when issuing a judgment, then the evaluation does not count. A remark is not viewed as indicative of malice or true sentiments if said within a framework of humor. Sheryl observes, "My dad used to say things like 'Don't be my fat little Jewish girl,' but he never said it in a mean way, only jokingly." Similarly, Janet indicates, "He never seriously criticized the way I looked. Sometimes he'd tease me and say, 'We'll have to widen the doors if you get any bigger,' but I knew he didn't really mean it."

In general, women criticize their fathers in very cautious terms. Unkind or insensitive treatment of family members is often noted, then followed with elaboration that places father's actions in a larger framework, wherein he becomes a sympathetic character. As in the case of anti-diets, father's behavior is likely to be viewed in a larger context of family or work relationships which often shifts the blame to external factors, thus father can be said to exist in a "sick" world, but he is not "naturally" diseased. Far more frequently than in discussions of mothers, women rationalize father's behavior: "He's an alcoholic and that's why he's mean sometimes;" "You really can't blame him because my mom was hard to live with;" "He was always under a lot of pressure at his job and anytime someone feels pressured he's likely to blow up, just explode, and say things he'll regret later."

An overall absence of sustained or serious interaction between fathers and daughters in the domain of appearance, combined with cultural depictions of appearance as a "women's issue," renders it easy to blame mothers for mixed or

negative messages. And it is true that women who exist in patriarchal arrangements pay a price for taking attractiveness standards lightly; mothers are not
afforded the luxury of joking about appearance. However, fathers and mothers
both work to oversee and normalize the bodies and behaviors of daughters.
Though mothers are seen to have a greater influence than fathers, the covert or
invisible impact of fathers may have more ideological import than the overt
influence of mothers. Daughters are very clear when speaking about maternal
expectations and demands; mothers are seen to make their standards and
values explicit. The normalizing standards of father, conversely, are often
given invisibility through compliments, joking, and an absence of overt statement. In turn, father's evaluations prompt an internal inspection on the part of
a daughter. She considers her own propensity for disease, rather than his, and
to retain his admiration, she must guard her capacity for evil.

The familial positions of mother and father, as described by women,
underscore the power of men within culture to retain bodily invisibility. In
part, invisibility is retained in a directly physical sense. In traditional house-
holds, father is not physically present on an ongoing basis. Further, his
interactions with the daughter work to conceal biases, rendering his values
and feelings unknowable to his daughter. She may struggle to please father,
never quite knowing him or understanding his responses. I am not suggesting
that fathers are wholly responsible for a daughter's sense of her own body, or
that fathers *consciously* withhold information from daughters. Rather, fathers
*and* mothers, themselves products of cultural institutions and practices, work
to supplant feminine eyes within the bodies of daughters.

## Chapter 5

# Women's Friendships:
## "Going Down to the Depths of You"

*If someone is an attractive person, but she is not nice on the inside, not friendly, warm, sensitive, and caring for others, I don't care if she looks like Christie Brinkley.*

*Nicole*

The negation of human attachment in anti-diets extends beyond family life. An unhealthy woman may remove herself from the domain of family and mother, turning to extra-familial relationships for support in her efforts to achieve health. But because she is defined discursively as unhealthy/unattractive, the diseased woman is likely to exist in a constellation of involvements in which her sickness is masked due to systemic diseases—networks of persons brought together and sustained by illness. Primary in the excessive woman's abnormal ties, not surprisingly, are relationships with other women. From a practical standpoint, as seen above, women are more apt to be overweight than men. Thus it is likely that alliances with women run a greater risk of containing illnesses pertaining to excess. More generally, if woman is positioned in the realm of marginality, that is, if woman *is* disease, associations with all women must be examined and ideally transcended. Woman's release from disease is contingent on a release from women.

Female friends, in particular, are often seen by dieting rebels to prevent body liberation and health by endorsing or promoting excesses. Jane Fonda's (1981) account of a formerly abusive relationship to her body, for example, includes descriptions of friendships in which dangerous and unworkable diets are pursued, along with extreme eating binges. With encouragement from friends who are equally troubled by their bodies, Fonda perpetuates a cycle of body abuse and personal constraint. Freeing herself from abuse entails recognizing and accepting responsibility for alliances steeped in disease. As Robert

Linn (1980) argues, persons who wish to achieve health and beauty may have to abandon former friends because permanent weight loss is easier if "you avoid associating with Fat Failures—people who have dieted, constantly, and failed, constantly" (p. 262).

An anti-diet accomplishment of women's health is reliant upon a capacity to see that friends are often motivated by a desire to legitimize their own excesses, just as diet promoters are often motivated by their own financial gain. Friends encourage unchecked consumption in others not due to unqualified acceptance, but because of a wish to draw others into their own deviance. Similar to an alcoholic who preserves an image of normalcy by mandating consumption of liquor as a condition of continued friendship, female friends may retain self-defined respectability by demanding excessive food consumption of others. Because an unhealthy woman is drawn into and perpetuates the disease of friends, she must confess to her own disease. Body liberation calls for a condemnation and ultimate expulsion of friends whose unconditional acceptance is informed by a subtext of self-interest.

Within the boundaries of the anti-diet, female friends play a role that is at once trivial and significant. Typically, women friends receive little attention by dieting rebels, except for periodic emergence as a divisive influence. To some extent, *all* others must be trivialized to achieve health because anything but total self-reliance complicates liberation. Yet, some persons are more likely than others to encourage health. When women are free from a life of binging and dieting through the aid of friends, it is usually a male friend, or a female friend who endorses prevailing images of feminine health/beauty, who provides assistance. Fonda (1981) frees herself from body abuse through her association with a male dance instructor and friend. Gabrielle endorses the validity of male assistance in body liberation as she delineates the negative effects of female friends and the positive effects of male friends: "If you want to be supported in your diet, go to a man, not a woman. Women want you to fail so you'll be like them. Men want you to succeed." Because women friends perpetuate disease and anti-diets are designed to combat disease, female friends play a minimal part in the accomplishment of health. To be sure, a newly healthy woman may find herself in the company of "better" friends overall. Alternatively, Judy Wardell (1985) writes, the secrets of liberated and slender women ought to be "shared with family and friends, who deserve to be set free from the tyranny of dieting" (p. 285). Prior to health, however, women friends are depicted in a uniformly negative light—as persons who *prevent* the beauty and well-being of one another.

A general absence of positive focus on women's friendships in body reduction discourse is linked intricately and subtly to cultural visions of feminine sexuality. A central and implicit assumption in the domain of women's beauty/ health is that the labors of appearance are in principle heterosexual. Rosalind Coward (1985) has made this observation in the context of fashion, noting, "To be fashionable now is, I think, to express a readiness to keep up with prevailing sexual ideals" (p. 34). The payoff for women in anti-diets is an unsolicited command of male attention and sexual interest. Because she loves *herself* when beautiful, the healthy woman establishes relationships by choice rather than need. The convoluted logic of heterosexual desirability through self-love is infused with mandates for a demonstration of love for men, not women. In the many dieting success stories presented by Judy Mazel (1982), for example, nearly all include some version of increased heterosexual attractiveness, but the explicit rhetoric of experience as described centers on self-love. One of Mazel's newly thin clients reports, for illustration, "I did it, and I'm totally in love with myself" (p. 2).

Female friends who permit excesses are given visibility in anti-diets through depiction as persons who prevent self-love by transgressing hetero-sexual mandates. Although the excessive woman and the liberated woman may appear to have managed equally to abandon concerns with the assessments and judgments of others, the excessive woman's disease is grounded in her desire to bring others down with her. Healthy women, Wardell (1985) suggests, assist in helping others to achieve salvation. In much the same manner as Eve in Christian doctrine, diseased women friends are generally evil forces, placing all women in moral jeopardy by encouraging the consumption of forbidden substances; healthy women work to normalize others. The unrestrained woman, in turn, is undesirable as a heterosexual partner because she threatens to expose the arbitrary character of distinctions in the domains of sexual differ-ence and disease. If women's pleasure is woman-centered, male sexual partners are potentially rendered unnecessary as a source of pleasure and impotent as a source of power.

Portrayals of women's friendships in anti-diets are grounded in more gen-eral cultural understandings of friendship as an institution. Both historically and cross-culturally, the sanctity of friendship is reserved for men. This is not to say that friendships among women do not exist; rather, that male bonds are viewed as being stronger and healthier than are those of women. Robert Bell (1981) highlights the strength and selflessness of male bonds, noting "when friendships among men have been romanticized and eulogized, they have been friendships reflecting bravery, valor, and physical sacrifice in coming to the aid of another" (p. 75). Countless male bonds have been cast in an almost spiritual light, for example, in literature, film, and television. Although researchers in recent years have seriously questioned the presumed closeness in male friend-ships by pointing to competition, a lack of disclosure, and homophobia as barriers to intimacy between men, the cultural mythology concerning healthy male bonding continues (Basow, 1980, p. 213).[1] Moreover, the multitude of research indicating high levels of intimacy among female friends has not found its way into prevailing cultural images of women's friendships.

A general devaluation of relationships and communication among women, combined with the attendant dichotomies of sexuality and disease, underpins cultural views of female friendships. Women often come to internalize negative views of women's relationships with other women, claiming proudly that their friends are male because women are too petty, too superficial, too "gossipy." Women are viewed as persons who expend energy on unimportant or self-interested tasks, men hold more significant, morally laudible interests. Further, since women often represent a "bad" influence, female friends may be untrustworthy and unreliable. As Ann Seiden and Pauline Bart (1975) suggest, women are generally seen within culture to dislike women due to a lack of trust, an inability to work together, and competition for men (p. 192). In comparison to the valor and sacrifice of male friendships, the capacity to transcend self-interest, female friendships appear to rest on shaky ground, consumed by petty concerns and an absence of trust. Women's friendships are rendered insignificant due to their highly precarious foundations, exaggerating the healthy stability of male bonds.

There is indeed evidence to suggest that women's friendships are less enduring than men's. The temporal instability of female relationships, however, is not based in an inherent inability to sustain attachments, but due to heterosexual mandates which require women to exhibit health by abandoning female friends. Culturally, Bell (1981) notes, it "has been traditionally assumed that women can have their needs for close interpersonal relationships satisfied through their family and kin relationships" (p. 59). Female sexual development culminates in an exclusion of extra-family intimacies. The process of exclusion begins relatively early in the lives of women. The onset of dating behavior in girls, Susan Basow (1980) observes, often means that the "capacity for closeness and intimacy developed in same-sex relationships begins to generalize to heterosexual relationships" (p. 212). As girls begin to display signs of sexual maturation, efforts are directed toward receiving male approval. An ability to gain male approval is tied culturally to a lessening of intimacy in same-sex friendships because male interest is comprehended as the ultimate form of recognition, the basis upon which female value is determined. Basow writes, "a female's identity has been determined by the status of the male to whom she is attached . . . thereby limiting friendships. Or they may view friendships with girls as unimportant, since no status accrues from such relationships" (p. 212).

A primary mechanism at work to undermine women's friendships, given the signification of health and morality through beauty, concerns competition in the domain of physical attractiveness. Women comprehend outward appearance as a primary factor in societal evaluations of feminine worth; women who conform to beauty ideals seem to be valued highly. A lessening of one's opportunities in the marriage market, Susan Brownmiller (1984) points out, is often connected to a failure to outdo other women in the game of attractiveness. In order to appear more attractive, and indeed, more *moral* than others, a woman takes up competitive sensibilities regarding herself in relation to other women. She must show herself to be unlike most (diseased) women so that she is worthy of salvation. Cultural perceptions of female rivals are predominant, for example, in advertising imagery, where women are encouraged to "beat the competition" by purchasing countless varieties of "beauty" products. A contemporary television promotion for diet soft drinks combines images of gossipy women and female competition. A slender, youthful, scantily clad woman, who unwittingly catches the attention of each male as she walks along a crowded beach, is displayed to the viewing audience; a voice-over consists of two women, talking about the third woman "behind her back," comparing themselves to her and realizing that they are less attractive than she. Implicitly, viewers understand that the two gossiping women are in fact filled with disease and envy. Without too much hesitancy, viewers imagine two *unattractive* women in the position of jealous voyeur and competitor.

Body size and shape are perhaps the most prominent areas of feminine rivalry depicted in American culture. Only with much searching can one locate a popular women's magazine that does not entice consumers with an article on weight reduction or body conditioning. With virtually no exceptions, such articles assume that women want to be thin and that current readers are not thin *enough* to meet cultural standards. As Coward (1985) points out, readers are not enticed by the promise of thinness per se, but by the healthy attitudes represented by thinness. Yet, Coward argues, appearance is in no way separate from attitude: "The emphasis on the right mental attitude and the route to good health are subordinated to an overall requirement: their end product is that we should look better" (p. 23). In order to compete effectively, women are not only encouraged to obsess over dieting and exercise, but to view women's unhealthy attitudes as the cause of female disease and competition.

The anti-diet context for female friendships suggests tremendous difficulty in women's abilities to negotiate intimate relationships with one another. And indeed, women point to considerable obstacles in efforts to sustain female-female friendships. As in previous chapters, however, women's voices both embrace and resist cultural constructions of feminine health and disease. Two pervasive anti-diet themes emerge from women's stories concerning friends. The first theme centers on a contrast between surface and depth, wherein the "outsides" and "insides" of women are taken up by women to differentiate unhealthy from healthy relationships. A second, related theme concerns female competition as a primary barrier to intimacy among women friends. As women articulate experiences in which both themes figure prominently, the operations of an anti-diet politics of female liberation are reproduced and challenged, rendered compelling and simplistic in the portrayal of the body's position in women's friendships.

## Superficiality and Depth in Friendships

Perhaps the most pervasive theme in discussions of friendship and appearance centers on a contrast between superficiality and depth. The surface-depth distinction combines the issues of relational definition, body appearance, and truth. In non-intimate friendships, women report high levels of attention to external physical features; in intimate friendships, as Angela observes, friends must "go down to the depths of you and accept what they find there." True friends do not base judgments on appearance alone because physical features are viewed as surface qualities, comprising only a minor and not very truthful part of a person's overall character. Ana states, "Anyone can look good, I mean if you try, you can always look good. But that just goes to show you that looking good doesn't say very much about what a person is really like. You have to go deeper if you want to find out about someone." Relationships based in disproportionate attention to physical qualities, in turn, are conducive to negative evaluations because they reduce the whole of a person to external appearance. Jean summarizes: "When you don't know people well, you're left with looking at them, just the outside of them. When that's all you have to go on, it's easy to pick them apart. I've seen it happen. But when you know someone and care about someone, there's just too much more to deal with than just the way that person looks."

Critical gazing with respect to a friend's body appearance may be contrary to women's definitions of intimacy, yet women are well aware of the cultural priority placed on appearance. Further, consistent with Mazel's (1982) characterization of body management as a "way of life" (p. xvi), women suggest a correlation between physical appearance and general lifestyle. Women are often quick to endorse the anti-diet assumption that external features permit a deeper, more accurate, more "truthful" reading of the internal dimensions of a person: "You can tell a lot about a person by the way she looks;" "I can look at the way a girl is dressed and tell you a bunch of information about her interests, her attitudes, her family background, just endless information;" "If a girl or a woman is really fat or not very pretty, you sort of know she's got problems and isn't very happy." In further questioning as to what can be gleaned from looks, dress, body type, and attractiveness level, women tend to draw from stereotypes found in anti-diets. As Gabrielle surmises, for example, "if a girl is fat, she will probably be dressed to hide herself, and that right there shows she is embarrassed and not proud of the way she looks. I mean, it's sad because you know she can't possibly be happy that way."

The apparent contradiction in women's views of the truth value in surface body characteristics points to a central contradiction in anti-diets. Beauty is cast as a sign of health that reveals much about a woman, but beauty is also superficial, revealing nothing of a woman's true character. Dieting is restricted to the accomplishment of beauty, but freedom from dieting, Wardell (1985) stresses, involves a concern with "body, mind, and spirit" (p. xiv). Freedom from dieting, paradoxically, is signified by beauty. Enmeshed in this contradiction by virtue of cultural membership, women, like men, learn to both prioritize and trivialize the informational value of female physical appearance. A concern with the whole person is pervasive in women's friendships, but tempered by a scrambling of boundaries between that which appears and that which is hidden.

A distinction between surface and depth is both antithetical to, and consistent with, many dimensions of women's friendships. Acquiring a deep understanding of another person involves talk in the form of immediate, unguarded self-disclosure, combined with reflective capabilities which enable humane, nonreactionary responses to another. Deep dimensions of women are often revealed mutually, without anxiety or relational intimacy as determined temporally. As a central premise, anti-diets assume grave difficulty in facing and communicating the dark and hidden features of existence. Health and beauty result from a harsh and unblinking self-evaluation, in which buried truths are uncovered. Returning to the confession, Michel Foucault's (1980d) analysis reveals a simultaneous demand on the confessing individual to hide and reveal secrets, to speak the unspeakable (pp. 60-61). A so-called difficulty in the speaking of the personal, however, is generally not characteristic of women's friendships. Feminist analyses of female friendship patterns reveal that, typically, women are not threatened by the prospect of a mutual sharing of personal information. For women friends, Luise Eichenbaum and Susie Orbach (1987) argue, "Sharing is not a concession, a particularly difficult struggle, an extraction; it is rather part and parcel of women's relating. . . . *Not* sharing feels odd, a holding back that feels almost like a betrayal" (p. 19). Although it can be argued, if Eichenbaum and Orbach are correct, that women demand disclosure as a condition of friendship, the demand is not fully confessional in character because disclosure does not proceed with self-conscious difficulty and is not one-sided. Sharon states, for example, "I tell my best friend everything, and it's not like I say to myself there is this list of things I can't talk about, and this list of things will be okay to talk about. She does the same with me. We're comfortable enough with each other to just say whatever is on our minds at the time."

A willingness on the part of women friends to discuss personal experiences and affective states, however, is not ever-present. Despite images of women as persons who "tell all" to friends and strangers alike, talk between friends is often censored. As Eichenbaum and Orbach (1987) point out, the highly disclosive character of women's friendship is tempered by a fear of confronting relational problems, particularly those problems about which a woman feels hurt or angry. A woman may experience unbearable anxiety over the actions or attitudes of a close friend, but "equally unbearable (or unthinkable) is the thought of talking directly to one's friend about the upset... within women's friendships there seems to be more fear in talking about anger or hurt than there is in a marriage" (p. 22). Speaking to another about relational discord establishes clear differences between participants, places the other at a distance, separates her from oneself. The accused partner is obliged to give an accounting of her actions or, if the speaker is communicating a wrong that she has committed, obliged to grant forgiveness. Confronting relational problems within the structural configurations of speech acts in dominant culture imposes a confessional format, wherein speakers attempt to clarify the positions of wrongdoer and judge. Insofar as women's friendships are grounded by equality, a confession of internal states that forges a hierarchical difference is a violation of the relationship.

The uneasy fit between women's discussions of surface and depth and those found in anti-diets can be clarified by returning to Carol Gilligan's (1982) analysis of female morality. Women are found to negotiate relationships through an ethic of care and connection, which assumes an in-depth consideration of multiple dimensions of life decisions. To judge self or other by considering only particular dimensions of person or context is immoral, one of Gilligan's respondents indicates, because it requires a person to "decide carelessly or quickly on the basis of one or two factors when you know there are other things that are important and that will be affected" (p. 147). Achieving health in anti-diets is indeed dependent on a thorough analysis of one's relational life and everyday circumstances, but the decisions made as a result of analysis are predetermined by the discourse (beauty equals health), rendering them "superficial" and immoral.

Women's friendships are impaired when one or both partners is compartmentalized or judged according to narrow criteria because care and moral decision-making are absent. A demand on women to reduce self or others to surface qualities contradicts the complexity of what Jane calls "the good messiness of the way things are with people." In Diane's description of her reaction to a social invitation, for example, a contrast between her "outside" and her "inside" reveals that one-dimensional relationships are generally not worth her energy because they display an absence of complexity and care:

> If a friend only complimented my outside, he wouldn't be a close friend of mine because those compliments are rewarding, but boring. I just got into a situation the other day where a guy obviously didn't like the person I was. He invited me to a dance and I asked him why he invited me. He said, "Well, I thought you were cute." I said, "Grow up." I think he thought he was complimenting me, but I just did not think of it that way at all. [Why did that bother you?] I want people to recognize that I have an inside, that I have something to say, that I feel things, that I have a brain. And if they want to

judge me as just an outside, fine, but don't take me somewhere because of my outside. That said very little for him as a person. It said he was only concerned with my outside and not concerned with me as a person.

Importantly, Diane implicates the character of her friend ("That said very little for him as a person.") rather than herself; his reduction of her to "cuteness" bespeaks moral impoverishment. Further, she does not render attention to "outside" features wholly insignificant, but emphasizes the need to exhibit concern for all aspects of another.

Responding to others in a non-reductive manner, for many women, is tied to personal maturity. Significantly, as Beth recalls, immature relationships are temporally contextualized in adolesence or youth, "In high school, how you looked mattered a lot. Every day a huge topic of conversation was the dress that so and so had on, or noticing that someone had gained or lost weight. When you start to grow as a person, those things don't matter as much because your real friends like you, not your new dress." An implied separation of inside and outside features, a frenzied and rule-bound compartmentalization of self or others, is required by the prescriptions of anti-diets, but, for women, points to immaturity and insecurity. Wardell (1985), like other anti-diet authors, encourages readers to isolate and record innumerable personal habits and rela-tional behaviors, and to determine the extent to which particular actions and attitudes are healthy or unhealthy. The acts of isolation and judgment con-cerning the behavior of self and others are contrary to women's visions of maturity: "When you're young, everything seems so ordered and neat. You have groups of people who have certain traits, and you see yourself and them in pretty black and white ways;" "Life is really complicated if you're going to be responsible about it because everytime you think you have someone pinned down, that person does something to make your way of thinking seem silly;" "My mother always said that being grown-up is being flexible. That makes a lot of sense to me now because you have to keep adjusting the way you think about things."

Women may equate morality with complex and shifting assessments, but women are also inscribed in a culture wherein deductive capabilities, truth, and finality are lauded as measures of sophistication and moral worth. The ideology of finality is played out fully in anti-diets. A final resolution to body problems, as seen in previous chapters, is promised in the form of an afterlife, of a complete detachment from the messiness of human existence. Wardell's (1985) book ends by equating final mastery with salvation: "You have mastery now, knowing exactly what to do to remain thin, satisfied, and filled with delight for the rest of your life. So take flight. The entire universe is your domain" (p. 284). Images of an afterlife are particularly compelling in the con-clusion of Mazel's (1982) book, where the author assures, "Tomorrow is here.

Here for you to celebrate. Could you have imagined getting on your scale and not having to lose one more pound? Could you have imagined being perfect?" (p. 230). Personal maturity does not automatically resolve appearance issues for women because they know that others, including themselves, make conclusive judgments based on attractiveness. Further, women understand, health is often measured by a capacity to render seemingly impartial and final assessments.

A promise of final resolution, final judgment, plays out in an uncomfortable fashion in women's body experience as contextualized by friendship. Although individuals presumably relish the opportunity for favorable assessment by others, women report uneasiness at the prospect of receiving assessments in which maturity and care are absent. An onslaught of self-consciousness often occurs as a woman has the sensation of being watched and evaluated by casual or potential friends, by persons who draw final conclusions *because* they do not care. Being watched in a reductive manner is often permeated with negative self-reflection and self-evaluation. Jane observes, "At a party, for some reason, people just think it's okay to stare you up and down, to give you dirty looks, and you know they're saying bad things about you. You start to feel like there's something wrong with you, like you've got your pants on backwards or something. Or maybe I forgot to shave my legs today. I hate it." The experience of being watched by persons who do not know Jane produces a feeling that "there's something wrong with you."

An anti-diet response to Jane's self-consciousness may be that Jane is unattractive by social standards. Success in the domain of beauty/health may be prescribed as the cure for Jane's "sickness." Yet, women indicate, unattractiveness as defined culturally does not necessarily diminish negative consciousness regarding appearance: "I might want to go to a party with friends and dress to the nines, knowing I look great, but then you have to deal with everyone staring at you;" "Being beautiful is not always an advantage. It means that people think it's okay to look at you and judge you, and usually they'll try to find something wrong with you;" "If you're out with friends and you look great, it sometimes makes it hard to talk because you're so aware of yourself." Attractiveness often "invites" the gazes of others, intensifying a woman's body consciousness and attendant anxiety.

Body consciousness often occurs not because a woman is unattractive/ unhealthy, but because primacy is given to physical appearance in her ability to communicate. The body is isolated from other dimensions of the person, and gazed upon as an object by self and others. Although women appear to embrace anti-diet prescriptions which demand an accounting of the whole person for an accomplishment of health, a reunion of mind and body, women diverge from the discourse of excess by suggesting that an absence of culturally defined beauty is not necessarily indicative of disease. When friendships are not based in complex visions of care, however, the fear of evaluation is present because women are well aware of *cultural* associations between disease and unattractiveness. Beth illustrates the duality of care and negative judgment in noting, "the nicest, most caring people are usually not the real attractive people, but they're not well thought of anyway because our society thinks it's sick to be ugly, I mean, that people would want to be beautiful if they could." Many women use the context of a party or informal social gathering to illustrate instances of negative body consciousness among acquaintances or casual friends. Here, objectification of the body occurs, in part, because there is not a shared history between relational partners. Paula describes a situation in which body consciousness is directly linked to relational superficiality:

> I was invited to a party and almost didn't go because I had gained about fifteen pounds. All my clothes looked like hell on me and I knew that I'd just stand out because, first of all, I barely knew those people, and second of all, because lots of those women are really skinny. Well, I said to myself, "Don't let them intimidate you," and I went. But as soon as I walked in the door, I asked myself why I came. Nobody knew me and nobody talked to me and I felt like a total nonentity. People looked at me and since they weren't talking to me, I thought they were judging me and thinking I looked like I wasn't a part of their group. Finally someone talked to me, but I knew she just felt sorry for me because I just stood there, looking lost. I left early. When I was walking out to my car, I felt like the ugliest creature God had put on this earth.

For Paula, being in the midst of people who do not know or speak to her heightens a negative evaluation of appearance: "I felt like the ugliest creature God had put on this earth." Undoubtedly, Paula's weight gain played a part in her experience, but in her description of the evening, the fact that nobody "knew me and nobody talked to me" engenders a sense of herself as a "total nonentity."

The sensation of negative self-consciousness is influenced by the appearance of persons who are seen as evaluators in a social setting. As Paula indicates, the presence of "really skinny" women can be unsettling if she is feeling unattractive. If those who stare evaluatively are perceived to be more attractive by cultural standards than the one who receives others' assessments, negative self-consciousness is more likely to occur than if evaluators are seen to be less attractive. In part, as Linn (1980) and other dieting rebels suggest, stares from attractive women may be uncomfortable because such women magnify the physical imperfections of other, less attractive women. And indeed, cultural images of women imply, beautiful women have the power to look down upon less beautiful women; beautiful women stand out from other women and value themselves as a result of their singularity. Yet, for Paula, a sensation of *ugliness* stems from "standing out" and "not being a part of their group."

Situations in which others are unknown do not always produce paralyzing self-consciousness. An absence of body awareness, moreover, is not always grounded in feelings of physical inferiority. Although many women evaluate their bodies negatively in the context of a social gathering initially, the evaluation itself is sometimes reassessed and shifted to a more positive view of one's appearance. In order for the shift to take place, however, women focus on *relational* dimensions of the experience rather than appearance. As Marsha indicates, for example, a favorable view of her body is possible with the realization that she is capable of interacting with others, that she need not be "reduced" to outward appearance:

> This past weekend I was invited to a beach party and I was feeling very fat. Some of the girls were incredible. [Meaning what?] Just really, really skinny. They were the kind that you look at in magazines and they can be really intimidating. At first I thought, God, maybe I should just keep on my shorts while I was there, on the beach. Then I said to myself, "Marsha, it doesn't really matter because whether you look like that or not doesn't mean somebody won't want to talk to you, or that you won't want to talk to anybody else." I realized that as a person I think I am pretty good, even if I do happen to be a little chubby. And if you think you're a good person, someone who's nice to be around and nice to talk to, then how you look isn't such a big deal. Anyway, it's then that you can make friends.

In order for Marsha to feel comfortable in the midst of "incredible" women, she reflects on physical features within a context of overall personal qualities. To say that she simply *rationalized* her deficiencies is simplistic. Reflection on her capacity to engage with others reduces the centrality afforded outward appearance, allowing her to see that, in the end, people ought to be more interested in whether "you're a good person, someone who's nice to be around and nice to talk to." Interacting comfortably with others is possible when appearance is dispersed as a primary issue because only through such de-emphasis are responsible friendships possible.

Comfortable interaction requires relational care, but does not preclude an active interest in appearance between women friends. Although women associate depth and complexity with intimacy, they also suggest that surface body characteristics play an important part in intimate friendships. Anti-diets often cast women in the part of voyeur with respect to other women, as persons who gaze critically and with envy at women. Linn (1980) suggests, for example, that women friends are a dangerous lot because they are often displeased by a friend's increased physical attractiveness (p. 261). Functioning as a voyeur, jealous or otherwise, holds the other at a distance, objectified and separate. Additionally, voyeurism implies inequality since detached assessment assumes superiority. For women, a key difference in dealings with appearance between close friends and acquaintances is an absence of *negative* body consciousness because, as Paula states, "you know your close friend cares about you and you care about her." Many women relay stories in which mutual and involved attention to the bodies of women friends is pleasurable: "[My best friend] and I love sitting around and doing our nails, doing each other's hair, and trying on each other's clothes;" "I have some real good girlfriends and a typical thing we do is sit around and talk about our bodies, and those are some of my best memories;" "It's great to have a close friend because you can share your insecurities about looks, and she listens and relates to you and doesn't think you're being stupid."

A close female friend, for many women, is the *only* person to whom one can turn for a complex, careful, discussion of body issues. Because women's beauty labors are both mandated and trivialized within dominant culture, it is often difficult to locate persons who will give serious attention to the complexity of female body appearance. Further, Brownmiller (1984) points out, women are required culturally to "hide" the labors of appearance, constructing beauty as a passive endeavor, in order to preserve the myth that women are "naturally" different from men (pp. 15-16). To express ambivalence about beauty, even though beauty, as we have seen elsewhere, brings its own forms of condemnation, is to signify a diseased female identity. Women may be the only persons capable of understanding the body experience of women because, as Jean suggests, "women are the only ones who can relate, really relate, to this impossible situation we're in. They're the only ones who know, from being in it too, that these body problems are not clear-cut."

To say that close women friends understand one another's body experience is not to say that women never feel negative body consciousness in the presence of intimate friends. Eichenbaum and Orbach (1987) provide analyses of women's friendship in which strained bonds between friends are traceable, in part, to physical appearance. Similarly, in Geneen Roth's (1982) collection of women's stories on the experience of compulsive eating, varying forms of female friendship surface implicitly as sources of body anguish. It is arguable that women become negatively aware of the body's appearance in intimate friendships when reminded of cultural standards, which proceed hierarchically and demand comparisons and judgments. Many women describe uneasiness in public situations with a close friend, for example, when others give greater attention to the friend: "It can be really terrible to be out with [my friend], who happens to be gorgeous, because I feel like a bump on a log;" "I feel awful for saying this because I love my best friend so much, but sometimes I don't like it when we go out because she is the one who gets all of the attention;" "It's hard not to feel inferior when you're out with a girl and everyone is talking to her and leaving you out." The cultural judgments made of women's bodies, the comparisons and determinations of attractiveness, are sufficiently pervasive to enter into women's most intimate friendships.

Attention given to a friend rather than to oneself often produces uneasiness or self-consciousness, but notably, women do not locate the problem in the friend's physical attractiveness. Rather, tension arises from the experience of being excluded, of having one's friend "taken away" by others, of feeling disconnected from a close friend. A profound sense of loss infuses experience of exclusion *and* attention. Linn (1980) reduces the complexity of this experience to a shared misery thesis, stating that when friends "see you happy, then they're left all alone with their problem . . . They're afraid of losing you now that you look so much better and are probably glowing with overall confidence too" (pp. 260-261). However, women report that the experience of *receiving* more attention than a friend can be equally alienating. Stephanie illustrates:

> For a long time my closest friend and I were the same size. We have been friends all through high school and college, and it's one of those relationships where you know you'll be friends forever. When we both got jobs in different towns, I went on a big diet and decided I was going to get thin, which I did. She came to visit me in the spring and hadn't seen me since the fall. She was really happy for me because I had lost a lot of weight—she praised me, asked how I did it, how I felt about it, just everything about it. But it ended up being an upsetting weekend. It's hard for me to say this, but I started noticing how people looked at me and not at her, and how a waiter or salesclerk would pay more attention to me. I wanted to scream at them for being so inconsiderate. It made me feel like I was being compared to her, like we were all of a sudden so different, like I was somehow better, more worthy or something. The whole thing was awful.

For Stephanie, misery results from receiving *favorable* attention from others. Her friend is not cast in the role of an embittered or hostile competitor, but as a supportive and enthusiastic relational partner. Stephanie's ability to "glow with overall confidence" is diminished *because* she, in Linn's (1980) words, looks "so much better" (pp. 260-261).

When disproportionate attention is given to women friends, they are placed in the positions of detached judges with respect to each other. They are jarred by the presence of socio-cultural evaluations and often uncomfortable with the criteria by which judgments are made. The friend receiving attention is suddenly confronted with her friend as only an "outside," a deficient and separate other, a characterization that is incompatible with the intertwining of lives in women's friendships. Perhaps this is why women express guilt over feelings of being ignored or attended to when in the company of a close friend; guilt arises from the sense of relational irresponsibility resulting from a sudden "reduction" of a friend or oneself to outside features.

Listening intently to women's body talk is a dangerous prospect due to its capacity to undermine prevailing images of women. As long as women's friendships are seen to be centered on discussions concerning the horror of breaking a fingernail, the devastation of a five pound weight gain, or the pros and cons of permanent waves, dominant imagery is preserved. Women then appear to be neurotic, insecure, vain, superficial: diseased. They are defined categorically and stripped of complexity; they are "reduced" to outward appearance. Yet, as women have suggested repeatedly, appearance is but one element in the context of friendships. Women's body talk then works as resistance to dominant images of women because it takes up *and* decentralizes appearance as an issue in the lives of women.

The forms of women's talk and the topic areas that are most trivialized, I believe, often pose the greatest threats to discourses of domination. As Dale Spender (1985) demonstrates in her analysis of cultural responses to women's consciousness-raising groups, the trivilization of such groups and their issues is belied by the frenzy with which male partners and husbands discourage the participation of their girlfriends and wives (pp. 108-114). Similarly, if issues of appearance are indeed trivial, it should please men to see women who give little thought or attention to presenting an attractive body. Such women are viewed negatively precisely because they defy male imagery and point to the artificiality of the so-called "natural" beauty of women.

### Rethinking Female Competition

Central to a cultural diminishment of female friendships are portrayals of women as highly competitive individuals in matters of appearance. Anti-diet discourse is pervaded by images of female rivalry which often leads to a deterioration of friendship. Invariably, as suggested by Fonda's (1981) discussion of competitive female friendships as part of her *past* life, competition in matters of appearance is seen to be destructive to intimate relationships. Competitive women are embued with excessive self-centeredness, a lack of concern for others due to a drive to be the best, the most superior, regardless of the cost to friendships. A recurring theme in discussions of women's eating obsessions combines frenzied self-centeredness with disease characterized by excess. On the cover of Roth's (1982) book, for example, an excerpt reads, "The inside of a food binge is deep and dark . . . A descent into a world in which every restriction is cut loose. Nothing matters—not friends, not family, not lovers. Nothing matters but food. Lifting, chewing, swallowing—mechanical, frenzied." Diseases pertaining to appearance render the formation of healthy relationships impossible because, in the effort to win at being most attractive, responsibilities to others are sacrificed for self-satisfaction.

A complex and paradoxical definition of female weakness, combined with images of feminine disease, informs anti-diet visions of competitive women.

Specifically, only strong and individualistic women are capable of forming healthy relationships, but women who are self-focused are indifferent to the needs of others and consequently diseased. Fonda's (1981) work is worthy of considerable attention because, within the boundaries of the text, the paradox of female health and disease becomes pronounced.

Notably, Fonda's present friendships are formed with women who exhibit physical strength, mental determination, self-confidence. In a chapter titled "Breaking the 'Weaker Sex' Mold," Fonda chronicles the lives and bodies of strong women, including professional athletes such as Evelyn Ashford, Beth Heiden, Mary Decker, Nadia Commaneci, among others, and pays homage to pioneer women and Rosie the Riveter of the World War II era (pp. 45–49). In the story of a friend and work associate, Fonda recalls a friend's physically disastrous accident, in which the friend was hit by a car and sent through a plate glass window, crushing her pelvis and breaking her legs. The story epitomizes the importance of female strength and determination. Fonda writes, "Even though she was confined to a hospital bed, she managed to devise a special exercise regime for her upper body and torso... The doctors and nurses were amazed at her determination—and how quickly she recovered" (p. 48). Fonda's account substitutes female weakness for female strength, enabling greater individual determination, but the women presented are also highly competitive in a blatantly *physical* sense.

The moral dimensions of female competition and strength are highlighted, again paradoxically, by Fonda's discussion of the weaker sex mold. Impressionable and weak women from the past are replaced by "strong and healthy" women who "are taking the initiative, they are not being manipulated" (p. 47). Healthy women aspire to self-development through fitness, but do not rely on others. Although Fonda discounts a correlation between strong women and superior morality, "I do not claim that a strong, healthy woman is automatically going to be a progressive, decent sort of person," she does note that "one's innate intelligence and instinct for good can be enhanced through fitness" (p. 49). By implication, unhealthy and unfit women are in danger of their innate goodness remaining dormant, underdeveloped and weak. In Fonda's vision, strong women are more attentive to their surroundings, responsible to others and the environment, and aware of women's exploitation. Yet, returning to Fonda's images of independent women, photographs depict women who signify singular attention to appearance, lives devoted to competition with other women, determination to win at all costs.

A distinction between healthy and unhealthy friendships blurs because self-centered competition points equally to illness *and* fitness. In anti-diets, the key difference between diseased and healthy women is that the former have not mastered the art of "fair" competition, resorting instead to underhanded and ineffectual means in the effort to win. Healthy women, by contrast, compete through sheer mental and physical stamina. But at base, both states of being signify separation from others and an accentuated sense of individuality.

A heightened capacity to compete in a healthy manner develops through an enhancement of individual attractiveness, trancendence of the barriers to female well-being. At the same time, disproportionate levels of beauty between friends is said to *instigate* negative forms of female competition. Linn (1980) warns that friends

> may be afraid of the physical competition the slim you would give to them. This problem often arises when two people of the same sex are friends, and one loses weight and the other can't . . . Women, when they lose weight and start to look attractive, are especially threatening to other women, including those whom they consider their closest friends . . . What used to be a friendly relationship may become a bitterly competitive and hostile one (pp. 260–261).

For Linn, like other proponents of anti-diets, beauty is the cause and the effect of female competition. A friend's increased physical attractiveness introduces relational tension; a desire to acquire beauty is based in competitive sensibilities with respect to other women.

The impossible paradox of the strong and moral woman is both articulated and critiqued as women describe female competition. Given the centrality of independence in anti-diet images of healthy women, manifested as physical attractiveness, and the importance of care and connection in women's friendships, women both take up and challenge dominant images of feminine health. Initially, nearly all women report that competition among women is particularly strong in matters of the body: "Women are just very competitive when it comes to looks;" "Being thin and in shape is something women strive for, and they're very competitive with each other over those things;" "You have to be careful with girlfriends because it is a fact that girls are really, really competitive;" "I hate to say it, but the bold truth is that women compete with each other a lot, and mostly they compete to be the prettiest, the skinniest, the most beautiful." Quite readily, nearly all women concur with anti-diet characterizations, reporting or suggesting that competition in the domain of appearance is often pervasive and destructive.

Women who compete in an unhealthy fashion are portrayed as unattractive persons in anti-diets, but, as seen above, attractive women are often equally bothered by the implied comparisons which ground competition. Machiavellian sensibilities infuse anti-diets insofar as only *successful* women, beautiful women, gain credibility through competition. However, for women, the means to achieving beauty are often seen to be incompatible with intimacy, regardless of external appearance. As Gilligan's (1982) work shows, women's choices are informed by an ability for "seeing consequences of action by keeping the web or relationships intact" (p. 59). Gabrielle combines an absence of relational care and competition in external appearance, observing, "our society pits women against each other and it doesn't really matter how you look or if you're pretty or whatever. You can't really get close to anyone if you're comparing yourself and trying to outdo that person. She just has to be a non-person to you because you can't care how mean you get." Seeing an other as a "non-person" requires a reduction to "outside" features only, cancelling possibilities for intimacy. Competition based in external appearance, within women's understandings of intimacy, is problematical not because of inequity in empirical measures of attractiveness, but because such competition is regressive, requiring meanness, abandoning the ethic of care.

The superiority over other women promised or implied in body reduction discourse stands in direct contradiction to women's linkages between morality, intimacy, connectedness, and attention to the whole person. Beauty permits one to be "above" others, women acknowledge, but points to impoverishment if it exists independently from other dimensions of the person. Women's observations are initially corroborated by anti-diets since, like women, dieting rebels such as Fonda (1981) condemn the reduction of persons to outside appearance. Through a careful hearing, however, it becomes clear that the point of disturbance for women rests in a false equation between beauty or "fitness" and moral superiority. Competition is often avoided, Nicole indicates, not due to an inability to compete successfully, but due to the isolation and emptiness signified by being above others:

> I don't like people competing with me. The way a person looks doesn't make the person, but lots of people want it to be that way. I don't, though, not because I can't, but because I have no desire to be up there and say, "Here I am, one of these great looking people." If I don't have anything inside of me, I'd rather develop that. When you're up there, above everybody else, your life doesn't mean anything. So what? You can be great looking and have nothing else going for you. You can't be that way and be close to people.

Great looking people, for Nicole, are "up there, above everybody else." Implicitly, she assumes a distinction between being above others and having an underdeveloped "inside."

Superiority resulting from reducing self or others to external dimensions represents a deficiency, a lack of complexity. Indeed, within culture beautiful women signify reduction, concealment, emptiness. In the domain of intimate female friendships, an absence of care is often signified by a building sense of rivalry. Nicole describes a pattern in her friendships with women, wherein the movement of the relationship regresses due to jealousy, moving from intimacy to distance:

The most frustrating thing is becoming involved with a girl and you really care about her, and you think you're such good friends. You talk about everything and you just love her. Then, you feel things start to turn. You feel things start to deteriorate when jealousy and competition start slipping in. You go out to bars and she says things to you. My girlfriend would say, "I don't like going out with you because you always have so much to say and I stand around like a real dummy. And I look stupid when I'm next to you." What am I supposed to say? She is giving you a compliment, but saying, "Just because you're good, I don't like you." . . . Even though I care about her, I can't change certain things about myself. I've tried really hard, but there have been lots of girls who were obsessed with this and almost ruin my life as a result. It starts building because I start realizing the problem, and they start realizing the problem, and I try to step back a little, but that frustrates me. I mean, I thought they liked *me*. Looks are dangerous in that respect. I think the whole thing in society makes it very difficult for women's relationships and friendships. Society reinforces a lot of backstabbing, a lot of shallow relationships, a lot of social relationships for women. I mean, you just can't care about someone a lot and compete with her. It just doesn't work because it drives a wedge between you.

The regression described by Nicole is grounded in her sense of relationships moving backwards, of slowly reducing Nicole to appearance, which promotes "backstabbing" and "shallow relationships for women." A similar scenario of regression is offered by Beth:

I used to have a real close girlfriend. We're not close anymore and the reason is that things became competitive. Jealousy and competition turned what we had into a failed friendship. We both acted very irresponsibly toward each other, as if we barely knew each other, or as if we hadn't been through all that we had been through. I mean, we were inseparable for a long time, and then all of a sudden, bang, we were trying to beat each other. We were like strangers by the last stages of the friendship. I just felt numb for a long time during and after that experience because it really hurts to find out that what you thought was so special and so together is really nothing.

Women's desires for noncompetitive female friendships often entail the formation of friendships with men as a means by which to alleviate direct comparisons, judgments, regression. Significantly, women who form close friendships with men are almost invariably young and unmarried. Due to societal suspicions which surround female-male friendship, sustaining an intimate friendship with a man is difficult. "Except during courtship," as Bell (1981) notes, "men and women are not expected to pursue interaction voluntarily with one another . . . Even when they are unmarried, they are usually not encouraged to form friendships, but to try and find a marriage partner" (p. 97). Given the priority of marriage in the socialization of women, females, who prefer males as friends may be doubly suspicious within culture. That is, such a preference implies at least temporary indifference to marriage at a time when women are supposed to give priority to finding a mate. In addition, because "good" women are expected to seek male companionship solely within the context of marriage, where high degrees of social regulation take place, a woman who elects to engage in friendships with men may be seen to exhibit deviant, uncontrolled sexuality. Bell observes, for example, "being lovers places some social controls over sexuality, while being friends does not" (p. 97). From the outset, given cultural characterizations of female-male inter-action, friendships with men risk the label of illness and threaten a reduction to singular (sexual) features of woman.

Initially, male friends appear to provide relief from competition among women in the domain of appearance. Men offer the possibility of escape from the beauty game because men are not socialized to judge friends based on physical beauty. If attractiveness is not based on external or fragmented qualities of the person in male friendships, alliances with men promise con-formity with women's definitions of intimacy, care, and morality. Nicole makes a connection between female competition and her choice of male friends:

> It's really one of the hardest things I talk about. One of the hardest things in friendships with women is competition in appearance, and that's why I usually have more friendships with men. There have been very few girls that I have known who don't get hung up on competing with me. And I don't feel that way. I don't want to do it. I don't think I'm attractive. I go down to Florida and I put on a bathing suit and it looks like hell. I look terrible.

Friendships with men undoubtedly alleviate competition over attractiveness in a directly comparative sense. Cultural constructions of difference in female and male bodies render impossible the task of judging female and male attractive-ness according to the same criteria. Men may afford the possibility of placing the body into a more general context of personal qualities, enabling the relationship to conform to women's definitions of intimacy.

Friendships with men provide additional rewards. A man's "willingness" to define a woman as his friend may function to elevate her credibility in the worlds of both women and men, thereby serving as a powerful form of recogni-tion. Tremendous female urgency is attached to the struggle for recognition, Andrea Dworkin (1987) argues, because as women, "we exist as persons to the extent that men in power recognize us" (p. 127). When men recognize women as friends, *and* promise an escape from the agonies of female competition, they may indeed become desirable friends. Nicole summarizes the benefits of male friendship, "With men, you're not competing so there is not much to fight about. He doesn't care if Billy so and so talks to you in a cafe because you don't have that kind of relationship. And it's sort of neat to have a guy friend. I mean, that he could enjoy having you as a friend."

Friendships with men, given the oppositional position of women and men within culture, are not free from problems. Many women describe the difficulty of maintaining cross-sex friendships, and, not surprisingly, locate problems in issues pertaining to attractiveness and sexuality. Indeed, if women are seen culturally to compete solely for the sake of gaining male recognition, and are perceived to announce desires for male attention through beauty, physical attractiveness/health complicates the establishment of platonic relationships. Further, returning to Basow's (1983) observations regarding the transfer of intimacy from female to heterosexual partners, women who seek male companionship may be seen to hold romantic interests. Bell (1981) summarizes a survey report in *Psychology Today* which analyzed women's and men's views of cross-sex friendship (pp. 98-99). Opposite sex friendships were seen by respondents to be very different from same sex friendships, most primarily, because in the former, "sexual tensions complicated the relationship" (p. 99). Bell argues that sexual tensions produce problems because while men may enter a friendship with a woman in order to pursue sexual activity without commitment, "many women see friendship with men as a prelude to a future love relationship and the potential for marriage" (p. 104). Implicitly, Bell's analysis underscores prevailing stereotypes by suggesting that many women seek intimacy, sexual involvement, and commitment with all men.

Women offer a very different account of the sexual tensions in their friendships with men than the one proposed by Bell (1981). Many women acknowledge the presence of tension resulting from issues of sexuality, attractiveness, and attraction, but do not suggest that friendship is a prelude to romance or marriage. Gabrielle wonders, for example, "Why would I want to marry a man friend any more than I would want to marry a woman friend? Why do men think that's what you want?" Although women indicate that romantic partners are also friends, they do not suggest that friends are, or will become, romantic partners. If anything, women often experience uneasiness when a male friend indicates a romantic interest. For example, Ruth correlates a desire to remain overweight to an alleviation of romantic interest in her friendships with men: "I think I get along easily with guys because I play around with them. But sometimes they take things the wrong way and think I want a romantic relationship with them. That has happened so many times with different guy friends, and I think that has a lot to do with not wanting to be thin." By making herself undesirable, according to traditional standards for female attractiveness, Ruth eliminates an obstacle in her friendships with men; her desire for male sexual interest is refuted by her body.

Many women echo Ruth's sentiments by describing situations in which a change in appearance led to uncomfortable attention from male friends. Laurie remembers how a negligible weight loss altered her friendships with men:

> I remember one summer I lost only eight pounds, and it didn't make much of
> a difference. But all of a sudden, guys would ask me out, even though I used
> to be just one of their buddies. And they would ask my advice about other
> girls—should they ask this one out, would she go out with them—they were
> always asking my advice about dating. I'm not sure if it's because I lost weight
> or because we were good friends, or if they just considered me a friend or as a
> romantic partner. You know, to all of a sudden talk about girls and romance as
> a way of getting me to notice them in that way . . . With my good guy friends I
> didn't want to have anything romantic, but they would tell me that so and so
> likes me and wants to take me out.

A striking parallel in the stories of Ruth and Laurie is that sexual tension and
romantic interest results from increased attractiveness; both women become
potential sexual or romantic partners *because* they are considered by former
"buddies" to be more attractive. If intimacy is defined as concern and connectedness with the whole person, a reduction to sexuality or appearance calls into
question the closeness of female-male friendship bonds.

In cross-sex friendships, as in friendships between women, female appearance plays a part in relational dynamics. Women may be perceived to be undesirable friends because undo emphasis is given to competition in the area of
physical attractiveness; men may be undesirable friends because, similarly,
physical attractiveness introduces relational conflict and tension. In either
case, discomfort resides in a pronounced focus on women's outward appearance. Moreover, both scenarios carry an implicit assumption that women tend
to their bodies in an effort to attract male attention. Friendships with women
and men must be potentially transcended in an effort to avoid preoccupation
with the surface of women, with the implied reduction to outside features.
Both types of involvement, as Nicole observes, are in danger of becoming diseased: "Having a guy friend being obsessed with your body is just as sick as
having a girlfriend do that. If they're just as obsessed [as girls], what's the point
of having any friends?"

A primary component of the morality characteristic of women's friendship
centers on an awareness that a person's self-image and sense of worth are tied
to the actions of others, whether others are female or male. The demand for
individuality in anti-diets, the transcendence of others' evaluations, connotes
a self-centeredness that is incompatible with women's visions of morality. Individuals not only have a responsibility to see that they affect others, but that
they are affected by others' assessments. A male friend who unthinkingly or
uncaringly reduces a friend to particular features is acting as irresponsibly as a
female friend who does so because, in either case, responsibility for the other is
disowned. As women indicate, a person does not exist in a vacuum, but
functions in relation to and with other people; a woman's view of herself is

dependent on the manner in which others treat her. Ellen states, for example,

> It's very clear to me that a lot of the way I feel about myself is extremely dependent on other people—how they respond to me and whether or not I think that they think I look good, or they like me, or they think I'm confident. Much of it is dependent on the messages that I either get directly or indirectly from other people.

Women are not reluctant to admit dependence on the evaluations of others because, as Lucy states, "if you're not affected by how people react to you, you're not alive." Because the impact of others on self-perception is unavoidable for "living" human beings, care must be taken in responding to an intimate friend because she is affected by the actions of her friendship partner.

Women report that friendship entails responsibility for another's sense of self and identity. Women do not speak simply of trying to make one another feel good or of a mutual bolstering of egos, but of a complex process whereby reciprocal responsibility must be taken for the establishment of identities-in-relation. That is, individual identities merge *and* function interdependently so that responsibility must be acknowledged for two separate persons who are intertwined through relational history. Once again drawing a distinction between inside and outside features, Diane delineates the responsibility of friends to acknowledge their reciprocal contributions to each other's identity:

> I'm somewhere in the middle of attractiveness and unattractiveness. I'm attractive, I think. Other people see my outside. People in a bar will judge you on first appearance, then they will get to know me. They will see that I'm a nice person, and I see that they are interacting me as if I'm a nice, loving person, not just a body. I internalize their attitudes toward me and it helps me to project a nice and loving outwardness . . . Telling someone about her outside is important, but when she starts internalizing the words, that's when you have to notice insides because you played a part in what's inside of her. That's when you have to start getting feedback and giving feedback to insides. If you just keep complimenting the outside of a friend, then it becomes superficial; it's nothing because you are basically saying, 'Hey, I'm not responsible for you.' You are saying she doesn't have an effect on you either; you're just not together and you don't affect each other.

Diane's description is complex and rich with insight. An acknowledgment of outside features only is correlated with irresponsibility, yet attention to outward features is included in responsibility for the other's identity. When others are responsive and behave with Diane as if she is a "nice, loving person," her "insides" are projected as a form of "outwardness." Friends who fail to acknowledge both insides and outsides, and the extent to which their actions "construct" the other, are "not together" and "don't affect each other."

When women encounter the rhetoric of anti-diets, reduction and irre-sponsibility are presented as the ingredients for liberating friendships. A reduction in body is a reduction of the person that requires distancing oneself from a web of relationships sustained by mutuality and care. As women have shown repeatedly, isolation from others, whether or not one conforms to cul-tural standards for attractiveness, is often an alienating, uncomfortable experi-ence. Images of confinement—being watched, assessed, and judged—surface as women relay stories in which they stand out from others. Feelings of abnor-mality result from being examined from a distance, prompting self-scrutiny: confession.

The confession demanded of women in anti-diets is contrary to visions of friendship and female identity. As seen throughout this chapter, intimate friendships promise the possibility of at least temporary escape from hierar-chical judgments which prompt confession. To occupy the dieting rebel stance of resistance, of accepting responsibility for oneself only, is impossible for women not only because it signifies irresponsibility, but because female stereotypes prioritize women's abilities to sustain relationships. The impos-sible position of women renders liberation difficult. Within the domain of anti-diets, the healthy woman questions and transcends attachments, but the healthy woman also acknowledges the importance of her relationships. The healthy woman readies herself for sexual attention, but the healthy woman does not require the sexual interest of others. The healthy woman does not need friends, but the healthy woman sustains healthy friendships. Totalizing confinement within the multiple paradoxes of women's "health," women understand, can be escaped temporarily through an *absence* of confession.

## Chapter 6

# Romantic Relationships: "Getting Him to See Me"

*I have always felt that men were attracted to good looking
women, and I have never changed my opinion of that.*

*Ellen*

The excessive woman who combats disease by releasing herself from the grips of oppressive attachments appears to ready herself for sexual or romantic relationships with men. Through a physical transformation from illness to health, displayed by conformity to cultural beauty standards, a woman becomes a desirable relational partner. Her conformity, by implication, endorses a masculine valuing of control and transcendence because, to achieve health, she has had to rise above the constraints of femaleness as signified by mother, friends, and self. A popular scenario in anti-diets centers on the diseased woman who fears or dislikes men and uses her unattractive body to keep them at a distance; failure to show an interest in men is a failure to exhibit control, an inability to separate from women. With remarkable frequency, for example, anti-diet authors who have cured themselves of weight problems establish an implicit correlation between achieving fitness/beauty and achieving healthy relationships with men (Fonda, 1981; Boone-O'Neill, 1982; Principal, 1983). Evidence for freedom from abnormality and disease appears in the form of romantic love.

The equation between women's health and romantic love is complicated in anti-diets by a concurrent demand on the diseased individual to rise above *all* constraining attachments. Rebels in the world of women's health stress repeatedly that efforts to achieve beauty must be individual in character, not reliant on others. To illustrate, cosmetic surgeon Jerrold C. Gendler (1987) argues, "it is important to realize that having cosmetic surgery done is a personal decision" (pp. 2-4). Rather than approval from others or satisfying

romantic relationships as the rewards of beauty, he underscores a "more positive mental attitude" as the "ultimate reason for improving your appearance"
(p. 2). A closer approximation to cultural beauty standards, provided it results
from an individual decision, alleviates disease in mind and body. "People who
are self-assured regarding their appearance," Gendler writes, "are often more
well adjusted than those who are not" (pp. 2-4). Thus, a key element in
women's health involves an identification and cure of disease which necessarily
transcends the influence of others.

A fairly transparent contradiction informs the anti-diet logic of individual
choice. Namely, if readers actually follow the advice of rebels in the world of
women's health, they will refuse the cosmetic alterations promoted by authors
such as Gendler because his images of beauty and acceptability must be
rejected, along with those of other individuals. Negotiating a solution to this
contradiction entails a distinction between persons who undermine and
persons who enhance the choice-making powers of the individual. In the
domain of romantic relationships, for example, only sick men are seen to
influence the choices of women. Importantly, sick men are often identified as
persons who sabotage a woman's efforts to achieve health. Robert Linn (1980)
calls up images of disease, abuse, and powerlessness, for example, in explaining the negative responses of romantic partners to a woman's increased attractiveness, "If you're not fat, they have less reason to use you, abuse you, or put
you down. Suddenly, you're far less vulnerable than you were, which may make
them feel more vulnerable" (p. 261). A healthy woman must see that men who
tolerate or encourage her excesses are themselves diseased; by contrast, men
who promote beauty and individuality are healthy. The advice of healthy men
can be accepted because they appear to be selfless in efforts to beautify women,
wishing not to abuse or exploit women but to enable independence and, in
Gendler's (1987) words, a "more positive mental attitude" (p. 2).

Healthy female rebellion in the world of appearance involves a realization
that men who encourage women's beauty are men who encourage women's
independence. Progressive men permit women to control their own bodies,
freed from the repressive mechanisms of imposed criteria for women's morality.
Yet, as Michel Foucault (1980b) observes, contemporary discourses of liberation proceed through a logic of "control by stimulation" (p. 57). Specifically,
intensified surveillance accompanies an "intensification of each individual's
desire, for, in and over his body" (p. 57). In anti-diets there is a seamless
blending of surveillance and desire because the demand of the individual
entails body empowerment, power from within rather than imposed externally.
A governance of bodies works to identify and watch persons who are in need of
escape from governance, whose bodies bespeak a lack of personal ownership
and control. As a discourse, anti-diets condemn both women and men who are
entrapped by power. Thus, men who have not managed an escape from repression, signified by an investment in individual abilities for body control, are

implicated on the grounds of illness. And indeed, women apply labels of illness and restraint to romantic partners who undermine female efforts to achieve beauty: "My best friend's boyfriend was really sick when it came to her looks. It was almost like he wanted her to be ugly;" "Men can be funny about good looking women because everyone thinks they want women to be great looking, but some men have a twisted desire for women to stay unattractive. I think they think you don't need them if you're attractive;" "You have to be careful when your husband criticizes you, especially when you know you look terrific, because he might just be afraid you look too good—like you'll leave him for someone else."

If women can be convinced that healthy men encourage female freedom and that female health is evidenced by beauty, healthy women will be drawn to relational partners who are attracted to beautiful women. For instance, Jane Fonda's (1981) marriage to Tom Hayden, a liberated, progressive man, materializes when she becomes independent, physically fit, and healthy. Yet, in the rhetoric of Fonda's liberation, physical fitness is subordinated to an overall sense of self-confidence—the fact that she is beautiful when she meets Hayden is incidental and/or irrelevant to relational instigation or success. Fonda is no longer controlled in *any* way by restrictive and sexually exploitive practices and relationships. At the same time, beauty as culturally defined points to Fonda's independence; beauty is a central factor in her ability to attract healthy men who do not impose their will on her.

Women's voices, given the politics of liberated romance in anti-diets, offer a complex assessment of heterosexual interactions. The freedom offered to women by way of health, in practice, gives legitimacy to an intensified cultural surveillance of women. Panoptic controls attain maximum efficiency and invisibility when guards are transformed into an enabling presence. Women's oppression can then be seen as self-imposed, as entirely disconnected from institutional restraints. To govern the lives and bodies of women through discourses of liberation exhibits extraordinary tactical finesse because then only repressed and sacrificial women are unconcerned with beauty and fitness. For example, Linn (1980) calls up images of constraint and repression when inviting readers to identify unattractive women, such as "a rotund older teacher who never married, a plain, grossly obese girl who stayed with her ailing mother instead of marrying or finding a career" (p. 74). Importantly, the relational status of Linn's female cases is identified and linked implicitly to the illness about which he writes.

I wish to address women's ideological placement in anti-diet images of romance by taking up two pervasive themes in women's stories concerning relationships with men. First, I return to the operations of the gaze, as outlined in chapter 2, to show how the cultural gazing power given to men permits a surveillance and judgment of female relational partners. Women locate the constraining elements of a so-called appreciation of women's freedom in anti-diets. The second theme centers on manifestations of masculine gazing power in the form of compliments. Specifically, when women speak of male partners, pronounced attention is given to experiences in which praise is offered by men to comment on attractiveness. Expressions of appreciation are important in the discourse of female body reduction because they appear to enable, to express acceptance. However, women suggest, compliments given by "healthy" men often function to constrain female choices. Pronouncements of women's acceptability/health can work to foreground physical attractiveness as a requirement for women's health and for relational health.

### Nonreciprocal Visibility

A central element in culturally inscribed gender positions is the compulsory visibility of women's bodies and the relative invisibility of men's bodies. As seen in chapter 2, by virtue of being labeled the "aesthetic" sex, women are gazed upon, assessed, and controlled within dominant culture (Coward, 1985, pp. 225–232). If the bodies of women are seen as inherently more desirable and more central to identity than the bodies of men, potential female and male relational partners will be selected by giving disproportionate amounts of attention to physical attractiveness. Women note frequently that appearance, and in particular body shape, plays an important role in female prospects for intimacy, but a relatively negligible one in those of men. In discussing possibilities for romantic involvement, Joan observes, for example,

> It doesn't seem as important for men to be thin. It seems they might have the same thing about being in condition that women have about being fat. But at the same time, men don't seem to be judged nearly as much if they have a bit of a gut or if their bodies don't look good. For example, if they were overweight when they were little and that carries over into adulthood. And you don't hear women saying, "Well, I'd like him, but he has a bit of a gut." You know, hardly ever do you hear that.

Pat extends Joan's point by suggesting that for men, "being a little on the heavy side is one thing, but a fat girl generally does not have a boyfriend. As much as I hate to believe it, it is true." Every woman who addresses differences between the role of physical appearance for women and men in male-female relationships concurs with the observations of Joan and Pat: the aesthetics of men's bodies matter far less than do those of women's bodies in the world of romance.

Women are *required* to be physically appealing in order to participate in romantic life. Indeed, women's thoughts are corroborated by countless studies of dating and marriage patterns, which suggest a male propensity to give far greater primacy than women to physical appearance in the selection of a partner (Phillips and Wood, 1983). Responses to one interview question, in particular, specify physical attractiveness as a precondition of romance for women. During each interview, I ask women to imagine two women present in the room with us; by cultural standards one is attractive, and the other is unattractive. Women are then asked to describe each woman. In addition to forming a number of visual contrasts—thin/fat, stylish/unstylish, fashionable/unfashionable, energetic/lethargic—many women connect visual imagery to relational prospects. In listening to the wording of women's links between physical appearance and romantic involvements, the mandatory quality of female attractiveness becomes apparent: "The ugly girl couldn't have a boyfriend because she sort of violates everything men demand from women;" "The one who's not as attractive would probably be lonely since she doesn't have any meaningful relationships, I mean, she couldn't probably get any men in her life;" "I would think the pretty one works real hard at being the way she is, and I would think she does this because she wants to attract men and because men expect women to be pretty;" "Let's face the sad truth. The attractive one would have one or many men thinking she's hot and the unattractive one would be ignored totally, like she doesn't even exist."

Virtually none of the women suggests a diminishment in men's relational prospects resulting from physical unattractiveness. Although there seems to be general agreement on this point, women have diverse ways of expressing the absence of relational demands on men to exhibit physical beauty. The diversity, in itself, reveals important insights regarding the extent to which women's bodies are made visible within dominant culture. As evidenced above, many women state explicitly, men are not expected to be physically attractive for the sake of relational involvement. Moreover, not one of these women provides an elaborate description of men's bodies, as is done frequently when discussing women's bodies. Though women may make a general comment about particular men—"he has a bit of a gut," "he's no god," "he's great looking," "he's cute"—at no point is a man's unappealing appearance established as a "sickness" and as a subsequent barrier to romantic relational possibilities within society at large. For example, Laurie speaks at length about a male friend's "terrible acne," but she does not suggest difficulty in obtaining female interest as a result. Instead, she wonders, "Why would he think people would reject him because of that? That would be stupid." Women often assist in preserving the invisibility of men's bodies, making no attempts to control men, limiting their choices, through body inspection, proclamations of disease, and judgment.

Women's descriptions of men are not entirely devoid of evaluations of appearance. When men are criticized for unattractive physical features, however, women usually indict *themselves* for rendering superficial or unfair judgments. Disease is located in women who discount men based on body aesthetics: "I know this says something weird about me, but I just don't like it when men have those huge, bulging, body-builder bodies. I just don't find that sexy;" "I dated a man once and it drove me nuts because he never, well almost never, washed his hair. Call me unreasonable, or picky, but I couldn't stand that;" One thing I really don't find attractive is when a man has a big beer gut that just hangs there. This is a problem I have, and I know it's petty to make something like that such a big time problem." Judgmental gazing on the part of women, significantly, is refocused on the self. By rendering women the objects of scrutiny when women assess men, a nonreciprocal gaze, once again, is preserved.

Further, women are generally hesitant to offer criticisms of male relationship partners or masculine relationship behaviors. *Women, in fact, are often made responsible for the negative actions of male partners.* By placing the blame for insensitive male behaviors on females, women reproduce the cultural politics of gazing in the field of sexual difference: the oppressive elements of gazing are located not in the source of the gaze, but in its object. As seen in Foucault's (1979) analysis of the panopticon, the tower and tower guards are not implicated socio-culturally in the restraint of convicts; rather, it is the crimes of convicts that render surveillance necessary. Within panoptic logic, the object of the gaze is imbued with the power to control and manipulate the gazes of overseers. For example, a pervasive source of insecurity and anxiety for women surfaces when male romantic partners spend considerable time staring at, and commenting on, the physical attributes of other women. Lucy explains, "There's nothing worse than going out with a man who makes a point of checking out every woman in a bar or wherever you happen to go. It makes a person like me feel like nothing." Yet, when asking Lucy why she is bothered by such behavior, she states, "Because I don't like to feel like I'm in competition with other women, and women are really good at making you insecure. They do things to grab the attention of every guy that walks in." Several women echo Lucy's sentiments by stating or implying that one must be wary of the manipulative and "false" nature of women: "You have to be really careful with girls; they can be really manipulative when it comes to men;" "All girls are out to do one thing and that is flirt with guys;" "Get a lot of girls around guys and they turn into total fakes. They say, 'Oh, hi fellas,' then turn around and start ripping some other girl apart."

A man's actions must often be seen by a woman to be extreme in order to receive the label of illness and, as a result, to receive criticism. Even in cases of overt relational violence against women, blame is often placed with the victim instead of the abuser (Brownmiller, 1975; Caplan, 1985). A particularly telling example of cultural efforts to spare an abusive man judgment by locating disease in the abused woman is seen in the public reaction to the biographies by Linda Lovelace (1980; 1986). Although Lovelace's husband and manager, Chuck Traynor, committed atrocious acts of physical brutality against his wife, little mention is made of him in popular discussions of her writings.[1] She is scrutinized for defects, for emotional and physical flaws; he retains invisibility.

In turn, her absolution is dependent on her willingness to confess weakness, vulnerability, sexual pleasure. Her assertive insistance that she did not enjoy sexual abuse renders her unforgivable and opens her to further scrutiny.

When men are implicated for unfair treatment of relational partners, a complicated version of forgiveness operates to both underscore and cancel the need for a confession of wrongdoing. Unkind or unreasonable male behaviors are sometimes noted, but rather than connecting them to illness, women often reframe the behaviors to reach a more innocuous conclusion. For instance, Laurie describes a situation in which a male friend dates her female friend. He begins to lose interest in his partner when she gains ten pounds. Although Laurie tells him he is overly concerned with weight, she ultimately dismisses his obsession with weight and physical appearance:

> One of my good guy friends goes out with another friend who I sort of know from my home town. He had been dating her all last year, and then he said he didn't want to go out with her anymore because she was too fat; he said she should lose ten pounds. I told him he was obsessed with weight . . . I told him I didn't want him to go out with her if only her appearance mattered because I didn't want him hurting her. You shouldn't base it all on physical appearance. If you really care about someone and you have a mutual agreement and the relationship is great, it should not matter that much if the person loses ten pounds . . . I told him she is the same person as before and that he must just be bored. He just must be bored with her.

Laurie's response is complex because although she clearly finds it unreasonable to "base it all on physical appearance" and tells her friend so, she retracts her criticism *of him* by suggesting that the real issue is boredom. He is neither obsessed or unreasonable, implying weakness or "sickness," but simply bored.

In a determination of boredom, a man is given tremendous gazing power. Indeed, anti-diets are filled with images of boredom and dissatisfaction resulting from an unattractive partner (Linn, 1980; Wardell, 1985). Boredom is a passive state, a presence of mind in which interesting or stimulating information is absent; alleviation is dependent on regenerated interest. If a male partner's boredom results from a female's inability or unwillingness to conform to cultural beauty standards, women are required to act, to engage in beauty labors to sustain or reinspire male attention. A man's ability to set boundaries and standards within a romantic relationship, while appearing passive, is important when considering that many women avoid criticisms of male behavior by subtly or overtly criticizing themselves. A man's power to see and not be seen is strengthened when women point to their own inadequacies to explain male actions. Many women compare themselves to other women, for example, concluding that they are less attractive and hence less desirable. Such conclusions grant legitimacy to male criteria female attractiveness, and permit men to determine the parameters of relational involvement. To illustrate, Ellen describes her belief that men are drawn to physically appealing women and her resulting experience of insecurity and implicit self-effacement:

> I have always felt that men were attracted to good looking women, and I have never changed my opinion of that. I have some good male friends and I know on a cognitive level that looks are not a big issue to them. But on another level, I still believe it's an issue to them. And that they will go through moments of thinking they wish they were dating someone more attractive [than myself]. Or, I bet he wishes he were married to someone who was more attractive. Gee, I wonder if he is noticing all of these attractive women who are coming in, and wondering what he is doing with me. And in romantic relationships with men this has always been a concern with me.

Although Ellen does not openly endorse the value placed on physical attractiveness in women, she assumes implicitly that male companions will find other women more attractive than she. In making her own physical appearance a key point in the story, male criteria and demands are not questioned, and male bodies retain their invisibility. Her own body, conversely, is scrutinized and judged; concomitantly, her desirability as a relational partner is suspect. When the potentially problematical dimensions of male relationship behavior are masked, women are obliged to testify to their own inadequacies, to *confess* weakness and unattractiveness.

The ideological mechanisms at work to preserve male invisibility in intimate or romantic relationships are multi-faceted. In their analysis of sexual politics in interpersonal relationships, Nancy Henley and Jo Freeman (1984) show how an intertwining of numerous socially endorsed male behaviors enables men to delimit and oversee the boundaries of relational intimacy. They observe, "The social rules say that all moves to greater intimacy are a male prerogative: it is boys who are supposed to call girls for dates, men who are supposed to propose marriage to women, and males who are supposed to initiate sexual activity with females" (p. 467). A capacity to set boundaries works ideologically to permit a determination of relational health, and the health of individuals. Within the field of sexual difference, unhealthy males are those who open themselves to scrutiny, males who, perhaps even consciously, invite the gazes of others. A man who takes obvious steps to render himself physically or interpersonally appealing is often "feminized" by male groups and rejected. A moralistic dimension is often added to perceptions of objectified men through the equation of feminized men and homosexuality. The "natural" male role, by implication, entails unilateral gazing power and indifference to the gazes of others. As Ruth describes female-male roles in advertising, for example, men are constructed as self-assured and choice-making individuals who need not worry about the evaluations of women:

In the advertising field, women's products are geared toward attracting men. As for men, it's the macho type who appears in beer commercials and always projects a very self-assured, self-centered image. He doesn't have to bow to anyone and especially not a woman. When it comes to advertising for women, it's all geared toward how to attract these men to you.

Women may work to make themselves attractive, but as Ruth suggests, it is men who are "attracted toward" women.

Cultural images of the "self-assured, self-centered" male create a complicated paradox for women in the context of romantic relationships. Important parts of the imagery include a complete lack of neediness, distance from any form of involvement, and indifference toward relational partners. The mystery of macho or "real" men rests in a refusal to be known, manifested silence, unannounced arrivals and departures, a categorical refusal to disclose personal information, and a gaze so powerful that it can stop enemies and women dead in their tracks. The qualities of "healthy" men are problematical for women, however, because they stand in direct contrast to women's definitions of intimacy. The reciprocity of gazing seen in women's intimate friendships is unacceptable in an economy of difference wherein the gaze and its object occupy mutually exclusive positions. The unknowable and unlovable man held up to women as desirable, is someone worth knowing and loving precisely because he represents opposition to the world of femininity; he cannot be known.

A significant twist in the imagery of real men entails the possibility of a breakdown in impassivity and indifference, a willingness to be known. Distant men may become open to involvement if women are sufficiently stimulating to jar a shift in male sensibilities. Paula Caplan's (1985) analysis of the "myth of the New Man" reveals a recent historical glorification of men who exhibit openness, respect for women's ways of establishing intimacy, and sensitivity (pp. 106–108). New men endorse women's equality and independence, as do the healthy men in anti-diets. The new man is often a reproduction of "real" men, a persuasive repackaging which makes constraint appear in the form of liberation. For example, Caplan examines the expressivity of the new man, concluding, "there is nothing new about men making their needs and feelings known to women . . . they have traditionally been better at making their own needs known than at responding to the needs of their women" (p. 106). The danger for women is that "we will mistakenly identify as 'new' the man who appears to be better than most at making *his own* needs or feelings clear but who is hopelessly bad at responding to ours" (p. 106). A principal luxury possessed by the new man is his ability to express blatant self-interest as evidence for his sensitivity to others.

Ideologically, the promise of new men works to further indict women because men appear to be lovable *if* women are sensitive enough or "liberated" enough to merit serious consideration. New man mythology, Caplan (1985) suggests, "plays into the handicap under which women are already operating —their tendency to take blame upon themselves" (p. 107). If men do not exhibit a capacity to love, as seen in chapter 3, it is due to women's regressive or "sick" approaches to relationships, not a pathalogical fear of intimacy on the part of men. The labors of women to be one of the "right" ones are accelerated with the promise of a new man's love. A woman must work harder than other women to make herself deserving of the much prized breakdown in male defenses, of male openness and commitment. She listens to the disclosures of men, she works diligently to attend to their needs, she supports their projects and understands their hardships. In other words, she intensifies all of the behaviors that define her as a woman. Gabrielle locates key points of inequality in relationships between women and new men:

> It's pretty funny how men are supposed to be liberated now, like they're all of a sudden open about their feelings, and they'll even say, "Oh, something awful happened to me today and I'm sad." I'm not making fun of them for that, I think it's good in a lot of ways. But all these men are all of a sudden talking about how they feel to me and my friends, and we just sit there and listen to them for hours on end. You kind of have to go along with it, I mean it wouldn't look good to say, "Your problems are nothing," because you want them to be open. But it's so rare in these conversations for the man to say, "And what about your life? How are you feeling these days? How is your job going? Are you happy in our relationship?"

The so-called newness of expressive males is questionable on historical as well as behavioral grounds. Although much cultural attention has been given to the changing roles of men, Foucault (1986) points out that the *Oeconomicus* of Xenophon emphasized the importance of dialogue between partners (p. 161). In marital relations, husband and wife are expected to support and encourage one another, making their union separate from all other relationships. The wife's duties involve listening to male disclosure, offering advice and direction, but she is not permitted to judge or to display superior knowledge. A male partner may reveal weaknesses or wrongful acts, yet his partner may not, without risking a label of illness, presume to operate from position of intellectual or moral exaltation. The "new" male cannot be said to operate confessionally since he runs no risk of reprisal.

Women who take an active interest in the needs of men, whether the men are old or "new," however, are often portrayed as undesirable relational partners. Men are often taught to be wary of overly enthusiastic women, of women who display an eagerness for involvement. In anti-diets, for example, healthy women do not need others and actively resist the relational boundaries established by self-interested others. Unhealthy women, due to their own desperation and neediness, not only allow themselves to be constrained by male demands, but use the *appearance* of compassion and sensitivity to induce male interest. Anthony Astrachan's (1988) analysis of contemporary male attitudes towards intimacy, for example, reveals a collapsing of the liberated woman and the demanding woman (pp. 269-271). Here, the woman who is open and expressive becomes interchangeable with the castrating women, whom one of Astrachan's respondents describes as "a woman acting like a traffic cop in bed" (p. 270). A "traffic cop" has the capacity to oversee and reprimand the actions of others, to legislate the boundaries of normality through the power of unilateral gazing.

The paradox for women is that they must work very hard to display a need for male companionship without appearing to need men. This is precisely the trick required in the world of dieting rebellion. Appearing healthy and self-sufficient entails no small amount of labor and strategy on the part of women. Perhaps most importantly, the task involves calculated indifference to the perceptions and needs of men which has as its basis heightened attention to cultural standards of attractiveness. Coward's (1985) examination of the transformation from smiling to scowling women in advertising imagery delineates the sexual politics of women who are valued for their independence. Coward points out,

> The look of defiance, the pouting and scowling faces, are part of the current tendency to represent women as attractive *whether or not they work at it* . . . We are meant to read off from the narrowing of the eyes, the perfection of the skin, the posture of the body, that this is a person confident of sexual response whether or not it is sought (p. 59).

The healthy woman, who is able to form relationships with healthy men, is the woman whose indifference signifies invitation, but expects nothing in return because, after all, the healthy woman does not need men.

### Body Compliments

The complex surveillance activities of men, particularly when they are aligned with masculine health, establish a hold over the domain of sexual identities. Power to dictate the boundaries of feminine health, and by implication, relational health, works to give the illusion that women enjoy the task of presenting absolute difference. As Susan Brownmiller (1984) points out, a central ingredient of femininity is the suggestion that the labor required for beauty is fun, pleasurable, and fulfilling. If women are presented as persons for whom the perpetuation of difference is synonymous with fulfillment, then men can select beautiful women as partners not because unattractive women are aesthetically displeasurable, but because attractive women are fulfilled. A woman who is fulfilled, in turn, does not need or make demands on men because she is confident in her difference. She is imbued with confidence and self-love.

Sustained confidence in a difference bound by cultural criteria for female health/attractiveness, however, cannot be achieved without approval. The scowling woman is permitted to scowl only on the condition that she receives male attention. A woman who is scowling and unattractive is not desirable, but viewed culturally as bitter, hostile, and unhealthy. For example, in the before and after photographs used to sell beauty regimes, both images may include the absence of a smile. Central to a differentiation between the women, through clothing, hairstyle, make-up, and demeanor is the message that the "after" image more closely approximates cultural requirements for hetero-sexual attractiveness. Male acknowledgment of women's beauty, then, is a central but implied element in portrayals of healthy women.

When women discuss male responses to an attractive female appearance, the subject of compliments emerges with tremendous frequency. Compliments are highly significant in the politics of women's health because, as in the case of fathers, they are seen to express approval, to acknowledge women's bodies and choices. As Gabrielle points out, "When someone says you look good, it's like that person is saying you're good, I approve of the person you are." Explicit verbal praise affirms individuality and, implicitly, enables a continuation of the behavior to which a compliment refers. To illustrate, April notes, "compliments are the opposite of criticism because a criticism says 'I wish you wouldn't do that' and a compliment says 'what you're doing is just fine with me'." Verbal acknowledgments of physical acceptability, women suggest, are pervasive, and often enabling, in relationships with men.

Praise directed at women's bodies is often experienced and reflected upon in favorable terms. When first inquiring about the experience of receiving com-pliments, women state in quite unqualified terms that compliments are power-ful affirmations of attractiveness. Ann observes, "When people say 'you look great' or 'I like your hair', they are saying something good about you. They are telling you you're attractive without coming right out and saying so in so many words." Several women, perhaps epitomized in remarks by Lucy, portray com-pliments on appearance as a *naturally* pleasant experience because praise affirms one's identity and one's value: "It's just natural that everyone likes to be praised, especially on your looks because that's so valued in our society for women. Even though we don't like to admit it, we are all dependent on others to validate who we are, and your body is just a big part of that. Compliments validate who we are in the eyes of other people." Ann and Joan speak for many women in defining praise directed at physical appearance as pleasurable, as an affirmation of one's social worth.

Indeed, when speaking about compliments or praise, women indicate a parallel to family and friendship relationships. As seen in chapter 4, women are quite critical of parents who do not praise their children. Similarly, with friends women suggest an obligation to support and affirm personal worth, which is often provided through praise or attentiveness. Compliments are often a form of positive attention, letting the recipient know that she is seen favorably, attended to, and appreciated.

Although women speak of compliments on physical dimensions in favorable terms, not all forms of seemingly affirming attention to outward appearance are enabling. For women, compliments are placed in the context of a particular relationship with the person who offers praise, along with reflection on the perceived motivation behind compliments. In questions of power in interpersonal involvements, Letitia Anne Peplau (1984) observes, it is particularly important to consider situation and motivation because "the context in which an action occurs and the intentions of the participants largely determine the meaning of the act" (p. 102). Women demonstrate an awareness of the potential power inequities communicated by praise. For illustration, when asking women to describe the highest compliment another person could give to them, responses include, "it depends on who's giving it," "first I'd have to know the situation I'm in," "it would be real different from a client than from my husband," "first I'd have to glean whether the person just wanted to get me to do something, like a favor." In addition, the timing of a remark, the specific situation in which praise is offered, and the affective state of the recipient all play a part in the experience of praise. Janet observes, "If I'm in a bad mood already, really stressed out on my job or something, and my boss comes in and says, 'You're a fox, and by the way, I need this report by 5:00,' I fume. I resent that kind of bullshit." In the remainder of this section, I delineate an overall framework for the complex experience of compliments as described by women. With remarkable acuity, women locate key points of contradiction and reversal in the anti-diet equation between health, beauty, and freedom from male evaluation.

In anti-diet images of health, women are portrayed as persons whose goal is to receive unsolicited acknowledgement from men, regardless of the relationship between the one who acknowledges and the one who is acknowledged. Advertising imagery, for example, often entices consumers by showing an attractively bold woman who is visually consumed by male onlookers. Part of the appeal, for women, is the possibility of involvements in which women are granted power by virtue of unbending self-assuredness. Indeed, as seen in Shere Hite's (1987) analysis of heterosexual intimate relationships, women are

often quite aware of, and bothered by, relational power inequities which diminish female confidence and assertiveness. The female pleasure derived from
such images, though, is often displaced by concomitant visions of women who
"invite" overt, sometimes forced, sexual involvement. As seen in earlier
chapters, one of the drawbacks of conformity to cultural standards for attractiveness is a threatening form of male attention. Lucy states, "Being real pretty
or slender is not always fun because men act different toward you and it can be
scary when they start coming on to you. You never know what they expect of
you, whereas if you're not pretty and you're fat, you know they don't want
anything."

The constraining elements of unsolicited male attention become especially pronounced when women describe the experience of receiving attention
from men who are strangers. In an analysis of rape, Dianne Herman (1984)
points out, women's movement in the public domain is always restricted due to
a keen awareness of location, time of day, and the forms of acknowledgment
received from men—all of which can place women in extreme physical danger
(p. 20). Further, Herman takes up Susan Griffin's notion of "mini rapes" to
illustrate instances of body surveillance in which women are made aware of
their subjection to male gazes and male control: "the pinch in the crowded
bus, the wolf whistle from a passing car, the stare of a man looking at her bust
during a conversation" (p. 20). Seemingly unsolicited male attention, women
understand, can as easily signify violation and degradation as adoration.[2]

Women are often uneasy about the implications of remarks characterized
by Beth as "shots out of the blue." Returning to Coward's (1985) analysis, the
presumed pleasure in images of scowling females who capture attentive gazes
is often transformed in women's experience into a violent invasion, an
unexpected "shot." Not a single woman expresses an unambiguously favorable
response to physical acknowledgment from men who are unknown to her.
Implicitly, women grasp the reductive or potentially violent elements of gazes
from strangers. When asked how overt attention to the body by strangers is
experienced, women answer with diverse, yet thematically connected, observations: "like I'm a piece of meat;" "as if I'm some kind of walking sex machine;"
"I'm confused by the experience because these men don't know anything
about me;" "I feel like it doesn't matter a damn who I am, as an individual,
because they do that to every woman that walks by;" "I feel sorry for the men
that do that because it makes a pretty sad statement about their lives, like the
only way they can endorse their manhood is by turning women into nothing
but tits and asses;" "I think it's something men do for each other, not for the
benefit of whoever it is that's walking by. It's a way of saying to each other, 'See
how macho I am,' or something, but it doesn't have too much to do with
women."

Not all women are uniformly negative in responding to their experiences of comments from strangers. However, most of the women who hold mixed feelings are cognizant of, and embrace, the views of women who experience such attention as hostile. Due to the reductive elements of comments that work to insure male bonding, women similarly remove themselves from the men who issue remarks. Women who take some satisfaction in comments from anonymous men, in other words, tend to disconnect statements from any particular man and thus diminish a sense of endangerment. The men become faceless voices, devoid of individual appeal or threat in much the same manner as the recipients of remarks from strangers. In fact, the male role in women's experience of pleasure in being recognized is not mentioned at all. When women discuss their pleasure in receiving comments, descriptions are largely self-referential: "It makes me feel like I look good;" "Sometimes when it happens, gee, maybe I don't look as old as I think;" "If I've had a bad day it sometimes picks me up;" "If I walk out of my house, wearing a skirt, and I think I look good, those whistles sometimes validate what I already sort of know."

Face-to-face interaction with men who are familiar, women suggest, often shifts the response to appearance compliments from negative to ambiguous. In the context of a conversation, favorable comments on physical appearance are often appreciated by women, but are also sometimes constraining. Most often, male attention to a woman's body is reported to be constraining when the context seems inappropriate for a focus on physical appearance. In work settings, for example, women indicate, remarks directed at outward appearance seem incongruous with both the interactional climate and the "professional" relationship. As in any employment setting, women expect assessments of job performance, but do not expect unsolicited assessments of physical beauty. Karla describes her sense of "panic," for instance, when reflecting on a job in which her male supervisor made continuous references to her attractiveness:

> I worked at an office once where my supervisor constantly gave me compliments on how I looked. Every day, it seemed, he would say how nice my dress looked, or my hair, or that I must have lots of guys after me because I'm so pretty. On Fridays he'd ask how many dates I had for the weekend. Every time I saw him I'd panic because the things he said made me feel really mixed up. I mean, here I am, at a job, but there he is, saying things about how I looked. It just didn't seem to fit together. At first I thought he might want to go out with me, on a date or something, but I never really knew for sure. Then I thought, oh no, he's just a letch—he does that to every girl. But I thought it was sort of crazy that he'd care so much about how many dates I had.

From Karla's perspective, an employer's attention to physical attractiveness is "crazy" because it is incongruous with both the context and the relationship between employer and employee. She struggles to determine the meaning of her supervisor's behavior, to "fit together" his comments and her professional role. A gaze pertaining to physical attractiveness is inconsistent with a gaze which oversees her professional duties.

A similar contradiction in boundaries is revealed when women describe dynamics in the work setting that combine a woman's sexual/romantic appeal with her professional actions concerning male business associates or clients. As Adrienne Rich (1980) demonstrates, the heterosexual attractiveness of women is taken into account within most places of employment. A woman's abilities to receive attention for competence are displaced by her value as sexual currency in exchanges between men. With keen insight, women often realize, equality in the workplace is diminished when women are "appreciated" as a component of male pleasure rather than as intellectual peers. Here, women are hired due to a presumed level of competence that is equal to men, but reminded, in Nicole's words, "that you're still a woman." Nicole provides a detailed description of the complicated and often subtle mechanisms at work to prevent women's equality in the workplace. In the same move, Nicole indicates, women are given equality and denied equality:

> I think men set up a major contradiction for women when they hire them in the business world. When they hire a woman, they're hiring her to do the same thing that a man could do. But then again, they want women to look good. They're saying, "Okay, we're hiring you as an equal, but don't consider yourself an equal because we're superior in some ways. So use the qualities you have, as a woman, to help us further ourselves in the business world ... But don't get too hyped up thinking you're any better and that you do a better job because we realize that you're still a woman." Men want women to look good in the business world so they can promote business and appeal to other businesses, and that's very hard for women to deal with. Because here they are, trying to do their job and be equal and just be themselves, and here is the boss, saying, "Well, I want you to sweeten up to Mr. Smith. I want you to look good for this meeting because these men are really important and I want you to look good. Not only that, but don't look too good because I don't want you to look too sexy or too attractive because that's not an asset."

Nicole's description locates a similarity between sexual remarks from strangers and an emphasis on appearance in the workplace. Specifically, in both cases, the behaviors of men have little to do with women, but rather promote good relationships among men. Whether a woman is used for lunchtime entertainment amidst a group of construction workers or used to solidify a business deal, her personal qualities or competencies are largely irrelevant. In a work setting, however, attention to appearance is experienced as more insidious than "street comments" because in the former, professional skills are presumed to be primary in securing employment. Messages from male employers are further mixed in professional settings when women are required, as Nicole suggests, to look attractive but not *too* sexually appealing. In combination, the elements surrounding workplace attention to appearance remind women that they are and are not aligned with male colleagues; that is, a woman's primary duty is to both capture and relinquish the gazes of men.

Calling attention to a woman's sexual appeal in the workplace not only raises suspicions regarding her intellectual or professional competencies, but implicates female sexuality as a distracting and potentially destructive presence. A strong analogy exists between depictions of women in the above discussion of boredom and workplace attention to appearance. Specifically, although one case involves a woman who does not meet cultural criteria for attractiveness and the other entails an acknowledgment of attractiveness, in both cases women's sexuality is viewed as something which acts upon men. Thus, women are typically held responsible for shifting the attention of male co-workers from professional goals to sexual desire. For example, in a recent court case in the state of Florida, a female prosecutor was dismissed due to unprofessional conduct, signified by revealing clothing, bleached hair, and heavy make-up. No suggestion of *male* inabilities to separate work from sexual desire is made in the public discussions of this case; rather, the woman's appearance is held responsible for preventing objectivity and professionalism in the courtroom. Implicitly, as in the cultural response to the Lovelace (1980; 1986) biographies, women are required to confess sexual deviance when men "cannot" control themselves.

A woman's opportunities for personal achievement or fulfillment are undermined by attention to her romantic/sexual potential because such "appreciation" functions to prevent a manifestation of female power. The presumably favorable attention to appearance serves to remind all workers of the incompatibility between work and sexual activity, and by implication, Peplau (1984) suggests, women's professional goals are suspect (p. 106). In an important study of sexual harassment, Billie Wright Dziech and Linda Weiner (1984) show that although masculine images of women work to dichotomize females into competent/nonsexual and incompetent/sexual realms, the distinctions between women blur *because* judgments of competence are connected to levels of attractiveness (pp. 147–162). As Lin Farley (1978) relays the comments of a male academic administrator who describes the treatment of an attractive female colleague, the impossibility of women's "health" by virtue of beauty and independence gains clarity:

> Here she was a Ph.D. and a woman with all kinds of strengths who also happens to be exceptionally attractive. All her colleagues were men and they just never gave her a chance because they thought she had been brought in to be the playmate of the man who hired her. It wasn't true at all, but she could never establish her credibility as a person. She finally confronted one of the

men because, although she was the official channel, they wouldn't come to her about things. He just said they thought she was only there for sex. She said that was completely false and he just said, "Well, you do lead us to that conclusion. You dress real nice and you have a very seductive voice." She eventually got a bad evaluation (qtd. in Dziech and Weiner, p. 152).

In viewing a professional colleague as a "playmate" or potential romantic partner within the dichotomy of competence/incompetence, a woman's professional capabilities are questioned, along with those of her unattractive/ unhealthy counterparts, and often discounted altogether.

When an involvement is viewed as potentially intimate, inclusive of respect and care, women's responses to compliments or attention to appearance are considerably altered. In new dating relationships, women are initially unanimous in identifying praise directed at physical appearance as a confirmation of attraction, particularly when the relationship has not reached a stage in which the degree of involvement can be discussed openly. With high degrees of consistency, women use compliments as a means of determining relational definition. According to Robert Bell (1981), men in relationships tend to be "outward oriented," and thus a man acts upon external stimuli but "reveals little or nothing about what is inside of him" (p. 77). Low disclosure is particularly pronounced in the beginning phases of a relationship. Given women's fears of being labeled pushy, demanding, or castrating, overt efforts to clarify male understandings of the situation are often risky. Rose describes this period as the "everything's up in the air phase" of a relationship in which men do not verbalize their feelings; compliments tell a woman indirectly that a man finds her attractive and wishes to share her company. Beth observes, for example, "When you don't really have a relationship established, and you're not sure what a guy thinks of you, you're sort of wondering a lot of the time what he's making of the situation. I mean, does he want a relationship or not? Most men won't say. If he makes nice comments about how you look, like 'You're really pretty' or 'You have a good figure,' then you're sort of reassured that, yes, he is interested in you."

As women discuss the continuation of new romantic relationships, they begin to express some uneasiness about what Joan calls "body boosting," defined as "the never-ending ego boosts about how you look." Given women's definitions of intimate friendships, continued attention to appearance as a key issue may well be seen as incongruous with developing intimacy. Most models of relational development support the definitions of intimacy proposed by women, suggesting a move from superficial information to an increasingly expansive and deep understanding of the other as relationships achieve greater intimacy (Altman and Taylor, 1973; Duck, 1976). Insofar as excessive attention to physical features is inconsistent with intimacy, "body boosting" may well call into question, rather than support, a man's romantic interest in a woman. Barbara echos a resounding theme in stating: "At first I loved it that he'd say, 'Oh, you have the best body' or 'Your skin is the softest' or 'You have the nicest breasts I've ever seen.' After awhile, though, I started to think, my God, doesn't he see anything else in me besides body parts and how they look?"

A focus on appearance in the context of multiple issues in a partner's life signifies a fragmentation of woman. The personal empowerment afforded by compliments is undermined through an implied reduction to external features. Experientially, the reduction brings a male partner in line with the stranger on the street; in both cases, woman is "only" a body. A fixation on the body works to hold another at a distance, thereby calling into question a man's degree of involvement. Ethel Spector Person (1988) finds similarity in female and male description of love, but points to affective and social differences. The blending of lives characteristic of women's love relationships is not well suited to the primacy placed on independence for men. Thus, she writes, "women are more at ease with the mutuality implicit in love, as well as the surrender, while men tend to interpret mutuality as dependency and defend against it by separating sex from love, or alternatively, by attempting to dominate the beloved" (p. 265). A focus on woman's body offers protection from mutuality, and a means by which to exert dominance in the form of objectification and judgmental gazing.

Dimensions of a woman's existence other than physical appearance, Lynn indicates, are often not acknowledged in dating relationships: "I can get a big promotion in my job, something really significant. I go out with a man and tell him about it and what does he say, 'You look beautiful tonight'. It's as if everything except how I look gets pushed to the background." Neither Barbara nor Lynn indicates that compliments are inherently negative, or that male attention to appearance is categorically unpleasant. Rather, uneasiness is experienced when appearance is the only dimension of themselves to receive explicit acknowledgment. Further, as in friendships, women do not render outward appearance irrelevant to intimacy; rather, they suggest, responding to another's physical features takes place within a larger context of behavior, beliefs, values, and relational history.

Many women imply a connection between pervasive compliments from intimate partners and overt prescription, a connection grounded in dominance. Although anti-diets portray healthy women as persons whose freedom is evidenced by positive remarks from loved ones, women suggest a correlation between compliments and constraint. Compliments directed at female appearance are viewed frequently as constraining when a man's attention to the body is experienced as an inspection. When speaking of compliments from male partners, for example, women often use metaphors that connote unilateral male gazing power: "you have to pass inspection," "he sees right through you," "he guards the way I look," "he doesn't miss a thing," "it's like I'm accountable to him." Images of an all-powerful other pervade women's experiences of inspection. During inspections, a man appears to fixate on a woman's body, noting minute changes in particular aspects of the body's appearance. Because the fixation is articulated as appreciation within cultural economies of difference, it should engender freedom and promote female confidence. Yet for women, favorable inspections imply rigid conditions for involvement, a pre-established "doctrine" of acceptability. Julia remembers an intimate relationship, for example, in which a man was obsessed with her body, making her feel as if she were "under a microscope":

> I went out with a guy once who was absolutely obsessive when it came to my body. This guy noticed everything, absolutely everything about me. He was always really flattering, but I just felt like I was under a microscope with him. If I wore a different color eyeshadow, he'd say something about it; if I trimmed my hair, he'd say, "Oh, you've done something to your hair. It looks good." It made me feel really uncomfortable. My friends would never understand why this bothered me, but to me, it was like he was obsessed. And I was always waiting for a time that I'd screw up and do something to my body that he didn't like. I just felt like he was setting some standards or something, always evaluating how I looked. I didn't like it at all.

Julia connects an obsessional attention to appearance with a fear that she may "screw up and do something to my body that he didn't like." Here, a man's compliments are seen to set parameters on Julia's choices of make-up, hair-style, and overall appearance. More generally, her mate's comments establish Julia's body as a central element of his involvement in the relationship: the attractiveness of her body is *required* in order to sustain his interest.

Women who question the empowerment afforded by an abundance of body compliments glean a significant reversal in discourses of female reduction. In anti-diets, healthy men acknowledge feminine beauty/health, diseased men work to undermine women's health through prescriptions and constraints (Linn, 1980; Mazel, 1981; Fonda, 1981). In either case, however, an inspecting gaze is operative and holds the other at a distance. A gaze that works on behalf of feminine beauty, women see, is still a policing, governing, controlling gaze. Similar to the prisoners in Bentham's plan, the overseeing gaze does not punish as long as order and conformity are retained within prison walls (Foucault, 1979). The conditional acceptance implied by compliments is articulated by Joan, for example, when she observes that her husband is "appreciative and complimentary" when she loses weight, but "says nothing" when she gains weight. Gaining explicit approval, then, is dependent on conformity to her husband's standards for acceptability. She must internalize his criteria and reproduce them bodily to guarantee acceptance, and to hold at bay his fear of mutuality.

The reversibility of female empowerment and constraint are particularly visible in stories which highlight a juxtaposition of compliments and criticisms. Intimate heterosexual relationships, women suggest, often contain praise *and* critical remarks regarding appearance. Louise's articulation of the juxtaposition epitomizes the experience of many women:

> My husband is really good about telling me I look beautiful, or thin or whatever. He is big on compliments and he often says he is proud that I am his wife. But sometimes I wonder if he is proud of me when I look a certain way, but embarrassed of me if I don't look the way he wants me to. He lets me know in no uncertain terms if I am wearing something he doesn't like, or if I gain weight on a vacation or something. I have a belt he hates and everytime I wear it, he says, "Are you really going to wear that thing?" Sometimes we argue about it and I think to myself, good Lord, is this belt such a big deal? The next time we go out he might tell me I look great, but somehow it makes me mad because I think, sure, now that you approve, I look great and you're proud that I am your wife.

In Louise's story, the legitimacy of body compliments is called into question by instances in which dimensions of her appearance are overtly condemned.

Excessive body criticism, even when tempered by periodic praise, produces resistance to the demands of the other. Defying the wishes of another both assumes and challenges the power of others to control and judge a woman's body and behavior, constituting a form of rebellion. Frequently, in fact, women link defiance and rebellion: "When he says, 'you shouldn't be eating those cookies,' I rebel and eat the whole bag;" "I am well aware that it's not good to consume sugar and greasy foods, and all that, so when my boyfriend tells me that, I know there's more to it and I rebel;" "If you defy someone, you're saying, 'I am a thinking person so don't treat me like you own me'." Joan makes an explicit connection between power inequity, criticisms, and defiance by connecting "judgmental hints" to her relationship with her mother:

> I always feel rebellious when anybody makes any sort of judgmental hints about either how I look or what I'm eating, and the obvious connection between the two. That just zips right back to my mother when people make judgments about me. I just stick my heels into the ground and go in the opposite direction. So when anybody does that I eat to defy them.

Prescriptions through compliments are difficult to confront in intimate relationships because praise is seen to constitute validation. A blatant setting of boundaries through criticism can be met with defiance because the source of constraining surveillance is clear. For this reason, compliments comprise a more effective form of control not only because they constrain by appearing to enable, but because if a woman objects, it is she who appears unreasonable, repressed, and "sick." A story told by Lucy illustrates:

> This is hard to explain. I've gone out with guys who pick apart everything I do, just everything. I know now that I don't want to be involved with people like that because why should I always feel like I'm the one who has the problem? I know now it's usually a guy's problem if he has a need to constantly point out how I'm messing up. So now I get involved with men who support me—that's a real important factor. He has to like and accept the person I am. But accepting someone can be complicated too because that can be manipulative. This might be unfair, but when a man starts praising me all the time, especially how I look, I instantly wonder what he wants from me. What does he expect? But it's hard to say to a man, "Listen, stop saying nice things because you're manipulating me." It's really hard to put this across in a way that doesn't make you look like a fool.

In Lucy's story, images of diseased and healthy men contain expectations and constraints. An important difference between the types of men described is the level of difficulty in overriding the prescriptions put forth by each man. The diseased man can be abandoned due to his blatantly restrictive behavior, but the healthy man operates in a manner that renders criticism difficult. A woman who expresses disapproval or uneasiness regarding the apparently supportive remarks of healthy man is indicted on the grounds of sickness; she is a "fool." She must confess to misguidedness, an inability to tell the difference between liberation and repression.

Sustained intimate involvement sometimes shifts compliments to aspects of a woman's life other than physical beauty. If women perceive an intimate relationship to be healthy, partners are assumed to offer reciprocal feedback on a number of issues, behaviors, and life choices. The responsibility described by women is rich in scope because it not only entails acknowledgment of personal complexities, but an abandonment of anti-diet associations between external appearance and health. Marion states, for example, "If a man loves you, he lets you know you're worthwhile and great and intelligent if you've gained, as well as if you've lost, fifty pounds." As in anti-diet discourse, a suspension of one's own interests is identified by women as a central factor in relational health, but women diverge from anti-diets by suggesting that a healthy form of relational liberation entails a shared acknowledgment of shifts and changes in the lives of partners. In Andrea's description of the relationship between herself and her male partner, health is signified by a reciprocal capacity to be "in tune" with one another:

> Having an intimate relationship with anyone is hard to achieve because you have to tune in to that person in a big way. I'm seeing a man now and I'm excited about him because he is really interested in the things that are

important to me, and vice versa. If I get a contract [at work] and I'm happy about it, he's happy. If I'm not happy about a contract, because of the terms or something, he shares that too. And I do the same for him. I'm just hoping we keep doing this, really tuning in to each other, because that's the closest two people can be and it feels great.

For Andrea, healthy attentiveness to another requires an intertwining of lives wherein both partners are obliged to abandon overarching criteria for "health" if they hope to understand one another.

The capacity to be "in tune" with an other, for women, is not akin to blind or uncritical acceptance of another's choices. Alternatively, the relational responsibility described by women is highly dissimilar to anti-diet characterizations of freedom in which the sanctity of the individual, separate from others, takes precedence over the inevitability of interdependence. Rather, women's visions of intimacy and health entail an ability to *connect* with another life and to acknowledge the connection. Women do not speak of a loss of individuality through connectedness, but an enriched sense of who they are in relation to diverse relationship partners. Lucy summarizes:

People don't like to think they need anyone but themselves; everything is geared toward the individual. I think that's sad because you miss a lot that way. It's good to see how you relate to people and how they affect you, and how you affect them. It gives you a chance to be a lot of different people, and to appreciate the people in your life. You're a better person for doing that. If you really and truly love someone with all your heart, and that person loves you back, you have to know you need each other. If it's just all me, me, me, then you don't have anything special.

According to Lucy, the sanctity of the individual *prevents* persons from knowing themselves and each other. If partners are truly intimate, by contrast, "you have to know you need each other." Acknowledging interdependence, in Lucy's description, *strengthens* relational partners and the relationship.

When empowerment is envisaged as interconnectedness between partners, the metaphors used to characterize relational health alter considerably. Images of panoptic inspection are replaced by images of identities that are at once separate and collapsed: "You should be free to express yourself and to know, at the same time, that you affect the other person;" "I might be thinking he's being ridiculous about something, but before I open my mouth and say so I have to think about it from his point of view, just like I expect him to do for me if we have a good thing going;" "You should both be strong as people, and that way you can have a good, close relationship." Further, women indicate, confessional mandates are reduced because labels of deviance and illness are not applied in a manner disconnected from and indifferent towards, relational history.

Attractiveness and empowerment are dependent on healthy relational interaction, not an approximation to objectified cultural beauty standards. For example, when asking women to describe instances or stages of relationships in which they feel most attractive, many women describe positive encounters with relational partners. By contrast, women report, unpleasant interactions produce a sense of unattractiveness. Ellen notes, for instance, "[if] I have a fight with my husband the night before I go to work, the next day I go into work and feel generally unattractive. If we went out the night before and had a good time and enjoyed talking, that carries over to the next day in terms of the way I feel about myself being attractive." Feeling attractive or unattractive is dependent on self, other, context, and relationship.

Relational health, in the lives of women, entails a move from independence and objectification of the body to interdependence and reciprocity of involvement. An "equal" relationship is one in which both persons behave attentively and responsibly by acknowledging, rather than overriding, their dependencies on one another. A healthy male partner demonstrates his respect for a woman's independence not by praising her attractiveness exclusively, but by relinquishing his panoptic power. In a lengthy description of her current intimate relationship, Ruth establishes clear connections between a reduction in body objectification and reciprocal communicative involvement:

> When I'm with guys I'm dating, especially if we haven't established a real friendship, it's hard to deal with my body. You have to establish a friendship to be secure in a relationship because before that happens, you always have the feeling of being abandoned for someone else. It's just very superficial. I've been dating a guy now and I feel more comfortable with him than I did in high school relationships because I was less mature about how relationships work. All of it seemed to ride on how you looked, so making yourself look good for the other person is what kept the relationship going. I think things have gotten better because recently I went to my boyfriend's house and said, "Look, this relationship is really bothering me. I feel like we don't have a basic friendship here because we don't communicate. You never ask questions about my life and it's driving me crazy. It's all one-sided." So things are working much better now. I feel better about myself and the relationship. I'm more secure with him because I could say that.

Relational security, for Ruth, entails "a basic friendship," which in turn involves mutual interest in the communicative lives of relationship partners. Seeing herself as more mature regarding "how relationships work," Ruth gains her sense of security and empowerment not through increased physical attractiveness, or her partner's willingness to offer a favorable assessment, but through a strengthening of relational ties that results from an assertion of her needs.

——————————————————————————————Part III

Wisdom from the Margins

## Chapter 7

## Seeing the Mythology of Resolution:
## "I Could Write a Book About This"

*You know, if you think about all of the things women do to*
*their bodies, you can't help picturing men.*

*Marsha*

The promise of transcendence in discourses of feminine health is central to a socio-cultural policing of women's bodies. An effective functioning of the discourse, in fact, is contingent on women's *failure* to achieve body liberation, on a continuous admission of deviance which legitimates surveillance. Promises of unveiling the beautiful woman imprisoned in an ugly body are belied by the existence of curative voices, the urgency with which others offer their assistance in liberating the real. That is, if women are "naturally" aesthetically pleasing and strong, the labor of discovery with the aid of a master voice is unnecessary, absurd. The countless consumer products and services designed to facilitate women's appreciation of the bodily constitute a pointless and nonproductive exercise. The extraordinary profits generated from a promotion of women's beauty, however, suggest that much can be gained from the construction of women's confinement as a prelude to women's liberation.

Efforts to free women's bodies from the confines of oppression, external ownership, exploitation, with each new master voice, underscore disease, entrapment, marginality. Jane Fonda's (1981) text provides a remarkable demonstration of the discursive fusion of women's health and disease. At every turn, self-acceptance is premised on change, activism is signified by conformity to cultural beauty standards, and health demands freedom from exploitation.[1] In a chapter titled "We Become What We Do," Fonda delineates her freedom from constraint, which is prompted by a specific incident. When watching a slide show on Vietnamese culture in 1972, she notes a billboard advertising the services of an "American plastic surgeon whose speciality was changing Vietnamese

155

women's eyes from their natural almond shaped to the rounder shape of the Caucasian eyes" (pp. 19-20). At that moment, she realizes her entrapment, her similarity to the Vietnamese woman whose body is altered at the hands of a profit-seeking physician. She resolves to take control of her own body, to become responsible to other women by ceasing to present herself as a sexual object, enabling the freedom of all women. The extensive instruction given to women who wish to be strong assumes women's weakness. Fonda's book, which has generated multi-million dollar sales, would not exist if women were truly or "naturally" strong.

The rebellion encouraged by dieting rebels constitutes an effective means of control precisely because it entails a negation of current identity. As diet book authors dissociate themselves from an identity of diet book author, female consumers dissociate themselves from women's bodies. As fashion designers and cosmetic surgeons dissociate themselves from those who demand conformity, female clients dissociate themselves from women's bodies. The dissociations are necessary for the construction of desire, and the concomitant pursuit of something else, something different, something missing. Premised on lack, discourses of feminine excess promise a version of completion that plays out as repeated displacement, an undermining of identity in order to achieve identity. Paula delineates the operations of identity and displacement:

> When you buy a magazine like *Cosmo* or *Elle,* you're sort of struck right off the bat by the women. They have all kinds of things that you don't have—not just nice clothes and jewels, and that kind of thing. They have a life [that] you don't have, they have everything that you don't have. You want to have what they have so you might go out and buy something small to bring you closer to them, but you know at the same time, right when you're standing at the cosmetics counter, that buying this lipstick will not make you like them. So you think, maybe if I buy a new dress *and* the lipstick, yeah, that's it. But then you're standing there in your new dress, realizing you really don't have what they have, and you never really thought you would. But wait, those shoes, maybe those shoes... (laugh).

Fashion models represent "everything that you don't have," prompting a desire to resist one's own life. Consumption is the cure for a deficient identity, but, at the same time, each effort toward the approximation of fulfillment reveals oneself as an impostor, as an illusion of "natural" health/beauty.

Women's confinement in discourses of excess is not reducible to a form of consumerism wherein needs are created and then satisfied with endless products. As Paula suggests, approximations to an ideal proceed both with and without hopes of success. Nor can it be said that women have merely been duped by capitalist beauty propaganda. To be sure, these explanations may constitute particular effects of discourse, but neither is adequate in understanding the complex interplay between body reduction texts and women's speech. Discourses of domination are desire-producing, but as Gilles Deleuze and Fleix Guattari (1983) point out, "Desire does not lack anything; it does not lack its object. It is, rather the *subject* that is missing in desire, or desire that lacks a fixed subject; there is no fixed subject unless there is repression" (p. 26). Promises of feminine health are enticing not because women are permitted to consume products and services, but because health is constructed as the precondition for an emergence of identity. Prior to health, women are invisible, empty, devoid of desirability; after, women are representationally complete, marked clearly, identifiable.

The completed world of a healthy woman is appealing not because she has managed to acquire objects—a perfect body, fashionable attire, but because she embodies mobility; she can choose her destiny, her subjectivity. Most contemporary health or beauty books, for example, offer success stories that are told by "real" women, such as Fonda (1981), whose lives and experiences are set free from the tyranny of others. Real women who embody a satisfaction of desire, whose lives are complete, provide incentive for the pursuit of health and beauty. Yet there is something unreal about the lives of such women, something too closed and too final, dissociating them from the lives of women who are motivated by them. The "real" women of fantasy life, though they are held up as convincing empirical evidence, symbolize a form of repression that is premised on choice-making. A continuous pursuit of health and beauty, for everyday women, entails repeated cohesion and disjunction between the lives of real and fantasy women—of never being absolutely sure where the dividing lines are between real and ideal.

I wish to trace the means by which women are constructed and construct themselves within dominant discourse to represent "woman," and to undermine her. In particular, I first analyze ideological relations which inform divisions between reality and fantasy as grounded in the socio-cultural field of sexual difference. The inscription of difference, marking bodies for self and others, conflates the boundaries between the real and the symbolic. In the case of anti-diets, the real and the symbolic are paralleled with earthly existence and afterlife. Second, it is shown that although images of the healthy female body appear to signify women's desires, the marks of otherness point to an economy of sexuality in which *male* desires are foregrounded; hence the persistent lack of fit between women and woman-as-represented. And finally, I reposition the symbolic construction of sexual difference in the division between dominant and muted or "other" groups within culture. Avenues for female empowerment are opened with the realization that women *already* occupy a position of critical resistance by virtue of symbolic body excesses, of double participation in dominant and muted cultures.

## The Lives of Dolls

A central aim in the discourse of women's health is to "enable" women to confront the truth about themselves, followed by a telling or a "confession" of the truth. Women are encouraged to look inward, deep inside themselves, and to demonstrate their strength through an admission of faulty reasoning, insecurity, deception, and all other indications of unhealthiness/unattractiveness. Gazing inward for the purpose of discovering truth/health is a complicated task because it is a gaze which is directed both inward and outward. It is by virtue of seeing the outside of oneself, as in gazing into the mirror, that a woman is able to prompt the inward, truthful gaze. Mary Ann Doane's (1987) analysis of "women's films" provides considerable insight into the concurrent inward and outward gazes of women. In reflecting on the predominance of film imagery that displays woman as one who gazes—off into the distance, at herself, at other people—Doane suggests, women are positioned "outside the arena of history, politics, production—'looking on'" (p. 2). At the same time, the outward gaze has an inward referent, that is, the spectator/woman desires entry into a world that places her in a position of exteriority by virtue of her identity. When an ordinary woman gazes at the adventurous and gutsy models in *Vogue*, for example, she is positioned culturally to covet the model's life as represented, and to gaze inward for purposes of more closely approximating the sensibilities of her spectacle. Woman does not engage in a narcissistic gaze of identification with images of ideal women, but, as Rosalind Coward (1985) observes, she *desires* them as one who looks on, as an outsider (p. 79). She "takes in" the model, performing adjustments on herself, confronting the truth about herself vis-à-vis the model woman.

Proponents of a holistic and "real" vision of female health, along with their female followers, are charged with a monumental task that meets with much historical baggage. Historical components of the process are important because, within the parameters of beauty/health discourse, women are encouraged, by way of outward/inward gazes, to dissociate themselves from body and cultural history. Specifically, they must abandon "before" pictures to reach an afterlife, and they must deny the notoriously *unending* character of beauty efforts in the pursuit of "health." Through truth telling, women are encouraged to enter a *fantasy* world, disconnected from the realities of everyday existence and body history, in which body and experience conjoin to form permanent bliss.

A cultural need to protect women from their own unreasonable and amoral tendencies through a confessional abandonment of past history is itself an historical phenomenon. That women must renounce their lives as women in order to gain acceptability or "insider" status within dominant culture is a pervasive theme throughout history.[2] To accomplish this feat, women are required to not only reject personal history, but to renounce identification with women generally. The so-called "health craze," for example, is often attributed to the particularities of contemporary women's lives: thus women who labor to extract the "natural" in themselves are different from the blatantly fabricated conceptions of beauty in earlier periods *and* different from their unhealthy contemporaries.

Yet, the project of teaching women to value the natural and the unique in themselves runs into a number of practical and ideological snags when placed in the context of consumerism. If women value themselves as they are *naturally,* of course, they will not spend millions of dollars in efforts to correct "defects." Also, if women are discouraged from modeling themselves after cultural images of woman, certainly a prerequisite for uniqueness, they are likely to see that imitation of another hardly testifies to individuality. Thus, built into systems of consumerism is a confusion of the real and the symbolic: the symbolic must be "mistaken" for the real. In the domain of women and beauty/ health, Lois Banner (1983) suggests a linkage between women's health and mass production, wherein confusion of the real and the symbolic finds a firm foothold. According to Banner, the beauty industry in American culture grew exponentially during the early 1900s, concomitant with a push toward advanced technology and a resulting capacity for mass production. The mass production of beauty products was associated primarily with women, implies Banner, because already in place within culture was an equation between beauty and woman: "personal beauty was defined as an attribute that only a woman could possess" (p. 9). Insofar as cultural visions of woman *mandated* female beauty by deeming it "natural," and, through sheer presence in the marketplace suggested that beauty was "absent" in women, the promoters of beauty found a ready and sometimes desperate audience for their products.

If the urgency of beauty is combined with concomitant images of female irrationality—an inability to distinguish reality from fantasy, women may well be seen as persons in need of help when confronted with the utterly strategic interests of big business. Implicitly, the protective stance of anti-diet proponents assumes the presence of a large and looming presence, from which women must escape, but cannot escape. A fetishization of women's helplessness is a critical component in anti-diet discourse. Each new dieting rebel spends considerable time *underscoring* women's confusion and collapse in the face of power. In the case of Robert Linn (1980), a detailed and brutal castigation of reader misguidedness and powerlessness is relentless, but a necessary component of "liberation." Infused with confessional sensibilities, anti-diets promise salvation through catharsis, cleansing, realignment with scripture. Feelings of despair, hopelessness, and isolation slowly vanish as women enter the world of dieting rebellion.

The dieting rebel signifies the possibility of an afterlife in which desire is satisfied and thus no longer operative. Through a mobilization of the will based in scriptural postulates, woman is able to accomplish a release from confine-ment. An over-arching master voice, as seen in Hunter's (1976) turn to the Holy Spirit, and in the appeal to a "higher power" in Overeaters Anonymous, enables freedom from the oppression of bodily desires. In his characterization of diet books as inspirational literature, for example, Richard Watson (1985) notes, texts assure the reader that "somebody cares, that there is a way, and that you can be saved" (p. 15). The afterlife is a world in which woman has vanished; she has been replaced by a perfected version of woman. She is no longer fleshy, wrinkled, and bodily, but ethereal, uncontaminated, and free. All signs of earthly involvement, signs of life, are erased. The saved woman is doll-like, a fantasy. Women describe the fantasy lives of women who have been saved: "If you can just get to the end and fix everything, your life would be perfect;" "You see models and you think to yourself, if I looked like that, I'd never worry about anything, ever again;" "I wish I could get over all this dieting and beauty stuff, I mean, there must be some point when you do. Maybe you have to be [the famous model] Paulina to feel that way."

The living and breathing bodies of "earthly" women are disqualified through an approximation to the fantastical woman. Desired women are those who *appear* to be something other than women, those who denounce them-selves in order to quell the fears associated with female bodies. The bodies of women are replaced with replicas or "fictions" of women. Fictionalized women do not require earthly pleasures for sustenance; instead, similar to the anorexic female saints described by Rudolph Bell (1985), fictionalized women signify a transcendence of desires. Female bodies are deadened, erased, in the creation of replicability, in the "promotion" of feminine beauty as liberation from the bodily. In functional terms, Susan Griffin (1981) points out, cultural images of women's bodies can be gleaned from the implications surrounding the porno-graphic doll: the doll is "an actual plastic copy of a woman, made to replace a woman, and to give a man pleasure without the discomfort of female presence" (p. 40).

The desired female body in discourses of excess is a dead body, a beautiful corpse. Andera Dworkin's (1974) analysis of fairy tale imagery clarifies the sex-ual politics of associations between femininity and death. Of the female character, she writes, "when she is good, she is soon dead. In fact, when she is good, she is so passive in life that death must be only more of the same" (p. 41). Images of death appear with remarkable frequency as women discuss partici-pation in beauty/health discourses: "You can diet until you're blue in the face, and still, it usually doesn't work;" "Going on a diet can be suicidal because you might know you're not ready to do it, but you do anyway, so you'll fail;" "She came in wearing a dress [that is] to die for;" "I'd give up life as I know it if I could lose the thirty pounds I've been trying to lose for the past five years."

Similarly, the lives of women who appear in accounts of anorexia and bulimar-exia are "deadened" to body sensation and need, sometimes reporting, as Marlene Boskind-White and William C. White (1983) find, that death is prefer-able to an unsatisfactory body weight. The dead body is not manifested through desire based in something missing, but in desire for something *less* than one is, a reduction of body and life.

Good women approximate the appearance of death because lifelessness, in dominant representations, is mistaken for female health. Kim Chernin's (1985) analysis of anorexic and bulimarexic girls, and in particular the lan-guage used by mothers and daughters to describe the bodies of one another, reveals images of concentration camps. Although the good daughter, in repro-ducing her culture's fear of female excesses, attempts body mastery, Chernin notes, "The vocabulary of women who suffer from eating disorders is filled with words like *shrunken, impoverished, exhausted, depleated, all used up, sucked dry, totally empty, all spread out*" (p. 62). Concomitantly, as the "mothers of anorexics describe their daughters as concentration camp victims," daughters "see death in their mother's faces" (p. 62). Both women, one who labors to create an ethereal, untainted body, and another whose body is acceptable because it has produced children, sense death, the shell of a life, in the other.

The good woman, in dominant imagery, is a reminder of woman in the form of an artifact, a remnant. Jean Baudrillard (1981) provides a compelling analysis of the construction of artifactual bodies and power relations in the context of consumerism. The artifactual is invariably taken as the real in systems of exchange. In his discussion, the discourses of consumerism are linked to the discourses of human identity in a highly complex and political fashion, displacing origins and closures. A key element in exchange economies is the establishment of difference through a proliferation of symbolization which offers countless *illusions* of difference. False differences are constructed, but become "realized" in an empirical fashion through artifacts and models. The models that are taken up and "taken in" by women are themselves symbol-izations, collections of signifiers which point to "woman," the good life, free-doom, a satisfaction of desire.

The pursuit of health, for women, entails going inside of oneself to dis-cover that insides are constituted by further symbolizations, each one pointing to yet another, and another. The "chaining" of needs in beauty discourse, for example, can occur only if women can be counted on to look within for a recog-nition of defectiveness. Baudrillard (1981) points out, within capitalist econo-mies, the concept of "need" arises in relation to internal propositions: "and thus, in order that [consumers] should experience this or any other particular need, the need must already exist inside people as a virtual postulation" (p. 71). The insides of woman spill onto the surface of woman and, in turn, point back to that which is under the surface and hidden, in need of extraction. Models of beauty, for example, open themselves fully to inspecting gazes, providing an opportunity for knowledge; at the same time, they hide the truth about themselves (through make-up, lighting, airbrushing, and so forth).

The mobility promised in discourses of women's health is illusory because beauty is profitable only on the condition that it can be mass produced. Progress toward freedom is made when a woman is consumed by systems of exchange, when each image of perfection is replaced by another image in which life and lifelessness are collapsed. The model, Baudrillard (1981) writes, exists in a discursive space characterized by "perfectionist vertigo and controlled narcissism" (p. 94). As women "take in" models, they enter dizzying and contradictory constructions which fuel a never-ending pursuit of health. The body acquires exchange value through its approximation to the *artifact,* rather than to an "original" vision of the body as a living, breathing, experiencing entity. Here, the female body is *consumed* by cultural economies and rendered harmless *as* a living body because the living body is taken as fiction. The discipline and maintenance required of "healthy" women entails continued participation in the very systems that have "deadened" women. Of the body's circulation in systems of exchange, Baudrillard observes an association between the body's subjection to discipline and the body's erasure:

> It is the final disqualification of the body, its subjection to a discipline, the total circulation of signs. The body's wildness is veiled by makeup, the drives assigned to a cycle of fashion. Behind this *moral* perfection, which stresses a valorization of exteriority (and no longer, as in traditional morality, a labor of interior sublimation), it is insurance taken out against the instincts (p. 94).

The body is marked by consumer artifices so that, in the final analysis, the signs of labor (lipstick, high fashion, expensive jewels) comprise the object of desire. Baudrillard thus argues that in the exchange economy of beauty *"it is the artifact that is the object of desire"* (p. 94).

Baudrillard's (1981) analysis is important because it addresses the ideological play between female body erasure, desire, and morality. Systems of domination are well served by constructions of women as persons who are both wicked and innocent, trustworthy and manipulative, reverent and contemptable. *All* women are "fictions" within the ideological interplay of gender and consumer economies: sickness and health are interchangeable. Life and death, as Paula observes, are synonymous: "If you're not beautiful and sexy and savvy, you don't have much of a life. If you are those things, you might not be well off either because people think you're sort of empty, just a doll to look at."

The mythology of female beauty serves androcentrism well for at least two interrelated reasons. First, male members of society escape responsibility for the construction of femininity. Because women are assumed to *choose* engagement with beauty pursuits, since beauty and woman constitute a "natural" correlation, men are seen to play no direct part in the exploitation of women via consumerism. Women often point out, for example: "Women are the ones who buy the creams, the diet pills, etc., so they only have themselves to blame;" "Girls have some kind of need to make themselves acceptable appearance-wise;" "Your boyfriend might say 'You'd look better with lipstick on,' but in the end, its you who goes out and plunks down the money for it." In fact, women indicate, men often stand back and wonder "why they do it to themselves" when confronted with the latest weight, cosmetic, fashion, or relational concern. Alternatively, as implied by the resistive elements in the discourse of women's health, male sensibilities work to aid women in seeing both the frivolity and exploitation of modern consumerism, all the while demanding consumerism.

A second function of feminine "falseness" is to evidence the so-called manipulative character of women in general. Beautiful women, then, can be castigated on *moral* grounds. As persons who manipulate the "real" or "natural" in order to appear as something or someone other than themselves, women are masters of deception, of hiding the truth under layers of cosmetic tricks. Indeed, in talking with women, I learn about endless "beauty secrets": "If you wear a lot of black, you look thinner;" "Someone told me that you can make high cheekbones if you can put your blush on right;" "I went to one of those fashion consultants where they tell you what to wear, and it really does make a difference." Thus, although female beauty signifies a deadening of the body, a reduction to complete innocuousness, it also signifies an active capacity for deception. The moral danger of women is in fact implicitly assumed in images of lifeless or doll-like replicas of female bodies. A body that is truly nonthreatening does not need to be rendered lifeless, having its history and its powers undermined permanently.

The strangely powerful and powerless qualities of femininity can be clarified through an examination of larger systems of difference which hold in place the precarious position of woman's relation to man within cultural discourse. In the discussion to follow, I consider the pursuit of beauty as motivated by a desire that shifts back and forth within the polarities of feminine and masculine, never fully resting on one side or the other. The instability of woman as represented highlights her moral excesses and her beauty. In turn, the instability of woman calls into question the sexual identity of woman as object of terror. Insightfully, Janet sees, "I think it's terrorizing for men to think that they can try to control women, but in the end they can't."

## Imagined Difference and Desire

The pursuit of beauty is infused with absolutist sensibilities regarding the differences between women and men. Ideologically, woman and man from the symbolic limits of numerous divisions, in turn representing and underscoring sexual difference. As noted in previous chapters, men signify "higher" dimensions of existence, including transcendence, reasoning power, strength of intellectual presence; women signify "lower" or oppositional elements in the range of human qualities, such as immanence, faulty reasoning, and strength of bodily or material presence. Woman constitutes a complex vision of otherness because she is not only different from man, but represents that which man must *not* become if he wishes to retain his position within socio-cultural hierarchies. Man's alignment with masculine identity is contingent on representing his opposition to woman for self and others. As Marilyn French (1985) observes, because woman is aligned with the bodily and the nonvolitional, she is precisely that which must be rejected in order to create a transcendent world (p. 103).

Discourses of feminine excess foreground many undersirable dimensions of masculine existence. Central to body reduction texts and programs is an absence of control, an inability to rise above everyday circumstances, immersion in filthy and deviant desires—all of which bring ridicule, moral contempt, and social condemnation. Invariably, successful dieters have taken control of their lives by way of reason and diligence, avoiding the temptations of quick and fraudulent solutions in exchange for momentary pleasure. Healthy bodies are not manipulated by the promises of charlatans; with insight, their inhabitants see, freedom requires knowledge, certainty, exactness. The implied contempt for persons who have not mastered existence is, implicitly, an expression of contempt for women that disguises a contempt for men. Women, after all, have never been aligned with reason.

The masculine labor of establishing a clear difference from the feminine is both complicated and intensified by the fact that men, too, are bodily. And because men are bodily, they are associated with nature, non-volition, and necessity. Michel Foucault (1985) examines the western preoccupation with mental control by taking the fall of Adam in Christian doctrine as articulated by St. Augustine, and establishes a clear linkage between man and non-volition. A male fear of the flesh, due to its propensity for moral transgression, infuses *masculine* accounts of losing control, of being caught off guard by bodily desires. Prior to Adam's fall from grace, his body "was perfectly obedient to the soul and the will" (p. 370). The fall not only signified a violation of religious doctrine, but a loss of *bodily* control: "His body, and parts of his body, stopped obeying commands, revolted against him, and the sexual parts of his body were the first to rise up in this disobedience" (p. 370). Sexuality, thus defined, is not perceived as a problematical interference involving another person, but as "the problem of the relationship of oneself to oneself, or more precisely, the relationship between one's will and involuntary assertions" (p. 371).

Male identity is divided internally so that a struggle between the flesh and the intellect informs male experience. The struggle itself is represented as a masculine/feminine one, but as Luce Irigaray (1985) points out, "Feminine sexuality has always been conceptualized on the basis of masculine parameters" (p. 23). Harmony in man's relationship to himself is threatened by bodily desires, by the body's capacity to undermine self-control. A loss of control, in turn, violates the doctrines of higher powers, the laws of masters, relegating the one who loses control to a space characterized by shame, filth, baseness. To guarantee salvation, man is required to marginalize the bodily, to both despise and expunge his propensity for transgression. A harmonious relationship with oneself (and with the Father) is symbolized by control over the body, manifested in strength of will and an ability to resist all sensual temptation.

The self-referential quality of masculine sexuality is veiled by a projection of all things bodily onto women. The anguish of male sexuality is not a product of feminine powers per se, but of the continual repression and silencing of the male body, the need to escape from that which cannot be escaped: sensation, feeling, vulnerability. As women observe: "A man has a need to prove that he doesn't feel anything;" "It's kind of sad about men because they have to walk around and act like nothing gets to them;" "Being a man is having an answer to everything, not being weak, and not being able to show emotion; this is the sign of being a real man." In the crime of rape, the very testimony of "defenselessness" in the face of a woman's body points an impoverished relationship between the rapist and his own body, an inability to be a "real" man. Paula Caplan's (1985) analysis of violence against women reveals a correlation between male aggression and a loss of control, both of which originate within an individual body (pp. 144-145). The expression of hatred and contempt which informs an act of rape is self-directed. That the particular characteristics of a woman are often irrelevant in a rapist's selection of a victim, for example, belies judicial defenses centered on a disparagement of the *victim's* character. Moreover, as Dianne Herman (1984) notes, rape is often viewed culturally, not as a violation of *women*, but as "an offense that one man commits against another" (p. 22). A rape victim's husband or lover is violated because in the taking of another man's woman, the rapist asserts control over the desires of men. The raped woman is clearly and brutally violated in the process, not because of who she is or anything she has done, but because she represents the contents of male projection: she signifies that which man despises not in women, but in himself.

The construction of gender difference conceals the self-referential character of masculine sexuality and begins with anatomy, in the realm of the visual. A cultural preoccupation with empirical assurance of difference is in fact grounded in a terror of sameness; in the possibility that women may not be fundamentally different from men.[3] The pervasive male insistence of female difference, going so far as to view women as incomprehensible ("Who can figure women?"), labors to produce evidence, verification, proof for fundamental differences between women and men. Ann Oakley (1981a) traces issues of human development in medical and psychological research, for instance, revealing that components of physiological functioning, even when few if any differences are revealed in females and males, are continually recast to highlight female/male *empirical* differences. And invariably, "significant" differences reinforce male strength and, by implication, female deficiencies.

The fury with which men project difference and deficiency onto women suggests that projection belies reality. French (1985) observes, in the relation between oppressor and oppressed, "All that the oppressed is, the dominator can deny being; this is symbolic truth, contradicted by reality" (p. 137). In writing about the field of the real and the imaginary, psychoanalyst and critic Jacques Lacan (1985) places the inscription of sexuality in the imaginary realm, where the phallus is seen as the (symbolic) mark of difference. Jacqueline Rose (1985), in an articulation of Lacan's positions, outlines the symbolic figuring of sexual difference. Rose explains that anatomical difference entails a visible referent, coded as sexual difference:

> Sexual difference is then assigned according to whether individual subjects do or do not possess the phallus, which means not that anatomical difference *is* sexual difference (the one as strictly deducible from the other), but that anatomical difference comes to *figure* sexual difference, that is, it becomes the sole representative of what difference is allowed to be (p. 42).

The figuring of sexual difference exists in the imaginary because the so-called "absence" or "lack" in female anatomy can only be defined as such "according to a pre-existing hierarchy of values" (qtd. in Rose, p. 42).

The hierarchy of values which holds in place the figuring of sexual difference represents woman as an untrustworthy other precisely because she threatens to complicate male projection: to mirror *man's* excesses. If woman refuses confinement in her symbolic place, the entire system of sexual differences is revealed as "imagined." Thus, the projected otherness of woman insures continuation in the production of symbolic differences that are mistaken for real differences. Rose (1986) writes, "Set up as the guarantee of the system [woman] comes to represent two things—what the man is not, that is, difference, and what he has to give up, that is, excess" (p. 219). The character of woman is excessive because she embodies the possibility of losing control, of a protest by anatomy as announced visually. Her signification of excess provides assurance that being "too much," exceeding the bounds of self-control, is far removed from masculinity.

The alien character of woman as represented establishes a practical problem for male projection and the power constructed for men by virtue of their place of privilege in systems of sexual difference. By virtue of her symbolic existence, wherein she is constructed as "other" and "not male," woman cannot be fully represented. That is, if woman is truly "other," then she cannot be wholly pinned down or comprehended; her difference is fundamental. Attempts to represent woman by way of compulsory visibility, as fully seen and known, are repeatedly usurped by woman's otherness. Irigaray (1985) points to the symbolic slipperiness of woman, "It is useless . . . to trap women in the exact definition of what they mean, to make them repeat (themselves) so that it will be clear; they are already elsewhere in that discursive machinery where you expected to surprise them" (p. 29). The very elements of woman that must be known and rendered safe, for example, the vulnerability of the flesh, are rendered alarmingly unknowable within dominant codes.

The fabrication of visible or "marked" feminine difference—through "make up" and other artifice—both symbolizes and erases the threat posed by female/male excesses. Dolls, while static and lifeless, are reminders of the flesh, substitutions for the flesh, and ultimately point to an owner who is fearstruck at the prospect of engagement with women/with himself. Doll and woman symbolize one another. Keeping one's distance from woman, gazing at her with fascinated eyes, provides an illusion of difference and power, an ability to differentiate between dolls and women. Indeed, speaking about the relation between spectator and spectacle, Irigaray (1987) points out, "More than the other senses, the eye objectifies and masters. It sets at a distance, maintains the distance" (qtd. in Owens 1983, p. 70). Yet, the object of mastery is not woman, but a facsimile of her, that is, woman as represented. Female conformity with dominant images, as we have seen throughout women's descriptions, is always precarious because as women move from one dimension of "health" to another, each promising wholeness, there is always more, always an "excess" not captured by representational boundaries. Woman is made safe *and* dangerous through the difference demanded of her within the symbolic order. The same signifiers point to good and bad women. For example, both mother and whore embody the capacity to consume, undermine, and render powerless.

The complex operations of male terror help to form women's body experience. Women labor on behalf of masculine fears by marking themselves as others. Indeed, Susan Brownmiller (1984) observes, femininity "must constantly reassure its audience by a willing demonstration of difference, even when one does not exist in nature" (p. 15). At the same time, the marking of difference represents the danger of woman, body, vulnerability. The cultural promotion of women's "health" is based in a fear of the corporal aspect of femininity that, in the final analysis, has little to do with women. Fears of losing control, of the flesh, and of disrespect for the self are masculine ones that women are required to take up, to embody: as fictions. The fictionalized body, safe and nonthreatening, is a *male* body. Monica states, for example, "Isn't it funny about how when you look at a beautiful girl or woman, you always picture a man in her life?"

### The Power of Woman's Intermediacy

Women in androcentric practices do not merely fall on one side of cultural polarities, but, as seen in chapter 5, function as *mediation* in the dichotomies of masculine and feminine, rational and irrational, transcendent and immanent, goodness and evil. Women's intermediate position requires a bridging of, and participation in, both sides of cultural dichotomies. Haunani-Kay Trask (1986) explains, because women obviously exist as members of society, "women cannot be wholly relegated to the realm of 'nature' or the 'natural' " (p. 16). Trapped in the interstice dividing culture and nature, woman's position in the symbolic order is precarious and slippery. She is "more or less" natural and "more or less" cultural, but the precise limits of her association with either are impossible to determine.

The control of women, epitomized in discourses of feminine health, is in fact dependent on an expropriation of women's intermediacy. A position of intermediacy imbues woman with masculine consciousness so that she is compatible with the inferiority of lower life forms and has *knowledge* of her inferiority. Without consciousness, woman would be unable to reflect on herself and her behavior: she would be incapable of seeing herself as "naturally" subordinate to man. There would be no capacity for confession, no ability to define transgression *as* deviance. A positing of consciousness in women enables affinity with symbolic constructions of woman, a blurring of boundaries between woman as constructed and woman as real. For those who occupy dominant positions, female consciousness works to keep women in a constant state of "pre-resolution;" never quite sure of her footing but sensing that her steps proceed from an estranged body, woman becomes infinitely maleable.

A lack of clarity surrounding the divisions between the "reality" of woman and symbolic representations of her, though, is also woman's power. Her vacillation within the symbolic order, traversing the boundaries of nature and culture, underscores woman's power and hence the double-edged danger she poses. Woman poses a danger to man because she behaves in a manner that is structurally akin to madness, that is, she demonstrates an inability to determine reality from illusion; she poses danger in the symbolic order because she is a product of its own "pre-existing" madness. Hélène Cixous and Catherine Clément (1986) explain the danger of woman's "symbolic mobility".

> Societies do not succeed in offering everyone the same way of fitting into the
> symbolic order; those who are, if one may say so, between systems, in the
> interstices, offside, are the ones who are afflicted with a dangerous symbolic
> mobility. Dangerous for them, because those are the people afflicted with
> what we call madness, anomaly, perversion...But this mobility is also
> dangerous—or productive—for the cultural order itself, since it affects the
> very structure whose lacunae it reflects (p. 7).

Positioned on the dividing line between culture and nature, reason and
madness, evidence for woman's easy slippage into unreason both thwarts and
underscores the divisions of the dominant.

Because woman reproduces man's struggle with himself, she is a fascinat-
ing, if not entirely trustworthy other. Male eyes fixate on woman's otherness;
when she is most "other" she is most dutifully watched. When she most
symbolizes the fragility of cultural divisions, she is most thoroughly a spectacle. In turn, the gazes of men, from the sidelines, function to extract knowledge, to re-cement symbolic divisions, and to reassert absolute difference.
Cixous and Clément (1986) suggest an important connection between knowledge and fascinated gazes in observing that an "audience ready to satisfy its
fantastic desire, is necessary for the spectacular side of sorcery and hysteria" (p.
10). A satisfaction of desire by way of distance, not coming too close to the
spectacle, is characteristic of male gazes: "inquisitors, magistrates, doctors—
the circle of doctors with their fascinated eyes, who surround the hysteric,
their bodies tensed to see the tensed body of the possessed woman" (p. 10).
Gazing from a distance underlines woman's otherness, her "possession" by
cultural divisions, and at the same underscores woman's power: one need not
retain distance from someone or something that presents no threat of harm.
Angela locates the contradiction of distance and terror in observing, "Men
usually take an active interest in what a woman does to her body, watching and
commenting when she gets ready for an evening out, and all the time, they're
saying, 'Why do you go to all that trouble? You're fine just the way you are'."

The distance implied by the fascinated gaze works to insure the domination of woman's bodies and the invisibility of masculine terror. Spectators
entrap woman in the realm of hysteria, bringing her under total confinement,
without laying a hand on her. Diffused gazes are seemingly passive witnesses
to the expropriation of wo/man's possession. And from the hysteric is
extracted a performance in which the character of woman struggles to release
herself from the wo/manly forces that hold her in their grip. Cixous and
Clément (1986) explain,

> Women's bodies must be bound so that the constraints will make the demons
> come out; then, when the spectators have gathered in a circle, when the lions
> have come into the ring, they are let go—the pleasure of danger, the raging

beauty of the wild beasts in constrained freedom, of the violent demoniacal forces gripping the woman; but no, they are no longer women, no longer girls. The female body is only an intermediary, prop, passage. Passage accomplished, that which is no longer woman but beast, devil, symptom is set free. The girls are not released, the demons are: the girls are *bound* (p. 11).

The pleasure of onlookers culminates with the setting free of wild forces and demons because, then, the image before their eyes is reappropriated within the symbolic order, bound by the sheer force of male power to underline its own categories and laws.

The dominant gaze, importantly, frees itself from madness through an appeal to women's well being or "health." Fascinated gazes surround sick or mad women, possessed women, for the sake of assisting her in the pursuit of freedom from her illness.[4] The ruse in the whole operation is that, indeed, the *illness* is freed, but not the girl-woman who mediates sickness and health. She remains after her performance, spent, but incidental to the fascination by spectators because it is not she that they are eager to expunge. Rather, pleasure ensues from the release of evil within the confines of an enclosed space, a space of terror over which spectators give themselves the illusion of control. It is the spectator who requires a release from the terror of his own body, the performing women, as bodies, are not essential to the catharsis.

The contemporary urgency surrounding a manifestation of women's health is indeed telling in the context of hysteria and the spectacular. Discourses of women's health function to encircle women in a space of confinement in which they are never directly disciplined or touched. Discursive elements overlap and reinforce one another, *surrounding* women, to see with fascination the madness of female illnesses and deficiencies. They "perform" voluntarily, with conviction. Women's willingness to enter the circle of hysteria/illness functions to support and condition cultural categories. All elements of the symbolic system must play their parts convincingly or the system breaks down. Foucault (1980e) observes that the exercise of domination is dependent on a "complex play of supports" in which all participants in the domain of a particular discourse further its ends. Here, the "summit and the lower elements of the hierarchy stand in a relationship of mutual support and conditioning, a mutual 'hold' (power as a mutual and indefinite 'blackmail')" (p. 159). A "healthy" woman is defined as such because she has exposed her illness, underscored her symbolic value for the pleasure of others.

A position of intermediacy and support requires women to live within both sides of cultural divisions, to live within the boundaries of dominant and marginalized groups. Elaine Showalter (1981) utilizes the anthropological model developed by Edwin Ardener to outline the positions of women in dominant culture. Ardener suggests that "women constitute a *muted group,* the boundaries of whose culture and reality overlap, but are not wholly contained by, the *dominant (male) group*" (qtd. in Showalter, P. 199). Women are both separate from, and inside, dominant culture. Men, conversely, are inside dominant culture, but alien to the marginalized space reserved for women. Thus, as Showalter writes, women are not "inside and outside the male tradition; they are inside two traditions simultaneously" (p. 202).

The "dual citizenship" of women within the symbolic poles of masculine and feminine, combined with the "symbolic mobility" of women, creates entrapment, to be sure, but constitutes the site of women's critical insight. As seen earlier, for example, women's reported immersion in cultural beauty/ health standards is accompanied by keen vision, as in "I could write a book about this." In critical terms, women are grounded in a type of *bilingualism* that permits simultaneous affinity with, and alienation from, the beliefs and values of dominant culture. The performances demanded and offered by women are sometimes given uncritically, but often, women sense and see constructed divisions between woman as represented and themselves. As Irigaray (1985) says of women, "they are already elsewhere in that discursive machinery where you expected to surprise them" (p. 29).

Women's assessments of their own bodies reflect an accurately precarious relation to cultural beauty/health stndards. With tremendous acuity, women see/sense the traps of attractiveness prescriptions *as* they both participate in them and refuse participation. Points of resistance and co-optation are revealed with equal conviction: "Sure, I buy all that junk for my face, you know, to make my skin softer, etc. I know it's all a game and there are times when I say to myself, 'why are you doing this?';" "I can just turn it off sometimes, all the attractiveness this and that. I flat-out refuse to put make-up on and the whole bit. It's mostly when I go out with men that I do all that stuff to my body;" "You get sort of stuck in it, all these products, one leads to another. But you can't win either way." Seeing that one "can't win either way" or that "it's all a game" emerges from persons who are required to live in the margins, as onlookers, and from persons who know that in the game of women's health, women do not win.

The masculine priority given to independent thinking and detached gazes is, for women, based in fiction. A seemingly unending female consump-tion of health and beauty books and programs, in which lives are closed and complete, may point to a few parallels in the lives of everyday women, but at the same time, women sense the fictitious components of the worlds given to them in the name of health. A capacity to detach oneself fully from others and from cultural practices is a game in which success is contingent on self-deception, on living a fiction in which life is death. If persons are seen to be enmeshed in the world around them, there are no final resolutions, no points of absolute closure. In speaking with women, it becomes clear that the experience of body satisfaction/completion is seen as possible and illusory. Although women often express a desire for slenderness and culturally defined beauty, their voices are rich in critical potential because, in the process of speaking, women deconstruct the mythology of body resolution. The cultural mechanisms in which women are trapped receive critical acknowledgment, along with the struggles within the discourses that make up female "beauty." Women sense that the closer they come to approximating beauty ideals, the more "unlike themselves" they become, perhaps. Georgia summarizes:

> I've thought a lot about all the things women do to themselves in the name of beauty, fashion, or whatever it is that we do. I sometimes really make an effort, a big effort, to make myself up and go out, feeling great about myself. But it can happen just as often that I do the same things to myself, and go out feeling terrible. There's just no way of knowing how it's going to go. People will think you're crazy if you say, "Well, I'm going to [a] nice restaurant and I don't give a damn about how I look." But it's just that all this thinking about what to do makes you unsure, like you don't have a brain in your head. Then again, you have to do it, and sometimes you want to do it because you want to enhance yourself, but it's interesting. It's just interesting. I think that's all I have to say.

## Chapter 8

## Political Solutions:
## "Wait a Minute, This is Crazy"

> *There are moments when you remember all that you've
> done to make yourself one of them, the beautiful people, and
> you burst out laughing.*
>
> *Jennifer*

Discourses of women's excesses constitute a theater in which a male terror of the bodily is performed and reenacted for countless audiences. A darkened room prevents the woman on stage from seeing the tensed muscles and sweating face of her voyeur, the body whose place in symbolic imagery is dependent on evidence for her sickness, her possession by demons. The woman screams and rages, pulling at her hair and mutilating her body, desperate for release. She bears witness to her own transgressions, pleads for forgiveness and vows to realign herself with scripture. Through her body he is able to exorcize the demons within himself. He is reassured by the performance: the woman on stage is other, consumed. He walks away without feeling the weight of his body, the earth under his feet, because, in watching her, his body is numbed. Watching her allows him to sleep peacefully, confident in his own salvation, at least until the next performance.

> ... these are sick girls, no question ... you're up there and people see you and
> evaluate you ... everything about you is wrong ... it's all a game but everyone
> acts like it's real ... this is serious business that we're doing ... you never
> know for sure ... I want to stop this craziness but what happens if you just
> stop?

Discourses of women's health preserve an unending supply of performances. Individually and collectively, women are positioned center stage, waiting for another curtain to rise. A desire for health assumes disease, a desire for reduction underscores excess, a desire for control announces impotence, a desire for rationality foregrounds madness. Female desires, Rosalind Coward (1985) reminds us, are not narcissistic, grounded in self-love, but in desire for identity, a desire to be something/someone else. A female inability to achieve identity, written as health, must be built into the discursive machinery or else the entire projectory apparatus breaks down. The problematic is posed endlessly: how might women become healthy? Women must be counted on to confess illness, undergoing operations on the body, to reinforce male transcendence, the power to be non-bodily.

> ...I know I'm not going about dieting in the right way...I've tried everything and nothing seems to work...this body won't do what I want it to...I want to be freed from all worry...the more you do...the more of you there is not to like...no matter what women do, it's too much...you can't help picturing men...

An expansion in the domain of women's health/disease appears at a time when women are purported to be taking control of their lives, making strides off stage, into the audience, with increasing confidence. In the name of liberation, the same women are encouraged to turn a critical lens on dimensions of experience ranging from sagging eyelids, to relational competencies, to business finesse. To illustrate, in an analysis of cultural transformations in the arena of feminine sexuality, Barbara Ehrenreich, Elizabeth Hess, and Gloria Jacobs (1986) observe, contemporary media have begun to "metamorphize the woman, who had been practicing her sexual negotiating skills throughout the seventies, into an old-fashioned girl looking for moonlight, flowers, and commitment. Women who didn't fit this new stereotype were portrayed as hopelessly misdirected" (p. 162). At the same time, an episode of "NBC Reports" presented an episode in which reporters began by noting that modern women are " 'fed up with modern American men, and modern morality' " (p. 172). In turn, women are expected, again in the pursuit of freedom, to dismantle obstacles to health through a recognition of disease/misguidedness, a realignment with sexual oppositions disguised as liberation.[1]

> ...people have such [an] interest in how women's lives are going wrong... you can think about all of these things until you die...I want people to see that I have an inside...it is true that you have more advantages if you're thin and healthy...being just thin isn't good anymore...you have to really watch yourself...something can always go wrong...if women are liberated now, why do I worry...more than ever?

Countless female body liberation discourses are informed by an assumption that women gain knowledge and power through an examination of the personal and the bodily. Barbara Sichtermann (1986) examines the political implications of a "reprivatization of the personal" in contemporary scholarship concerning women's oppression (p. 3). She considers the tactical dilemmas in resistive efforts wherein the "personal is political" is lauded as a mandate of liberation. Positioning women in the domain of the everyday experience, does not represent a convincing departure from the rhetoric of women's excesses. Sichtermann writes, "The personal sphere is something directly political for women because it refuses to leave them alone, because they cannot rid themselves of responsibility for personal matters" (p. 2). The political call for a scrutiny of the personal and the bodily in women's experience assumes that, typically, women engage the world mindlessly/without insides, without political consciousness. Given a precarious and shifting position in discursive regimes, women have never had the luxury of mindless engagement.

> ... we thought about weight, morning, noon, and night ... I've spent so many hours and days, thinking hard about all of these things ... I think it's true that women notice more because we have to pay attention to what other people want from us ... you can't do anything without thinking about the consequences ... if you blow it, you just have to do better next time ... the kind of life you lead is very important ... have you been a good person?

A revolt against women's ignorance or entrapment as a prelude to liberation is a risky enterprise. In an impressive analysis of the tactical interplay between power, knowledge, and ignorance, Eve Kosofsky Sedgwick (1988) argues, "The angles of view from which it can look as though a political fight is a fight against *ignorance* are invigorating and maybe revelatory ones but dangerous places for dwelling" (p. 104). Characterizations of ignorance, Sedgwick writes, are not unveiled as "pieces of the originary dark," disconnected from knowledge, but are "produced by and correspond to particular knowledges and circulate as part of particular regimes of truth" (p. 104). Women's proposed/prescribed ignorance of the bodily corresponds with knowledges in whose parameters the bodies of women cut, starved, tortured, and bloodied— all in the name of knowledge, all designed to procure feminine salvation.

> ... you have to really get in touch with who you are ... you can't fool yourself in the end ... I know by now what all of my behavior means, I've read so many books ... eight hundred calories a day and I watch what I eat ... I feel like I'm dying, like I'll starve to death, but that's a problem with me ... you can't deal with false information ... when I'm dying to eat, I just remind myself of how

good I'll feel if I don't give in...I know everything there is to know about losing weight, so why do I look like I'm still in the dark?

A political solution to women's health problems wherein a privileging of women's experiential knowledge appears center stage is the counterpart to arguments centered on female ignorance. Sedgwick (1988) warns us to be wary of one "who appeals too directly to the redemptive potential of simply upping the cognitive wattage on any question of power" (p. 104). Jane Fonda (1981) offers experiential knowledge and encourages other women to take up her own life in efforts to see and resist oppressive cultural practices. An array of exploitive practices are paraded before our eyes in super-market fashion, ranging from oppressive family environments to air pollution. In the prologue, Fonda writes, "I decided to write this book, not because I consider myself an expert, but because I want to share what I've had to learn the hard way with other women" (p. 10). Implicitly, the call for a legitimization of women's lived experience as a source of knowing is opposed to, fundamentally different from, the wisdom of experts. Given the cures offered in the discourse of women's excesses, women are poorly equipped for helping others not only due to lacking expertise/genuine knowledge, but because the experience of women is positioned in the domain of illness.

> ....if you want to be supported in your diet, go to a man not a woman...girls get sucked into a lot of dangerous diets...girls encourage each other to overeat and break diets...you have to stand back and look at everything realistically...you should ignore what your body is saying to you if it's telling you to have that pizza...a lot of women are misinformed when it comes to losing weight...I'll be sick if I eat what I'd personally like to eat...it's hard to trust yourself...I could write a book about this...

A refusal to accept the political impossibility of disengagement with regimes of truth is yet another manifestation of discourses on women's excess. In numerous conversations with men on the politics of women's bodies and cultural practices, I am advised to find an answer, an inroad to liberation. My work, they say, will not "help" women if I do not propose an alternative to current images of femininity. I need to recognize that women are duped, exploited, and made to look silly by androcentrism. And from here, as a woman, I must provide release, catharsis, something they call power. I am an expert, I am told, with credentials suggesting a capacity to think, to rise above the world of everyday women. My power to present the truth, I glean, is dependent on my disengagement with women.

> ...other people are always telling women what to do...women can't do anything right...no matter who you are, how good or how smart you are, it

doesn't matter in the end... women can be very sick when it comes to appearance... go to a man, not a woman...

Others tell me that men are exploited, too. I am advised to consider the recent attention given to an aesthetics of male bodies, or my work will be biased, nonrepresentative, partial. Men are now becoming "reduced" to the pursuits of femininity, and should this not cause alarm? Am I not bothered politically by male cosmetics, high fashion in the world of masculinity, plastic surgery for men? Responding is difficult because, implicitly, I am cast in the role of a disease-free woman who must acknowledge the diseased character of women. Were it not for a beauty industry supported by women, men would not now be experiencing its effects. As a woman, I am held accountable, I must exhibit fairness toward men. Evidence for my objectivity (/illness) surfaces when I say, "Indeed, men are now suffering from the sickness of femininity."

... my boyfriend is really concerned about the way he looks... men do not have to care as much as women about appearance and weight... men are too busy to worry about trivial, ditsy things... my brother says girls are vain but he cares about how he looks... it's sick to think that men are getting caught up in the same obsessions as women... if a man starts buying all kinds of junk to make himself attractive, you know there's a woman in the picture somewhere...

Within the discursive interplay between personal experience, knowledge, and ignorance, a *solution* to women's excesses invites intensified visibility, inspection, confession. Each proposal for a move outside the realm of political praxis may rearrange the characters on stage, but attentive presence is mandatory, the script does not change significantly. A mastery of lines, the words of others spoken as our own, persuasively, preserves the illusion, our sense of distaste for these words and our urgency in speaking them. Each word must be heard, felt, by the audience. I think they call it projection. We collapse on stage, a curtain falls and we get up, the audience leaves and we take off our masks. And if we are good they believe we are dead, but until the next performance, they cannot be sure.

... these aren't the things that are going to dig my grave and shut me into an area that I don't want to be in... everything starts closing in and you want to break away... who said women always have to be onstage anyway... you decide to do it and you can't look back... thinking about beauty and health and everything is not healthy... you have to be health-conscious these days ... women are smart people... go to a man, not a woman... I didn't have a weight problem until I started dieting... it makes you wonder...

# Appendix

During the past five years, I have conducted fifty audio-taped interviews with women as a means by which to examine in a more systematic fashion, women's involvement in the discourse of dieting/health.[1] Gaining access to fifty women who were willing to talk openly about their bodies proved to be quite easy. All volunteered as a result of hearing about my research interests, or hearing me speak publicly on the topic of women and appearance. At the close of four public presentations I invited audience members to talk with me further about the topic during a tape-recorded interview, or to invite friends who were not in attendance to contact me for purposes of an interview. In some cases, the friends of women in attendance suggested that other friends call me. Unfortunately, time did not permit me to interview all of the women who expressed an interest in the study.

I did not presume from the outset that I needed to deceive women as to the "true" nature of my research or my position in order to obtain their views on the topic.[2] I felt it necessary to be open regarding my purposes if I were to expect openness from them. Also, primarily for two reasons, I wanted women to approach me, rather than the other way around, to offer their participation in the study. First, I did not want to speculate, in advance, about the "type" of woman who is interested in issues pertaining to body appearance or weight loss. I wanted women to identify themselves as persons who had a lot to say about issues pertaining to appearance. Second, given the extraordinary self-consciousness that often accompanies a sense of body unacceptability, I did not want to approach women with my request, who may in turn become anxious, nervous, or embarrassed.

The fifty volunteers comprise a fairly diverse group. The age distribution ranged from sixteen to fifty-four, with an average age of twenty-four. Women in the group represented diverse geographic locations, including western, mid-western, eastern, and southern regions of the United States. Occupationally, thirty volunteers were employed in the following professions: teacher, beautician, waitress, housewife, dancer, actress, accountant, manager, lawyer, research assistant, teaching assistant, sales clerk. In many cases, women described themselves as having more than one occupation, for example, "I'm a housewife and a teacher," "I'm an actress and a dancer." Twenty-two women at the time of the interview, were undergraduate students at either a small private university or a large public university. Twenty-two women were married at the time of the interview, and twenty-eight were single.

I viewed each interview as a personal conversation between two women. Sharing stories and views concerning one's body is often an intensely personal and sometimes awkward experience, which is rendered all the more difficult by a detached or disinterested interview. In addition, talking about personal issues is often done, between women, in a context of friendship wherein responsiveness, reciprocity, and equality are established as implicit responsibilities.[3] I did not find it appropriate to maintain strict hierarchical divisions between researcher and respondents, which grants power to the former and powerlessness to the latter.[4] Further, instead of conducting interviews so that I retained a position of silence while demanding high disclosure from respondents, I answered their questions and, when asked, offered my own views. In essence, I attempted to avoid a "confessional" format for interviewing.

The protocol used in conducting interviews followed the general structure of an "open-ended topical" format as suggested by Michael Quinn Patton (1980), in which a researcher brings a list of topics to the interview setting and develops particular questions during the process of interviewing (pp. 200–205). Three topics were selected based on a survey of dieting/health literature and research. I chose topics that are afforded much attention in the views of "experts" in order to see how everyday women encounter and live the discourses of weight loss and health: cultural standards for female appearance; body alteration activities, and the influence of others on body perception. All interviews, then, contain topical similarities, but there is much diversity as well because I asked questions based on the discussions or stories offered by each respondent. Both parties had a voice in determining the direction of the interview, the particular questions asked and answered, and the length of time given to each topic or issue.

The time scheduled for each interview was forty minutes. However, many interviews exceeded the stipulated length by a minimum of ten minutes and a maximum of fifty minutes. In addition, each respondent was invited to ask questions prior to and after the interview. Nearly all respondents asked questions both before and after the interview, mostly for purposes of clarification regarding the nature of the study and their participation. All respondents were assured of anonymity, and are thus referenced in my analysis by pseudonyms. Further, I have substituted the names of geographically specific organizations, stores, bars and restaurants, weight loss methods, and so forth, with a generic reference.

An analysis of data was conducted initially by noting thematic patterns in the responses given. In particular, I noted recurring topics and issues, the general themes and images used to characterize a particular experience, and similar thematics in the "speaking" of body issues. I examined language choices, metaphors, and imagery in each interview-text. I also paid close attention to the ways in which topics were "expanded" by respondents, that is, the giving of narrative structure to their experience and the "breakdowns" or disruptions in narrative. For example, many women began to tell a story and in the midst of speaking said such things as, "No, that's not it," "Wait, there's more to it than that," or "Let me back up." An analysis of thematics and narration allowed me to examine the means by which women align themselves with discourses of weight loss/health, along with points of resistance, digression, rearticulation, rethinking, and tension.

In conducting an analysis of the data, my goal was to see how women position themselves within the terrain of health discourse. I did not wish to place the women into categories such as healthy or unhealthy, fat or thin, liberal or conservative. That is, I did not wish to simply reproduce the dichotomies in which women live. Rather, I wanted to see if and how women "fall between" the oppositions presented within culture. I also wanted to examine the extent to which women have internalized cultural health representations, and the "fit" between women's lives and their internalized representations.

# Notes

## Chapter 1

1. Bayrd (1978) notes that the efforts of many Americans to lose weight is "evidenced by the fact that the diet industry has become a multibillion-dollar business" (p. 10).

2. In reading my criticisms of Stillman and Atkins, a friend advised caution in suggesting that these physicians had "intentionally" promoted dangerous diets. As physicians, I believe, Stillman and Atkins have a responsibility to present medically sound advice because they use their credentials as members of the medical community to profit from consumers. In a very real sense, medical credentials help to insure consumer trust, which in turn promotes sales.

3. Shulamith Firestone (1971) addresses the indispensibility of men as perceived within patriarchy and the relative interchangeability of women. She utilizes concept of "sex privitization" in the context of female "beauty" labors to illustrate the means by which women are stripped of individuality through the promise of individuality. The political function of sex privitization is greater ease in stereotyping women *in general:* "When women begin to look more and more alike, distinguished only by the degree to which they differ from a paper ideal, they can be more easily stereotyped as a class: They look alike, they think alike, and even worse, they are so stupid they believe they are not alike" (p. 152). A side-effect is that "men appear more individual and irreplaceable than they really are" (p. 151).

4. For an excellent re-reading of so-called "women's diseases," and the purposes served by masculinist ideology in the link between women and disease, see Paula Caplan's (1985) discussion of women's bodies (pp. 113-132).

## Chapter 2

1. See, for illustration, Linn (1980), pp. 87-97; Mazel (1982), pp. 215-233.

2. It is perhaps noteworthy that "Be all that you can be" is the recruitment slogan for the United States Army.

3. My own experience of being "constructed" within the domain of cosmetic surgery, and the political import of a "chaining" of disease within that environment, appears in Spitzack (1988a).

## Chapter 3

1. Young, Leplante, and Robbins (1987) attribute the premises of their views to Lemert's (1964) concept of value pluralism. Drawing from Lemert's work as a means by which to discuss the white ethnocentrism imposed on American Indian culture, the authors note that "value pluralism arises when the dominant values of a culturally distinct group are extended to become a basis of normative regulation of minority subcultures having divergent values" (p. 60).

2. Sonja Johnson (1987) argues that within patriarchal cultures, the power afforded to women is bound up with a rejection of traditionally feminine behavior. For example, a "career woman" is successful only if she does not exhibit feminine traits. The rewards for women who have rejected femininity, Johnson writes, are "feelings of being powerful, as well as of being 'on the right side,' which unconsciously means the men's side against women; the momentary feeling of not being like other women, not being a woman at all, not a slave like them, removed from the degradation of our caste altogether; the incredibly heady feeling of escape from the bondage of our gender" (pp. 56–57). The underside of freedom from bondage is that this form of power requires a condemnation of oneself, a renunciation of "womanhood."

3. Undoubtedly, Cowan and Kinder (1985) would claim that they are not asking women to limit their ambitions or to "settle" for an undesirable relational partner. As we have seen, the ideology in their brand of female confession promises liberation and expanded possibilities. Chapter titles such as "Freedom from Love Obsessions" and "Letting Go of Expectations" suggest that readers become healthy by confronting an obsessional and demanding disposition. Perhaps the most revealing connection between traditional femininity and confession is communicated in the title of Chapter Twelve, "A Fresh Look at 'Femininity': The Magic of Strength and Tenderness, The Courage to Express Yourself."

4. Hunter (1976) explains her title, the dual messages of "lose" and "loose," in stating, "Loose the bondage of self appeasement and the fat will go. Loose the power of God in your life and give him your appetite. Loose it and lose it—for Jesus!" (pp. 44–45).

5. It is perhaps noteworthy that both in structure and content, Hunter's (1976) book wholly endorses an anti-diet perspective. Her opening chapter, "The Great Christian Fib," begins with a litany of failed diets (p. 9). Hunter, like numerous diet book authors, links suffering and deviance to weight loss efforts, and indicates that a release from the bondage of dieting is imperative if one hopes to achieve permanent slenderness. Her realization of the futility of diets is documented in a chapter title, "The Great Awakening!" (pp. 15–25).

6. For an extended discussion of the before/after imagery endemic to body reduction formulas, see Millman (1981), pp. 192-208. An alternative, though not inconsistent, reading of before/after images appears in Spitzack (1987), pp. 357-370.

7. Marsha contrasts the experience of shopping for bathing suits when fat to shopping for bathing suits when thin. She explains that, when thin, store clerks bring out "a couple of bikinis," indicating that she is not overweight and need not hide her body.

8. The theme of "body as other" is also examined in Spitzack (1988b), p. 66.

9. The *Oxford American Dictionary* defines asset as "any property that has money value, especially property that can be used or sold to pay debts," or "a useful or valuable quality or skill, a person regarded as useful" (p. 36).

10. Brownmiller (1984) explains the biological changes that accompany reproductive maturation: "Triggered by estrogens, the adolescent girl's genitals increase in size and sensitivity, her mammary ducts enlarge, her uterus expands and her pelvis widens. Her ovaries and Fallopian tubes ready themselves for their reproductive function and menstruation begins" (p. 27).

11. Among other charts and records, Wardell's (1985) book includes the "Thin Within Observations and Corrections Chart," "Thin Within Food Log," and the "Fat Machinery Log." In nearly every chapter, Wardell also offers space for readers on which to record information about thoughts and desires that are connected to consumption.

## Chapter 4

1. Preserving the family in oneself, for Laing (1972), entails a preservation of a *shared* sense of the family. An expression of differences between family members is often destructive because it destroys the illusion of perfect alignment and agreement between members. Thus, mechanisms are concealed by family members in order to avoid the destructive outcomes of difference and division within the family. For elaboration, see Laing's discussion on the defensive function of the family, pp. 12-15.

2. McFarland and Baker-Baumann (1988) attribute their discussion of the perfect family to a text titled, *Bulimia: A Systems Approach.*

3. Weitzman (1984) attributes the latter finding to a study by Evelyn Goodenough (1957).

## Chapter 5

1. Eichenbaum and Orbach (1987) observe, "The tremendous importance of women's relationships may not be prevalent in everyone's mind, so that many women continue to be isolated, but these relationships are generally acknowledged and accepted" (p. 9). The authors point out that television programs such as "Rhoda," "Kate

& Allie," and "Mary Tyler Moore" exhibit cultural attention to women's friendships. The cultural acceptance of women's friendship, however, is often dependent on coherence with dominant images of women. For example, Rhoda is obsessed with dieting and weight, Kate and Allie are almost invariably involved in issues pertaining to child-care, men, and the difficulties encountered by women who work outside the home, and Mary Tyler Moore is a woman who functions largely to negotiate relationships between difficult men through women's intuition (not highly developed reasoning capabilities).

## Chapter 6

1. I qualify my discussion of reactions to Lovelace's work with the word 'popular' because I wish to exempt many of the excellent feminist analyses of Lovelace's place in the world of pornography. See, for example, Steinem (1983, pp. 243-252); MacKinnon (1987, pp. 127-133).

2. Woman's fear of sexual exploitation in the context of everyday actions is examined thoroughly in Sheffield's (1984) discussions of "sexual terrorism" (pp. 3-19). Sheffield's analysis is useful in understanding the female paralysis mandated by a so-called glorification of women's bodies. Placing women's experience of body acknowledgement in the language of "terrorism" shifts the sensations of being watched and pursued from pure pleasure to fear, an absence of control, and ever-present guardedness.

## Chapter 7

1. Jane Fonda (1981) begins the *Workout Book* by describing the destructive path she followed when allowing others to influence her notions of beauty and health. The transformation contained within textual boundaries is perhaps best captured in contrasting the title of the first chapter, "A Body Abused," with that of the last chapter, "Being Strong."

2. Gaining recognition within the boundaries of dominant culture through an abandonment of "womanhood" is prevalent, for example, in the domain of rhetoric. In an analysis of the place of great women speakers in the domain of rhetoric, Carole Spitzack and Kathryn Carter (1987) argue that "great" women are placed in a practical dilemma because they "are presumed to be atypical, and simultaneously they are thought to represent the concerns and styles of women" (p. 405). Here, it is a failure to identify with women that qualifies women for greatness.

3. The fear of suggesting that men and women may not constitute a strict opposition is seen in countless research studies. For example, Mary Ann Fitzpatrick (1983) examines a study designed to test male and female perceptions of relationships. She notes that although only two differences were found, among the ten dimensions measured, "the entire discussion section of the paper focused on the two differences discovered between males and females" (p. 75). We would do well, in fact, to view

research designed to identify sex differences with caution because it can work to further polarize female and male identities, thereby underscoring the legitimacy of cultural oppositions.

4. For an excellent analysis of the fragile distinctions made between "good" and "mad" women, see Jill Matthews (1984). Within the cultural division between sanity and insanity, Matthews conducts a careful examination of femininity as constructed in twentieth century Australia.

## Chapter 8

1. A classic case of cooption in the domain of women's relational knowledge can be gleaned from cultural responses to the publication of Shere Hite's (1987) examination of women's experiences of love relationships. Because Hite's respondents revealed that all is not blissful in the terrain of relationships between women and men, the author's credibility was questioned on every conceivable ground. Reporters, talk show hosts, editorialists, cartoonists, among others, speculated ad nauseam on the research tactics used by Hite, on her marriage to a younger man, on the possibly embittered, and thus presumably non-representative, character of respondents, and so forth. Cultural voices insisted that Hite reveal her research tactics, ignoring the thirty-four page discussion of them in her book. The frenzied attempts to falsify Hite's research provide tremendous insight into the means by which women's words and lives are represented by dominant culture. By scrambling to show that Hite's research tactics, her life, and the lives of her respondents are "sick," the illnesses of the dominant retain invisibility. The fury with which women must be realigned with illness, however, is only necessary if women show signs of strength.

## Appendix

1. An abbreviated analysis of the first thirty interviews is provided in Carole Spitzack (1988b), pp. 51-74. In my initial analysis I followed the procedures entailed in a phenomenological method. Working with the data more extensively and conducting additional interviews required some modifications in my initial choice of methods. The analysis offered in this work is to some extent informed by phenomenology, particularly the analysis of themes, but departs from the premises of traditional phenomenology by abandoning a search for essential structures.

2. Traditional guidelines for the conduct of scholarly investigations dictate a "cover story" to insure replicability and objectivity in research. Recently, many scholars have examined the ethical questions raised by, in effect, lying to subjects. See for example, James Anderson's (1987) discussion of ethics and research practices.

3. A study on female friendship patterns by Fern Johnson and Elizabeth Aries (1983) shows that women's interaction patterns are characterized by horizontal power relations, mutual trust, and mutual conversational contributions (pp. 353-361).

4. Many feminist scholars have questioned the feasibility and the ethics of strict hierarchical relationships between researchers and their subjects. Ann Oakley (1981b) provides a systematic examination of the "breakdown" of traditional research guidelines in the context of her study of women's experience of being pregnant and giving birth (pp. 30-61). See also Kathryn Carter and Carole Spitzack (1989) for an anthology devoted to critiques of traditional methodological and theoretical assumptions in the domain of scholarly research, and alternative approaches to investigation.

# References

Altman, Irwin, and D. A. Taylor (1973). *Social Penetration: The Development of Social Relationships* (New York: Holt, Rinehart and Winston).

Anderson, James (1987). *Communication Research: Issues and Methods* (New York: McGraw-Hill Publishers).

Appleton, Willian S. (1981). *Fathers and Daughters: A Father's Powerful Influence on a Woman's Life* (New York: Doubleday and Company).

Astrachan, Anthony (1988). *How Men Feel: Their Responses to Women's Demands for Equality and Power* (New York: Doubleday).

Banner, Lois W. (1983). *American Beauty* (Chicago: University of Chicago Press).

Barthes, Roland (1985). "The Shape I'm In: Interview with French *Playboy.*" In *On Signs,* ed. Marshal Blonsky (Baltimore, MD: Johns Hopkins University Press), pp. 33–34.

Basow, Susan (1980). *Sex-Role Stereotypes: Traditions and Alternatives* (Monterey, CA: Brooks/Cole Publishers).

Baudrillard, Jean (1981). *For a Critique of the Political Economy of the Sign,* trans. Charles Levin (St. Louis, MO: Telos Press).

Bayrd, Edwin (1978). *The Thin Game: Dietary Scams and Dietary Sense* (New York: Avon Books).

Bell, Robert (1981). *Worlds of Friendship* (Beverly Hills, CA: Sage Publications).

Bell, Rudolph (1985). *Holy Anorexia* (Chicago: University of Chicago Press).

Berger, John (1972). *Ways of Seeing* (London: British Broadcasting Corporation).

Boone-O'Neill, Cherry (1982). *Starving for Attention* (New York: Continuum Publishing Company).

Boskind-White, Marlene, and William C. White (1983). *Bulimarexia: The Binge-Purge Cycle* (New York: W. W. Norton and Company).

189

Brownmiller, Susan (1975). *Against Our Will: Men, Women and Rape* (New York: Bantam Books).

Brownmiller, Susan (1984). *Femininity* (New York: Fawcett-Columbine Books).

Bruch, Hilde (1966). "How Psychology Can Help the Overweight Patient." *The Physician's Panorama* 4: pp. 5–12.

Bruch, Hilde (1979). *The Golden Cage: The Enigma of Anorexia Nervosa* (New York: Vintage Books).

Bruno, Frank J. (1972). *Think Yourself Thin: How Psychology Can Help You Lose Weight* (New York: Barnes & Noble Books).

Caplan, Paula (1985). *The Myth of Women's Masochism* (New York: E. P. Dutton).

Carter, Kathryn, and Carole Spitzack, eds. (1989). *Studying Women's Communication: Perspectives on Theory and Method* (Norwood, NJ: Ablex Press).

Carter, Steven, and Julia Sokol (1987). *Men Who Can't Love: When a Man's Fear Makes Him Run From Commitment* (New York: M. Evans and Company).

Chernin, Kim (1981). *The Obsession: Reflections on the Tyranny of Slenderness* (New York: Harper-Colophon Books).

Chernin, Kim (1985). *The Hungry Self: Women, Eating and Identity* (New York: Harper and Row).

Chodorow, Nancy (1978). *The Reproduction of Mothering* (Berkeley: University of California Press).

Cixous, Hélène, and Catherine Clément (1986). *The Newly Born Woman*, trans. Betsy Wing (Minneapolis: University of Minnesota Press).

Cowan, Connell and Melvyn Kinder (1985). *Smart Women, Foolish Choices* (New York: Signet Books/New American Library).

Coward, Rosalind (1985). *Female Desires: How They are Sought, Bought, and Packaged* (New York: Grove Press).

Daly, Mary (1978). *Gyn-Ecology: The Meta-Ethics of Radical Feminism* (Boston: Beacon Press).

Deleuze, Gilles, and Félix Guattari (1983). *Anti-Oedipus: Capitalism and Schizophrenia*, trans. Robert Hurley, Mark Seem, and Helen R. Lane (Minneapolis: University of Minnesota Press).

Diamond, Harvy, and Marilyn Diamond (1985). *Fit for Life* (New York: Warner Books).

Doane, Mary Ann (1987). *The Desire to Desire: The Woman's Film of the 1940s* (Bloomington, IN: Indiana University Press).

Dowling, Colette (1988). *Perfect Women: Hidden Fears of Inadequacy and the Drive to Perform* (New York: Summit Books).

Duck, Steve (1976). "Interpersonal Communication in Developing Acquaintance." In *Explorations in Interpersonal Communication*, ed. Gerald Miller (Beverly Hills, CA: Sage Publications), pp. 127-148.

Dworkin, Andrea (1974). *Woman Hating* (New York: E. P. Dutton).

Dworkin, Andrea (1987). *Intercourse* (New York: The Free Press).

Dziech, Billie Wright, and Linda Weiner (1984). *The Lecherous Professor: Sexual Harassment on Campus* (Boston: Beacon Press).

Ehrenreich, Barbara, Elizabeth Hess, and Gloria Jacobs (1986). *Re-Making Love: The Feminization of Sex* (New York: Anchor Press/Doubleday).

Eichenbaum, Luise, and Susie Orbach (1987). *Between Women: Love; Envy, and Competition in Women's Friendships* (New York: Penguin Books).

Farley, Lin (1978). *Sexual Shakedown: The Sexual Harassment of Women on the Job* (New York: McGraw-Hill Publishers).

Firestone, Shulamith (1971). *The Dialectic of Sex: The Case for Feminist Revolution* (New York: Bantam Books).

Fitzpatrick, Mary Ann (1983). "Effective Interpersonal Communication for Women in the Corporation: Think Like a Man, Talk Like a Lady." In *Women in Orgainzations: Barriers and Breakthroughs,* ed. Joseph Pilotta (Prospect Heights, IL: Waveland Press), pp. 73-84.

Fonda, Jane (1981). *Jane Fonda's Workout Book* (New York: Simon and Schuster).

Foucault, Michel (1979). *Discipline and Punish: The Birth of the Prison,* trans. Alan Sheridan (New York: Vintage Books).

Foucault, Michel (1980a). "History of Sexuality." In *Power/Knowledge: Selected Interviews and Other Writings by Michel Foucault,* ed. Colin Gordon, trans., Colin Gordon, Leo Marshall, John Mepham, and Kate Soper (New York: Pantheon Books), pp. 183-193.

Foucault, Michel (1980b). "Body/Power." In *Power/Knowledge: Selected Interviews and Other Writings by Michel Foucault,* ed. Colin Gordon, trans Colin Gordon, Leo Marshall, John Mepham, and Kate Soper (New York: Pantheon Books), pp. 55-62.

Foucault, Michel (1980c). "The Politics of Health in the Eighteenth Century." In *Power/Knowledge: Selected Interviews and Other Writings by Michel Foucault,* ed. Colin Gordon, trans. Colin Gordon, Leo Marshall, John Mepham, and Kate Soper (New York: Pantheon Books), pp. 166-182.

Foucault, Michel (1980d). *The History of Sexuality, Vol. 1: An Introduction,* trans. Robert Hurly (New York: Vintage Books).

Foucault, Michel (1980e). "The Eye of Power." In *Power/Knowledge: Selected Interviews and Other Writings by Michel Foucault,* ed. Colin Gordon, trans., Colin Gordon, Leo Marshall, John Mepham, and Kate Soper (New York: Pantheon Books), pp. 146-165.

Foucault, Michel (1985). "Sexuality and Solitude." In *On Signs,* ed. Marshall Blonsky (Baltimore: Johns Hopkins University Press), pp. 365-372.

Foucault, Michel (1986). *The History of Sexuality, Vol. 3: The Care of the Self,* trans. Robert Hurley (New York: Vintage Books).

French, Marilyn (1985). *Beyond Power: On Women, Men, and Morals* (New York: Ballantine Books).

Gendler, Jerrold (1987). *Cosmetic Surgery: In Search of Perfection* (ISBN 0-937043-07-9).

Gilligan, Carol (1982). *In a Different Voice: Psychological Theories and Women's Development* (Cambridge, MA: Harvard University Press).

Griffin, Susan (1981). *Pornography and Silence: Culture's Revenge Against Nature* (New York: Harper-Colophon Books).

Henley, Nancy (1977). *Body Politics: Power, Sex, and Nonverbal Communication* (Englewood Cliffs, NJ: Prentice-Hall).

Henley, Nancy, and Jo Freeman (1984). "The Sexual Politics of Interpersonal Behavior." In *Women: A Feminist Perspective,* 3rd. ed., ed. Jo Freeman (Palo Alto, CA: Mayfield Publishing), pp. 465-477.

Herman, Dianne (1984). "The Rape Culture." In *Women: A Feminist Perspective,* 3rd. ed., ed. Jo Freeman (Palo Alto, CA: Mayfield Publishing), pp. 20-38.

Hite, Shere (1987). *Women in Love: A Cultural Revolution in Progress* (New York: Alfred A. Knopf).

Hoffnung, Michele (1984). "Motherhood: Contemporary Conflict for Women." In *Women: A Feminist Perspective,* 3rd. ed., ed. Jo Freeman (Palo Alto, CA: Mayfield Publishing Company), pp. 124-138.

Hunter, Frances (1976). *God's Answer to Fat... Loøse It* (Houston, TX: Hunter Ministries).

Irigaray, Luce (1985). *The Sex Which is Not One,* trans. Catherine Porter with Carolyn Burke (Ithaca, NY: Cornell University Press).

Janeway, Elizabeth (1980). "Who is Sylvia?: On the Loss of Sexual Paradigms." In *Women: Sex and Sexuality,* eds. Catherine R. Stimpson and Ellen Spector-Person (Chicago: University of Chicago Press), pp. 4-20.

Johnson, Fern, and Elizabeth J. Aries (1983). "The Talk of Women Friends," *Women's Studies International Forum,* Vol. 6, No. 4: 353-361.

Johnson, Sonja (1987). *Going Out of Our Minds: The Metaphysics of Liberation* (Freedom, CA: The Crossing Press).

Lacan, Jacques (1985). *Feminine Sexuality,* eds. Juliet Mitchell and Jacqueline Rose, trans. Jacqueline Rose (New York: W. W. Norton and Company).

Laing, R. D. (1972). *The Politics of the Family and Other Essays* (New York: Vintage Books).

Lakoff, George, and Mark Johnson (1980). *Metaphors We Live By* (Chicago: University of Chicago Press).

Langlois, Judith H., and A. Chris Downs (1980). "Mothers, Fathers, and Peers as Socialization Agents of Sex-Typed Behaviors in Young Children," *Child Development,* Vol. 51: pp. 1237-1247.

Lemert, E. (1964). "Social Structure, Social Control and Deviation." In *Anomie and Deviant Behavior,* ed. M. Clinard (Glencoe, IL: The Free Press).

LeShan, Eda (1981). *Winning the Losing Battle: Why I Will Never be Fat Again* (New York: Bantam Books).

Linn, Robert (1980). *Staying Thin* (New York: Zebra Books).

Lovelace, Linda, with Mike McGrady (1980). *Ordeal* (New York: Berkley Books).

Lovelace, Linda, with Mike McGrady (1986). *Out of Bondage* (New York: Berkley Books).

McFarland, Barbara, and Tyeis Baker-Baumann (1988). *Feeding the Empty Heart: Adult Children and Compulsive Eating* (New York: Harper/Hazelden Books).

MacKinnon, Catharine A. (1987). *Feminism Unmodified: Discourses on Life and Law* (Cambridge, MA: Harvard University Press).

Maddox, George L., and Veronica Liederman (1973). "Overweight as a Social Disability with Medical Implications." In *The Psychology of Obesity: Dynamics and Treatment,* ed. Norman Kiell (Springfield: Charles C. Thomas), pp. 84-91.

Martin, Emily (1987). *The Woman in the Body: A Cultural Analysis of Reproduction* (Boston: Beacon Press).

Matthews, Jill Julius (1984). *Good and Mad Women: The Historical Construction of Femininity in Twentieth Century Australia* (Sydney: George Allen and Unwin Publishers).

Mazel, Judy (1982). *The Beverly Hills Diet* (New York: Berkley Books).

Millman, Marcia (1981). *Such a Pretty Face: Being Fat in America* (New York: Berkley Books).

Moynahan, Paula A. (1988). *Cosmetic Surgery for Women: A Revolutionary Approach to Image Enhancement* (New York: Crown Publishers).

Mumby, Dennis, and Carole Spitzack (1983). "Ideology and Television News: A Metaphoric Analysis of Political Stories," *Central States Speech Journal,* Vol. 34, No. 3: pp. 162-171.

Oakley, Ann (1981a). *Subject Women* (New York: Pantheon Books).

Oakley, Ann (1981b). "Interviewing Women: A Contradiction in Terms." In *Doing Feminist Research,* ed. Helen Roberts (London: Routledge and Kegan Paul).

Orbach, Susie (1979). *Fat is a Feminist Issue: A Self-Help Guide for Compulsive Eaters* (New York: Berkley Books).

Owens, Craig (1983). "The Discourse of Others: Feminist and Post-modernism." In *The Anti-Aesthetic: Essays on Post-modern Culture,* ed. Hal Foster (Port Townsend, WA: Bay Press), pp. 57-82.

Palmer, R. L. (1980). *Anorexia Nervosa: A Guide for Sufferers and Their Families* (New York: Penguin Books).

Patton, Michael Quinn (1980). *Qualitative Evaluation Methods* (Beverly Hills, CA: Sage Publications).

Peplau, Letitia Anne (1984). "Power in Dating Relationships." In *Women: A Feminist Perspective,* 3rd. ed., ed. Jo Freeman (Palo Alto, CA: Mayfield Publishing), pp. 100-112.

Phillips, Gerald, and Julia Wood (1983). *Communication and Human Relationships: The Study of Interpersonal Communication* (New York: Macmillan).

Principal, Victoria (1983). *The Body Principal: The Exercise Program for Life* (New York: Simon and Schuster).

Rakow, Lana (1986). "Rethinking Gender and Communication," *Journal of Communication,* Vol. 36, No. 1: pp. 11-16.

Rich, Adrienne (1980). "Compulsory Heterosexuality and Lesbian Existence." In *Women: Sex and Sexuality,* eds. Catherine R. Stimpson and Ethel Spector Person (Chicago: University of Chicago Press), pp. 62-91.

Rose, Jacqueline (1985). Introduction to Jacques Lacan, *Feminine Sexuality,* eds. Juliet Mitchell and Jacqueline Rose, trans. Jacqueline Rose (New York: W. W. Norton and Company), pp. 27-58.

Rose, Jacqueline (1986). *Sexuality in the Field of Vision* (New York: Verso Books).

Roth, Geneen (1982). *Feeding the Hungry Heart: The Experience of Compulsive Eating* (New York: Signet Books).

Sedwick, Eve Kosofsky (1988). "Privilege of Unknowing," *Genders,* No. 1: pp. 102-124.

Seiden, Ann M., and Pauline B. Bart (1975). "Woman to Woman: Is Sisterhood Powerful?" In *Old Family/New Family,* ed. Nona Glazer-Malbin (New York: Van Nostrand Publishers), pp. 189-228.

Sheffield, Carole, J. (1984). "Sexual Terrorism." In *Women: A Feminist Perspective,* 3rd. ed., ed. Jo Freeman (Palo Alto, CA: Mayfield Publishing), pp. 3-19.

Shephard, Bruce D., and Carroll A. Shephard (1985). *The Complete Guide to Women's Health* (New York: Plume Books).

Showalter, Elanie (1981). "Feminist Criticism in the Wilderness," *Critical Inquiry,* Vol. 8, No. 2: pp. 179-206.

Sichtermann, Barbara (1986). *Femininity: The Politics of the Personal,* ed. Helga Geyer-Ryan, trans. John Whitlam (Minneapolis: University of Minnesota Press).

Sontag, Susan (1978). *Illness as Metaphor* (New York: Vintage Books).

Spector Person, Ethel (1988). *Dreams of Love and Fateful Encounters: The Power of Romantic Passion* (New York: W. W. Norton and Co.).

Spender, Dale (1985). *Man Made Language,* 2nd. ed. (London: Routledge and Kegan Paul).

Spitzack, Carole (1987). "Confession and Signification: The Systematic Inscription of Body Consciousness," *Journal of Medicine and Philosophy,* Vol. 12, No. 4: pp. 357-370.

Spitzack, Carole, and Kathryn Carter (1987). "Women in Communication Studies: A Typology for Revision," *Quarterly Journal of Speech,* Vol. 73, No. 4: pp. 401-423.

Spitzack, Carole (1988a). "The Confession Mirror: Plastic Images for Surgery," *Canadian Journal of Political and Social Theory,* Vol. 12, No. 1-2: pp. 38-50.

Spitzack, Carole (1988b). "Body Talk: The Politics of Weight Loss and Female Identity." In *Women Communicating: Studies of Women's Talk,* eds. Barbara Bate and Anita Taylor (Norwood, NJ: Ablex Press), pp. 51-74.

Steinem, Gloria (1983). *Outrageous Acts and Everyday Rebellions* (New York: Holt, Rinehart and Winston).

Stuart, Richard (1983). *Act Thin, Stay Thin* (New York: Jove Books).

Sutton, Remar (1988). *Body Worry* (New York: Penguin Books).

Trask, Haunani-Kay (1986). *Eros and Power: The Promise of Feminist Theory* (Philadelphia, PA: University of Pennsylvania Press).

Wallach, Janet (1988). *Looks That Work* (New York: Penguin Books).

Wardell, Judy (1985). *Thin Within: How to Eat and Live Like a Thin Person* (New York: Pocket Books).

Watson, Richard (1985). *The Philosopher's Diet: How to Lose Weight and Change the World* (Boston: The Atlantic Monthly Press).

Weitzmen, Lenore J. (1984). "Sex Role Socialization: A Focus on Women." In *Women: A Feminist Perspective,* 3rd edition, ed. Jo Freeman (Palo Alto, CA: Mayfield Publishing Company), pp. 157-237.

Young, Thomas, Charles LePlante, and Webster Robbins (1987). "Indians Before the Law: An Assessment of Contravening Cultural/Legal Ideologies," *Quarterly Journal of Ideology,* Vol. 11, No. 4: pp. 59-70.

# Index

Accountability: and deviance, 78-79; and dieting, 75-76. *See also* Confession

Aesthetics: of self-improvement, 47-48; of slenderness, 64-65; of women's health, 2, 37, 44. *See also* Health Discourses

Aging, 38-39, 185n10. *See also* Cosmetic Surgery

Altman, Irwin, 146

Anderson, James, 187n2

Andreadis, John, 14-15

Anorexia nervosa, 12-13, 28, 85

Anti-diets: as body-mind reunion, 16-17, 49-50; and individuality, 17, 19-20, 120; as resistance, 11-12, 17, 156

Appleton, William, 100-101

Ardener, Edwin, 170-171

Aries, Elizabeth, 187n3

Astrachan, Anthony, 139

Atkins, Robert, 22-23, 183n2

Baker-Baumann, Tyesis, 85, 93, 99

Banner, Lois, 15, 159

Bart, Pauline, 108

Barthes, Roland, 75

Basow, Susan, 107-108, 125

Baudrillard, Jean, 161-162

Bayrd, Edwin: on diet industry revenues, 9, 183n1, on dieting scams, 14, 20-22; on physiological imbalances, 12

Beauty: as death, 160, 167; as fabrication, 45-46, 110-111, 163; and heterosexuality, 70-71, 106-108, 126; as mythology, 162-163; as natural, 139-140

Bell, Robert, 107-108, 123-125, 146

Bell, Rudolph, 64, 69, 160

Berger, John, 34, 51, 53

Body alienation, 49-50, 66-67

Body consciousness, 46-47

Boone-O'Neill, Cherry, 84, 129

Boskind-White, Marlene, 161

Brownmiller, Susan: on beauty and youth, 38, 71, 185n10; on competition, 108; on fashion and restriction, 40; on femininity and self-love, 35, 117, 139-140, 167; on rape, 51, 134. *See also* Beauty

Bruch, Hilde, 13, 23, 85. *See also* Anorexia nervosa

Bruno, Frank, 17, 29

Bulimarexia, 161

Caloric intake. *See* Dieting

Cancer, 28-29

Caplan, Paula: on masochism, 79, 134; on the new man myth, 137-138; on physiological changes in female maturation, 10-11; on violence and volition, 165; on women and disease, 183n4

Carpenter, Karen, 13, 85

Carter, Kathryn, 182n2, 188n4

Carter, Steven, 63

Chernin, Kim, 13, 69, 95-96, 161

Chodorow, Nancy, 87-88

Cigarette smoking, 27-28

Cixous, Hélène, 168-170

Clément, Catherine, 168-170

Compliments: from acquaintances, 143; in intimate relationships, 146-149; in professional settings, 143-146; from strangers, 141-143

197